ORPHAN DANIEL RAND EARNED THE POWER OF THE IRON FIST IN THE MYSTICAL CITY OF K'UN LUN. AS AN ADULT, DANNY OVERSEES THE RAND CORPORATION AND MOONLIGHTS AS IRON FIST: KUNG FU DEFENDER OF THE INNOCENT.

PRISONER LUKE CAGE WAS SUBJECTED TO EXPERIMENTS THAT GAVE HIM SUPERHUMAN STRENGTH AND DURABILITY. AS POWER MAN, HE'S BEEN A HERO AND AN AVENGER, AND NOW A HUSBAND AND FATHER.

ONCE UPON A TIME, THEY WERE THE HEROES FOR HIRE.

CIVIL WAR II

THE EMERGENCE OF A NEW INHUMAN — AN INHUMAN WITH THE POWER TO PREDICT THE FUTURE — HAS SAVED MANHATTAN FROM CERTAIN CALAMITY! BUT IN THE AFTERMATH OF THIS TRIUMPH, FACED WITH THE REALIZATION THAT THEY NOW POSSESS THE ABILITY TO FORECAST TOMORROW, EARTH'S GREATEST CHAMPIONS ARE FORCED TO MAKE A CHOICE: PROTECT THE FUTURE...OR CHANGE IT?

BACK TOGETHER AS THE HEROES FOR HIRE, LUKE AND DANNY WERE JUST GETTING USED TO BEING A TEAM AGAIN. NOW IT LOOKS LIKE THEY'LL HAVE TO CHOOSE SIDES IN A WAR.

DAVID F. WALKER
WRITER

ISSUES #6-9 **SWEET CHRISTMAS ANNUAL #1**

FLAVIANO
ARTIST (#6-9)

SANFORD GREENE
ARTIST (#7-9)

SCOTT HEPBURN
ARTIST

JOHN RAUCH
COLOR ARTIST

SANFORD GREENE
COVER ART

MATT MILLA
COLOR ARTIST

JAMAL CAMPBELL
CVER ART

VC'S CLAYTON COWLES
LETTERER

KATHLEEN WISNESKI
ASSISTANT EDITOR

JAKE THOMAS
EDITOR

JENNIFER GRÜNWALD COLLECTION EDITOR
CAITLIN O'CONNELL ASSISTANT EDITOR
KATERI WOODY ASSOCIATE MANAGING EDITOR
MARK D. BEAZLEY EDITOR, SPECIAL PROJECTS

JEFF YOUNGQUIST VP PRODUCTION & SPECIAL PROJECTS
DAVID GABRIEL SVP PRINT, SALES & MARKETING
ADAM DEL RE BOOK DESIGNER

AXEL ALONSO EDITOR IN CHIEF
JOE QUESADA CHIEF CREATIVE OFFICER
DAN BUCKLEY PUBLISHER
ALAN FINE EXECUTIVE PRODUCER

POWER MAN AND IRON FIST VOL. 2: CIVIL WAR II. Contains material originally published in magazine form as POWER MAN AND IRON FIST #6-9 and SWEET CHRISTMAS ANNUAL #1. First printing 2017. ISBN# 978-1-302-90115-8. Published by MARVEL WORLDWIDE, INC., a subsidiary of MARVEL ENTERTAINMENT, LLC. OFFICE OF PUBLICATION: 135 West 50th Street, New York, NY 10020. Copyright © 2017 MARVEL. No similarity between any of the names, characters, persons, and/or institutions in this magazine with those of any living or dead person or institution is intended, and any such similarity which may exist is purely coincidental. Printed in the U.S.A. ALAN FINE, President, Marvel Entertainment; DAN BUCKLEY, President, TV, Publishing & Brand Management; JOE QUESADA, Chief Creative Officer; TOM BREVOORT, SVP of Publishing; DAVID BOGART, SVP of Business Affairs & Operations, Publishing & Partnership; C.B. CEBULSKI, VP of Brand Management & Development, Asia; DAVID GABRIEL, SVP of Sales & Marketing, Publishing; JEFF YOUNGQUIST, VP of Production & Special Projects; DAN CARR, Executive Director of Publishing Technology; ALEX MORALES, Director of Publishing Operations; SUSAN CRESPI, Production Manager; STAN LEE, Chairman Emeritus. For information regarding advertising in Marvel Comics or on Marvel.com, please contact Vit DeBellis, Integrated Sales Manager, at vdebellis@marvel.com. For Marvel subscription inquiries, please call 888-511-5480. Manufactured between 1/13/2017 and 2/14/2017 by QUAD/GRAPHICS WASECA, WASECA, MN, USA.

10 9 8 7 6 5 4 3 2 1

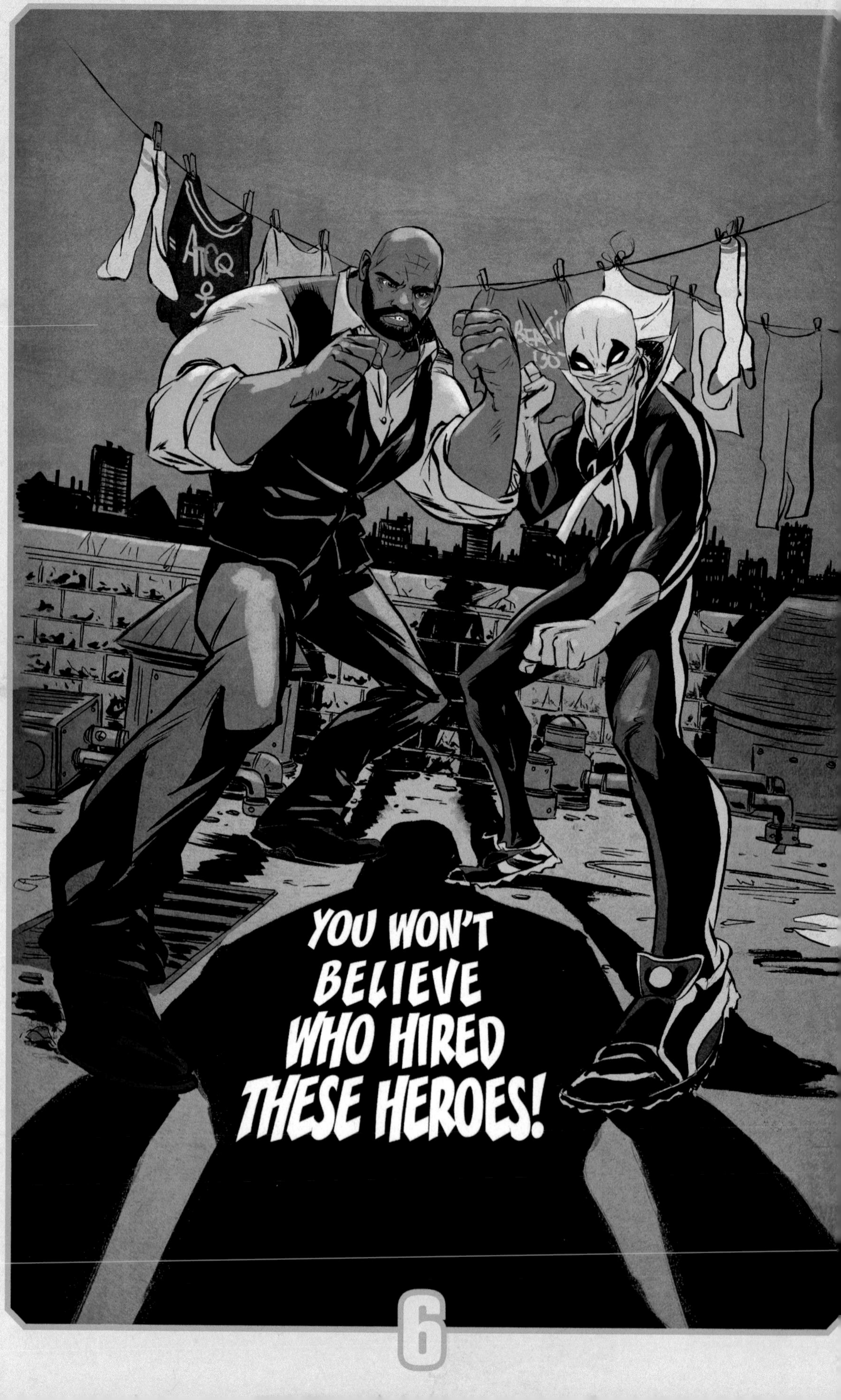
YOU WON'T BELIEVE WHO HIRED THESE HEROES!
6

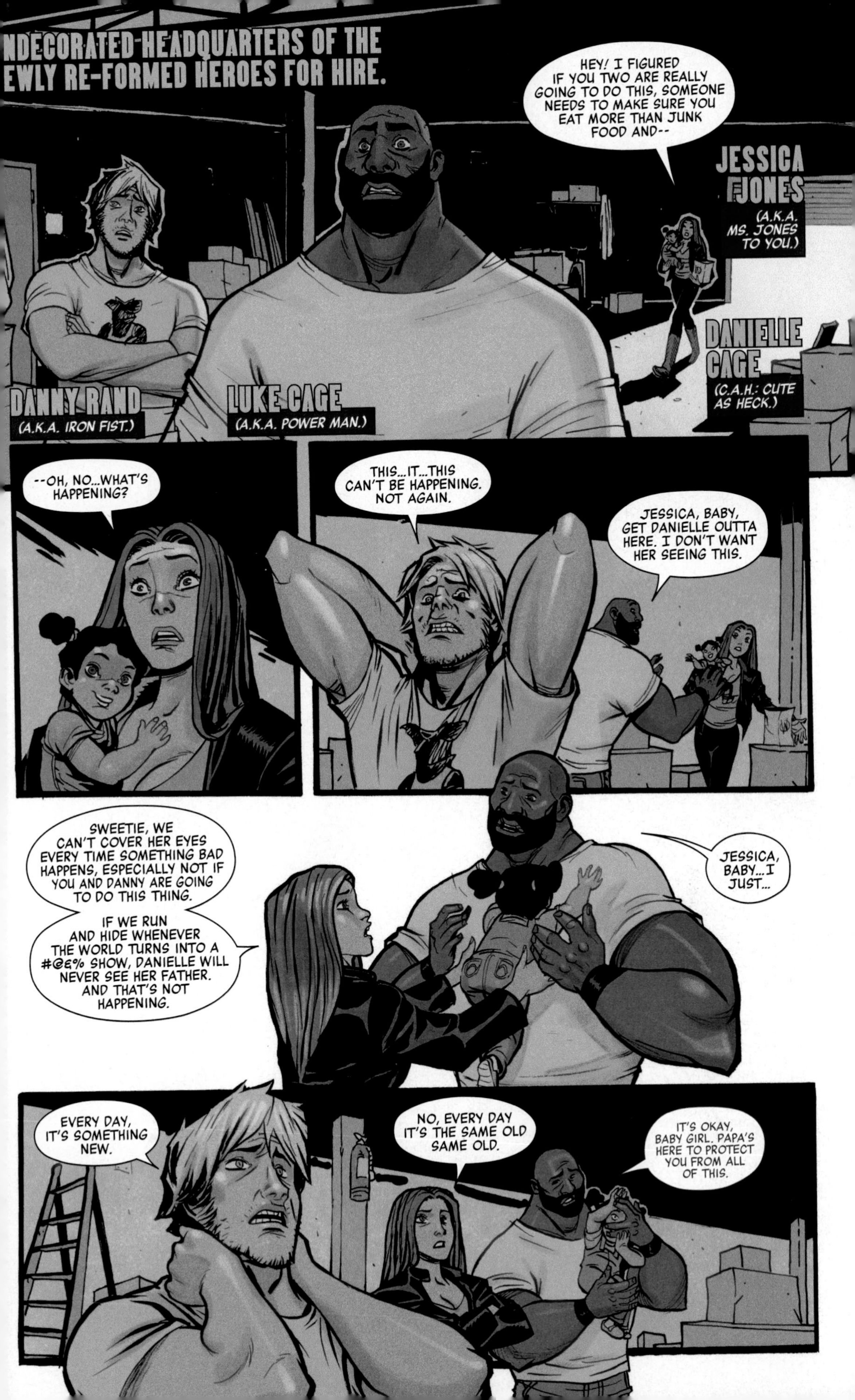
NDECORATED HEADQUARTERS OF THE
EWLY RE-FORMED HEROES FOR HIRE.
HEY! I FIGURED IF YOU TWO ARE REALLY GOING TO DO THIS, SOMEONE NEEDS TO MAKE SURE YOU EAT MORE THAN JUNK FOOD AND--
JESSICA JONES
(A.K.A. MS. JONES TO YOU.)
DANIELLE CAGE
(C.A.H.: CUTE AS HECK.)
DANNY RAND
(A.K.A. IRON FIST.)
LUKE CAGE
(A.K.A. POWER MAN.)
--OH, NO...WHAT'S HAPPENING?
THIS...IT...THIS CAN'T BE HAPPENING. NOT AGAIN.
JESSICA, BABY, GET DANIELLE OUTTA HERE. I DON'T WANT HER SEEING THIS.
SWEETIE, WE CAN'T COVER HER EYES EVERY TIME SOMETHING BAD HAPPENS, ESPECIALLY NOT IF YOU AND DANNY ARE GOING TO DO THIS THING.
IF WE RUN AND HIDE WHENEVER THE WORLD TURNS INTO A #@&% SHOW, DANIELLE WILL NEVER SEE HER FATHER. AND THAT'S NOT HAPPENING.
JESSICA, BABY...I JUST...
EVERY DAY, IT'S SOMETHING NEW.
NO, EVERY DAY IT'S THE SAME OLD SAME OLD.
IT'S OKAY, BABY GIRL. PAPA'S HERE TO PROTECT YOU FROM ALL OF THIS.

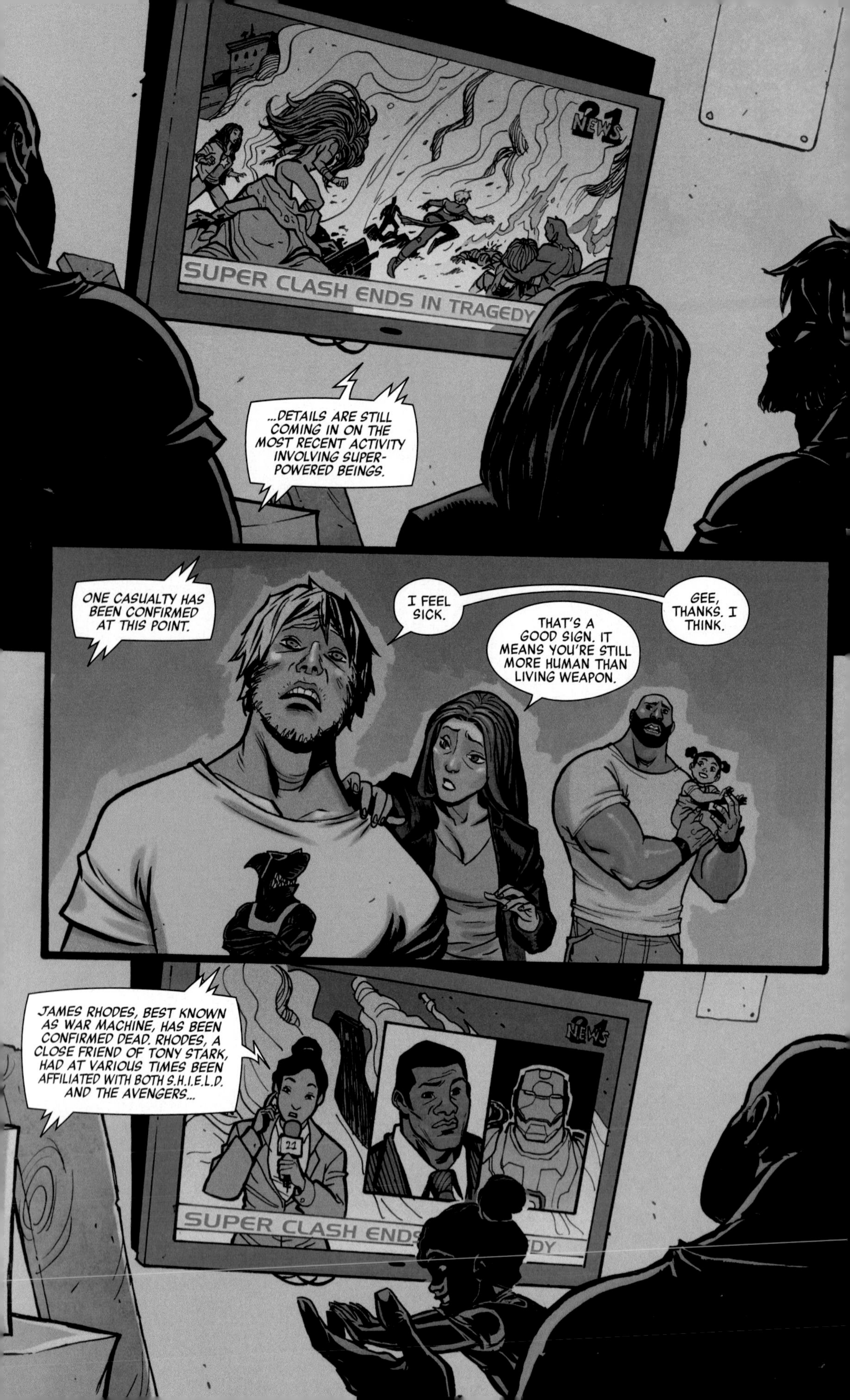
21 NEWS
SUPER CLASH ENDS IN TRAGEDY
...DETAILS ARE STILL COMING IN ON THE MOST RECENT ACTIVITY INVOLVING SUPER-POWERED BEINGS.
ONE CASUALTY HAS BEEN CONFIRMED AT THIS POINT.
I FEEL SICK.
THAT'S A GOOD SIGN. IT MEANS YOU'RE STILL MORE HUMAN THAN LIVING WEAPON.
GEE, THANKS. I THINK.
JAMES RHODES, BEST KNOWN AS WAR MACHINE, HAS BEEN CONFIRMED DEAD. RHODES, A CLOSE FRIEND OF TONY STARK, HAD AT VARIOUS TIMES BEEN AFFILIATED WITH BOTH S.H.I.E.L.D. AND THE AVENGERS...
21 NEWS
21
SUPER CLASH ENDS

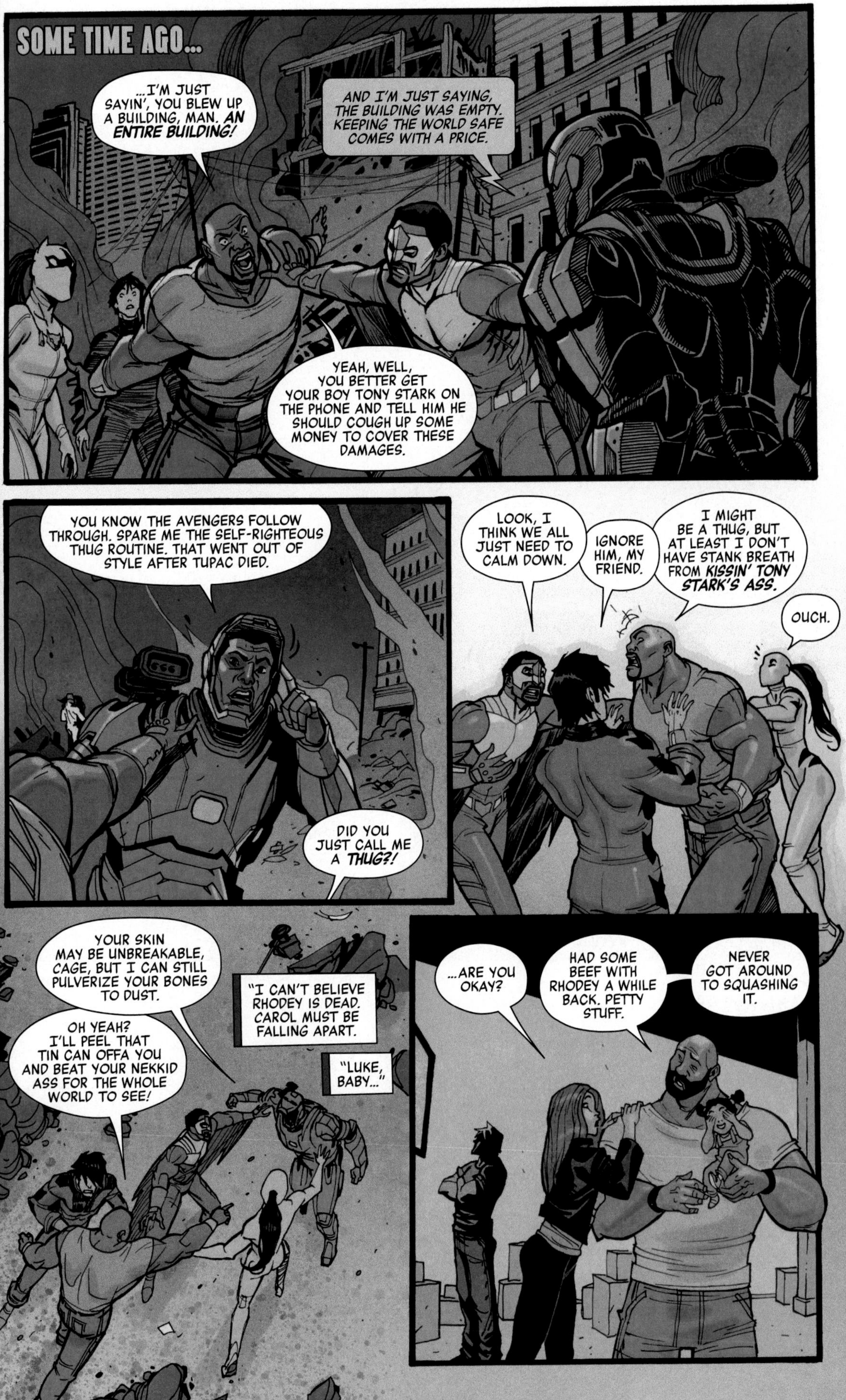
SOME TIME AGO...
...I'M JUST SAYIN', YOU BLEW UP A BUILDING, MAN. AN ENTIRE BUILDING!
AND I'M JUST SAYING, THE BUILDING WAS EMPTY. KEEPING THE WORLD SAFE COMES WITH A PRICE.
YEAH, WELL, YOU BETTER GET YOUR BOY TONY STARK ON THE PHONE AND TELL HIM HE SHOULD COUGH UP SOME MONEY TO COVER THESE DAMAGES.
YOU KNOW THE AVENGERS FOLLOW THROUGH. SPARE ME THE SELF-RIGHTEOUS THUG ROUTINE. THAT WENT OUT OF STYLE AFTER TUPAC DIED.
DID YOU JUST CALL ME A THUG?!
LOOK, I THINK WE ALL JUST NEED TO CALM DOWN.
IGNORE HIM, MY FRIEND.
I MIGHT BE A THUG, BUT AT LEAST I DON'T HAVE STANK BREATH FROM KISSIN' TONY STARK'S ASS.
OUCH.
YOUR SKIN MAY BE UNBREAKABLE, CAGE, BUT I CAN STILL PULVERIZE YOUR BONES TO DUST.
OH YEAH? I'LL PEEL THAT TIN CAN OFFA YOU AND BEAT YOUR NEKKID ASS FOR THE WHOLE WORLD TO SEE!
"I CAN'T BELIEVE RHODEY IS DEAD. CAROL MUST BE FALLING APART.
"LUKE, BABY..."
...ARE YOU OKAY?
HAD SOME BEEF WITH RHODEY A WHILE BACK. PETTY STUFF.
NEVER GOT AROUND TO SQUASHING IT.

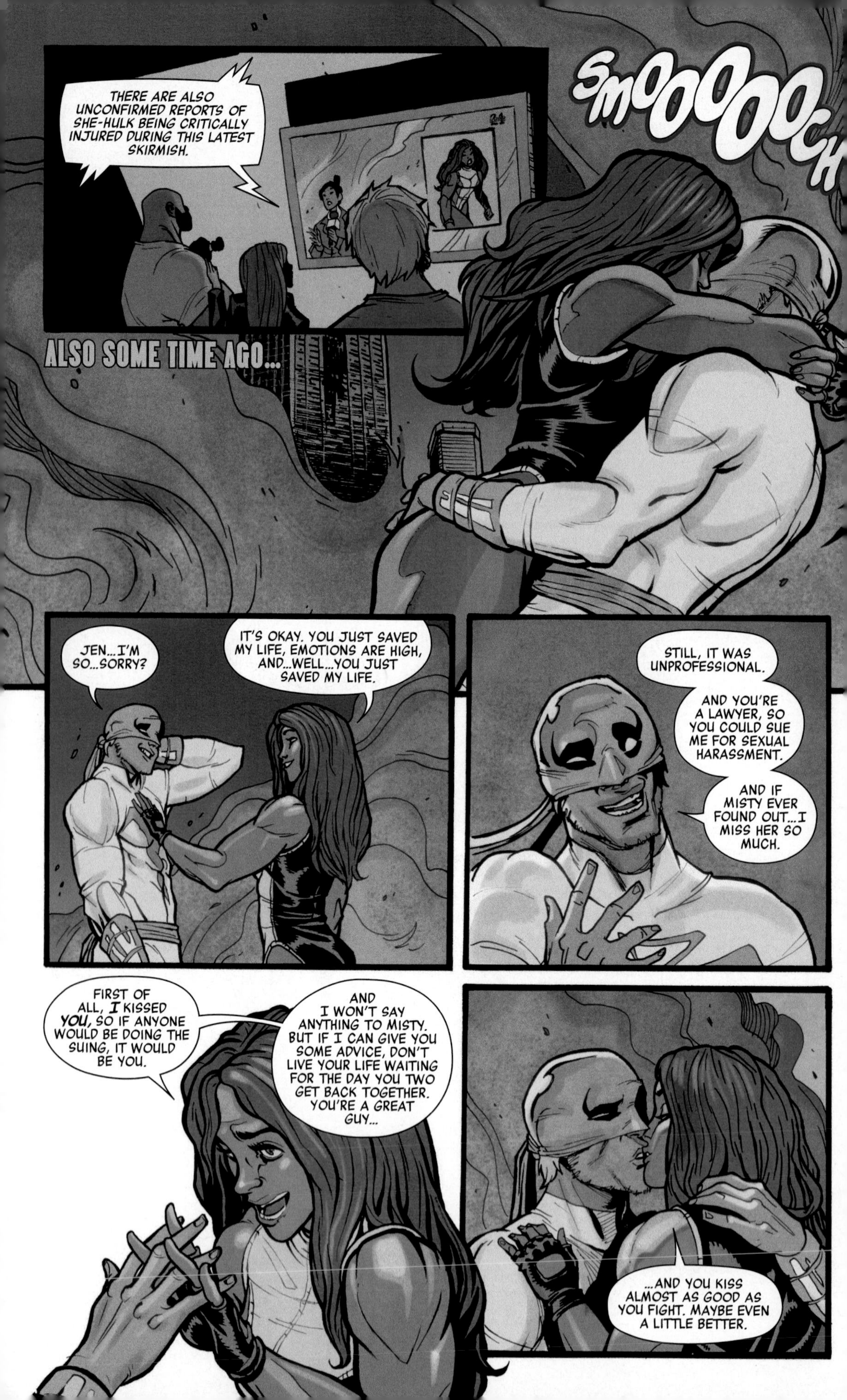

THERE ARE ALSO UNCONFIRMED REPORTS OF SHE-HULK BEING CRITICALLY INJURED DURING THIS LATEST SKIRMISH.
SMOOOOOOCH
ALSO SOME TIME AGO...
JEN...I'M SO...SORRY?
IT'S OKAY. YOU JUST SAVED MY LIFE, EMOTIONS ARE HIGH, AND...WELL...YOU JUST SAVED MY LIFE.
STILL, IT WAS UNPROFESSIONAL.
AND YOU'RE A LAWYER, SO YOU COULD SUE ME FOR SEXUAL HARASSMENT.
AND IF MISTY EVER FOUND OUT...I MISS HER SO MUCH.
FIRST OF ALL, I KISSED YOU, SO IF ANYONE WOULD BE DOING THE SUING, IT WOULD BE YOU.
AND I WON'T SAY ANYTHING TO MISTY. BUT IF I CAN GIVE YOU SOME ADVICE, DON'T LIVE YOUR LIFE WAITING FOR THE DAY YOU TWO GET BACK TOGETHER. YOU'RE A GREAT GUY...
...AND YOU KISS ALMOST AS GOOD AS YOU FIGHT. MAYBE EVEN A LITTLE BETTER.

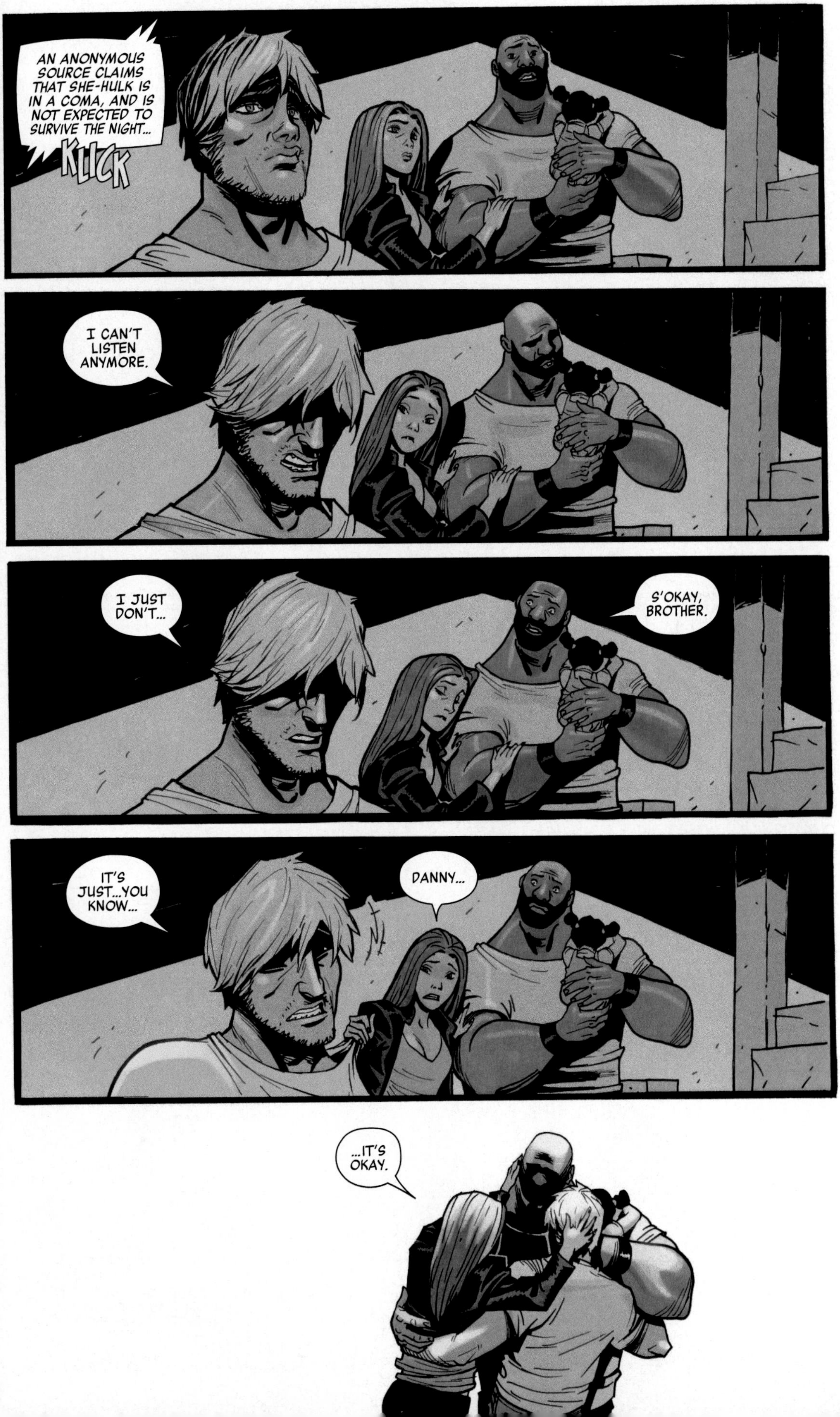
AN ANONYMOUS SOURCE CLAIMS THAT SHE-HULK IS IN A COMA, AND IS NOT EXPECTED TO SURVIVE THE NIGHT...
KLICK
I CAN'T LISTEN ANYMORE.
I JUST DON'T...
S'OKAY, BROTHER.
IT'S JUST...YOU KNOW...
DANNY...
...IT'S OKAY.

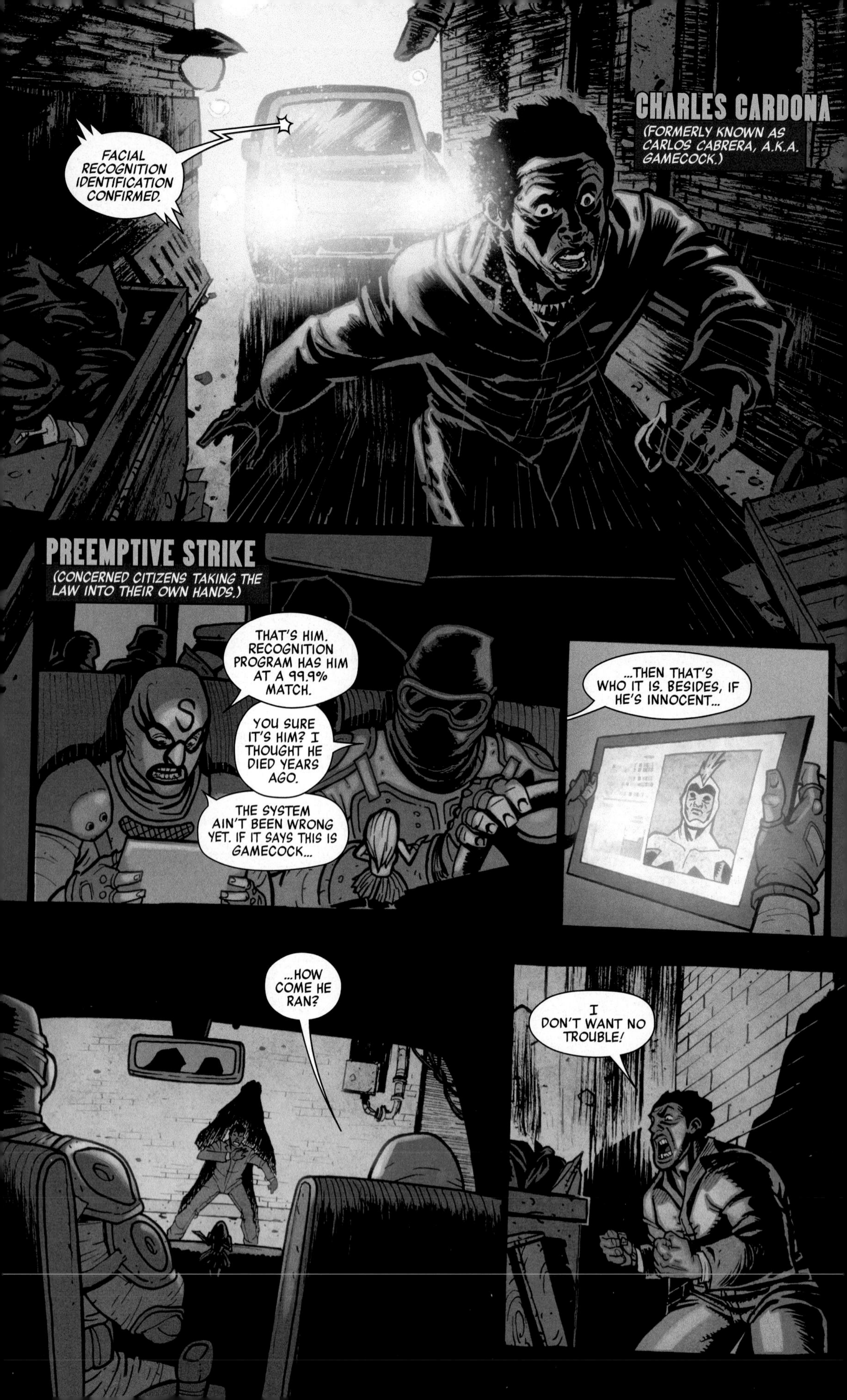
CHARLES CARDONA
(FORMERLY KNOWN AS CARLOS CABRERA, A.K.A. GAMECOCK.)
FACIAL RECOGNITION IDENTIFICATION CONFIRMED.
PREEMPTIVE STRIKE
(CONCERNED CITIZENS TAKING THE LAW INTO THEIR OWN HANDS.)
THAT'S HIM. RECOGNITION PROGRAM HAS HIM AT A 99.9% MATCH.
YOU SURE IT'S HIM? I THOUGHT HE DIED YEARS AGO.
THE SYSTEM AIN'T BEEN WRONG YET. IF IT SAYS THIS IS GAMECOCK...
...THEN THAT'S WHO IT IS. BESIDES, IF HE'S INNOCENT...
...HOW COME HE RAN?
I DON'T WANT NO TROUBLE!

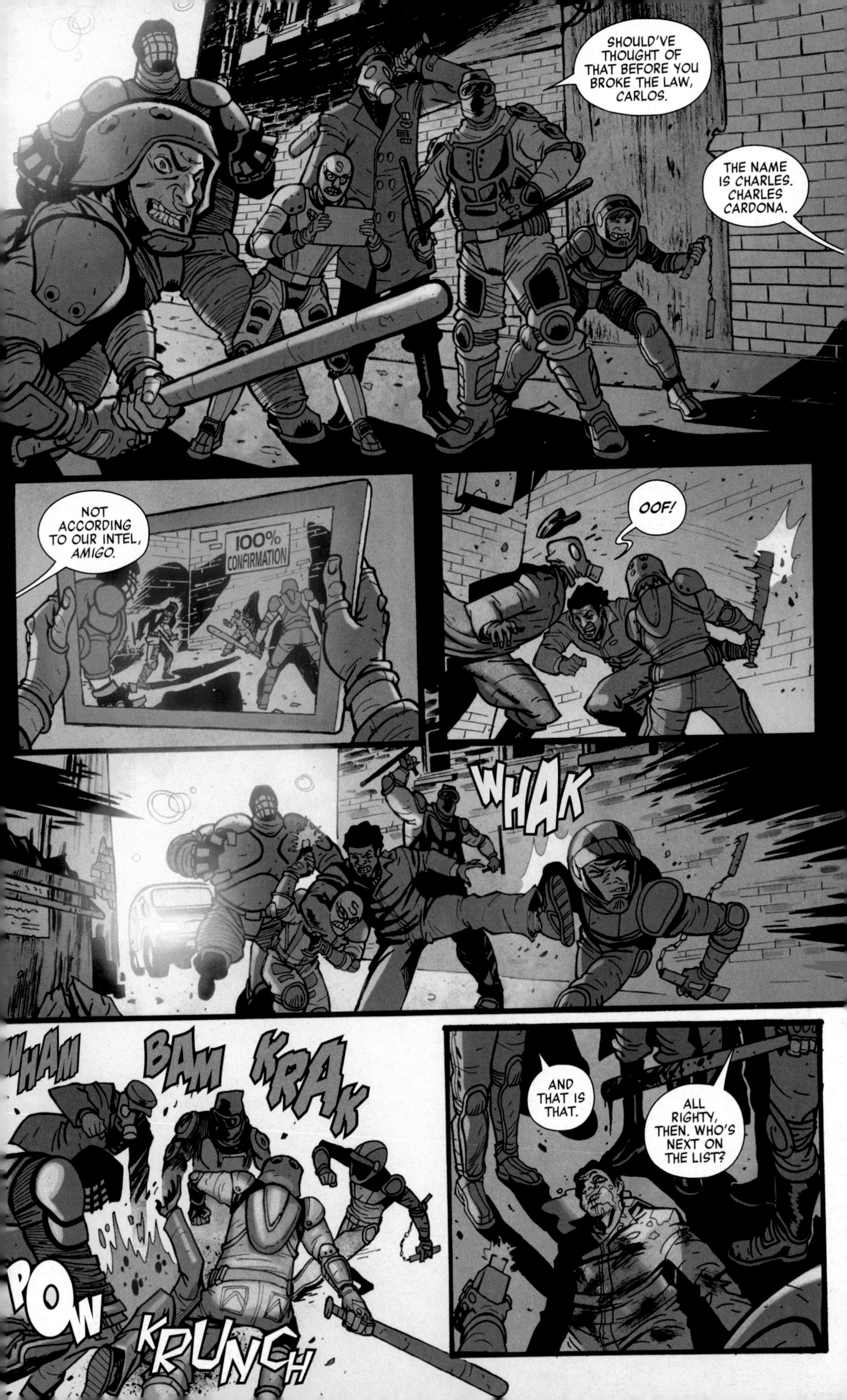

SHOULD'VE THOUGHT OF THAT BEFORE YOU BROKE THE LAW, CARLOS.
THE NAME IS CHARLES. CHARLES CARDONA.
NOT ACCORDING TO OUR INTEL, AMIGO.
100% CONFIRMATION
OOF!
WHAK
WHAM
BAM
KRAK
POW
KRUNCH
AND THAT IS THAT.
ALL RIGHTY, THEN. WHO'S NEXT ON THE LIST?

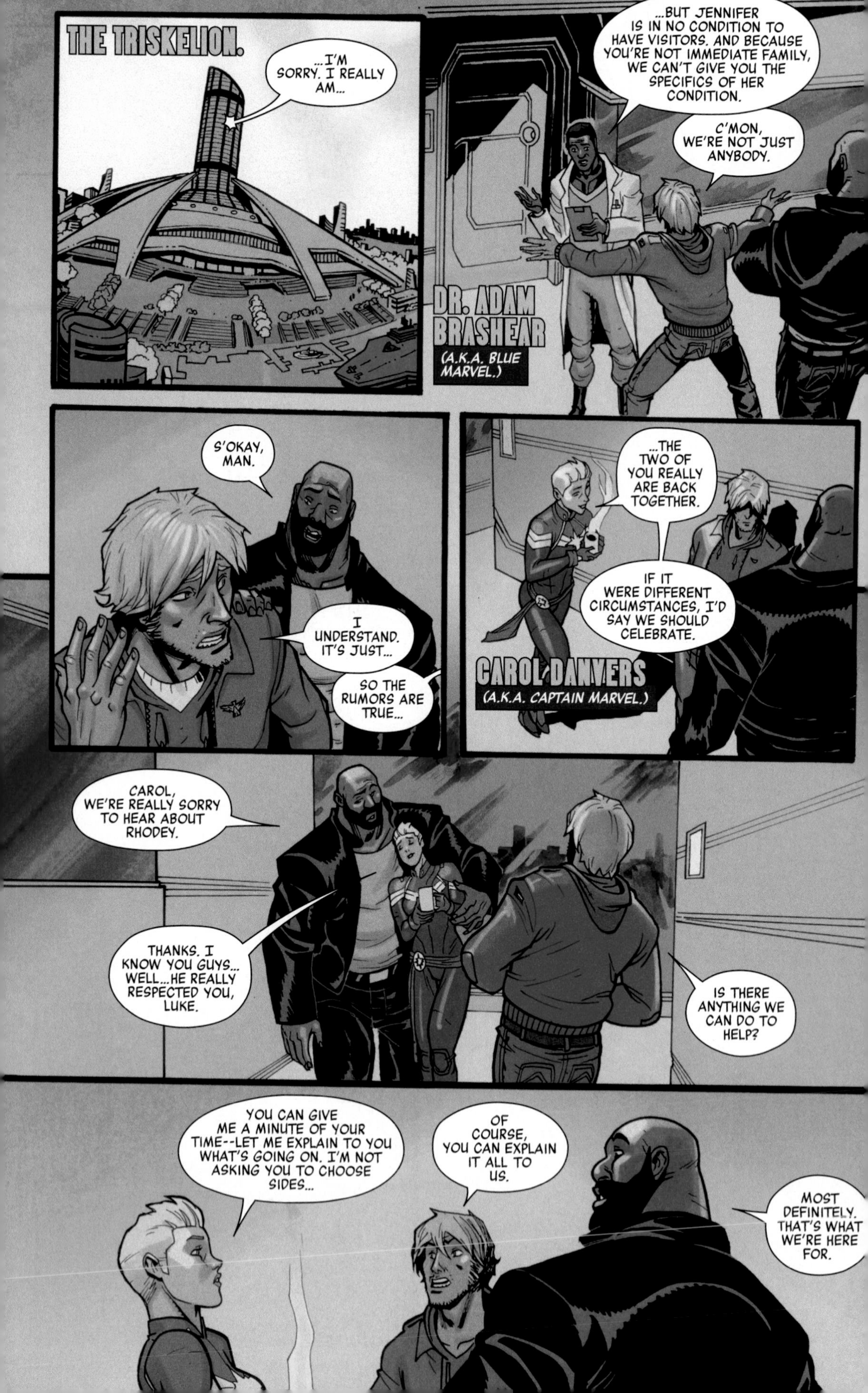
THE TRISKELION.
...I'M SORRY. I REALLY AM...
...BUT JENNIFER IS IN NO CONDITION TO HAVE VISITORS. AND BECAUSE YOU'RE NOT IMMEDIATE FAMILY, WE CAN'T GIVE YOU THE SPECIFICS OF HER CONDITION.
C'MON, WE'RE NOT JUST ANYBODY.
DR. ADAM BRASHEAR
(A.K.A. BLUE MARVEL.)
S'OKAY, MAN.
I UNDERSTAND. IT'S JUST...
SO THE RUMORS ARE TRUE...
...THE TWO OF YOU REALLY ARE BACK TOGETHER.
IF IT WERE DIFFERENT CIRCUMSTANCES, I'D SAY WE SHOULD CELEBRATE.
CAROL DANVERS
(A.K.A. CAPTAIN MARVEL.)
CAROL, WE'RE REALLY SORRY TO HEAR ABOUT RHODEY.
THANKS. I KNOW YOU GUYS... WELL...HE REALLY RESPECTED YOU, LUKE.
IS THERE ANYTHING WE CAN DO TO HELP?
YOU CAN GIVE ME A MINUTE OF YOUR TIME--LET ME EXPLAIN TO YOU WHAT'S GOING ON. I'M NOT ASKING YOU TO CHOOSE SIDES...
OF COURSE, YOU CAN EXPLAIN IT ALL TO US.
MOST DEFINITELY. THAT'S WHAT WE'RE HERE FOR.

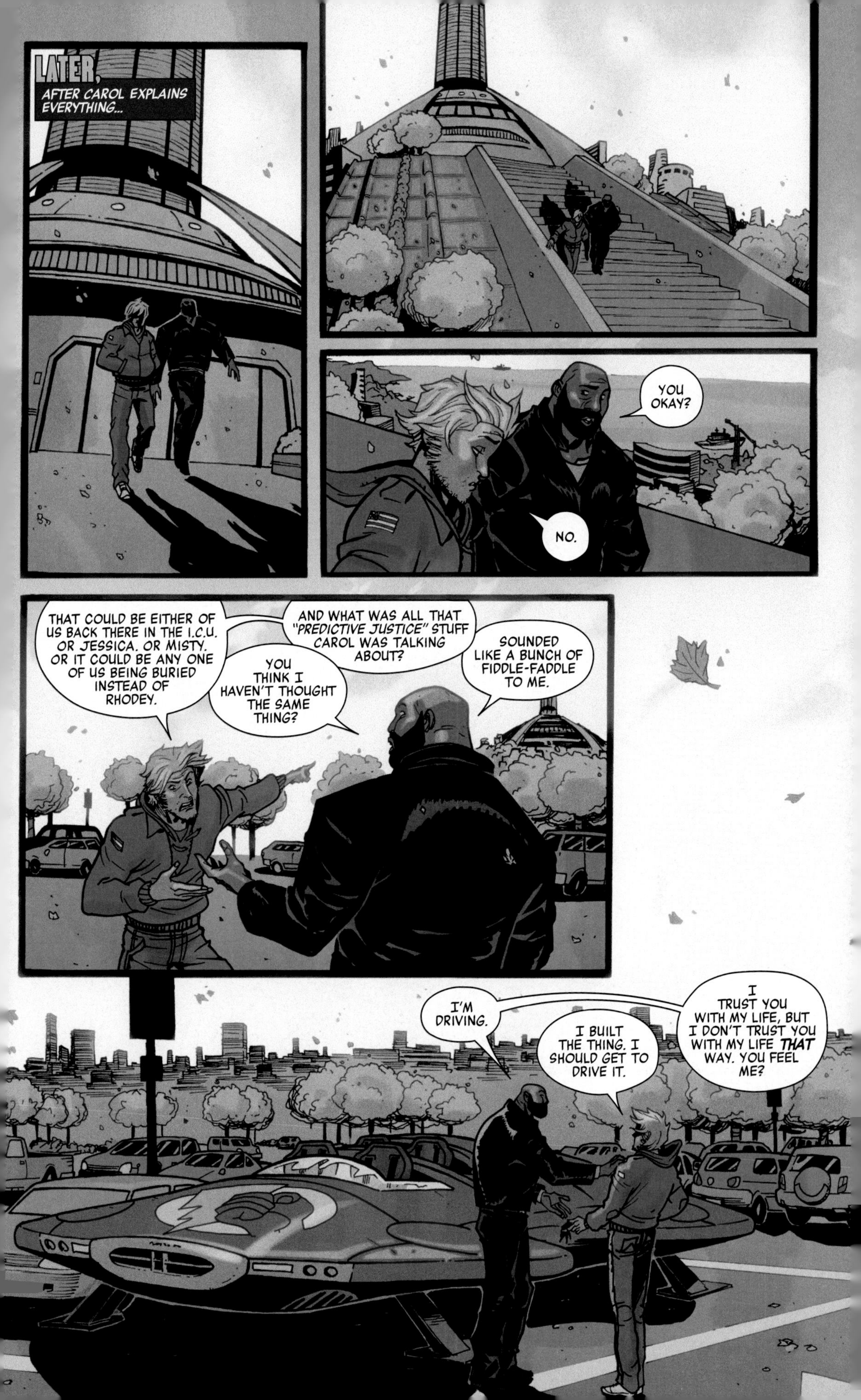
LATER,
AFTER CAROL EXPLAINS EVERYTHING...
YOU OKAY?
NO.
THAT COULD BE EITHER OF US BACK THERE IN THE I.C.U. OR JESSICA. OR MISTY. OR IT COULD BE ANY ONE OF US BEING BURIED INSTEAD OF RHODEY.
YOU THINK I HAVEN'T THOUGHT THE SAME THING?
AND WHAT WAS ALL THAT "PREDICTIVE JUSTICE" STUFF CAROL WAS TALKING ABOUT?
SOUNDED LIKE A BUNCH OF FIDDLE-FADDLE TO ME.
I'M DRIVING.
I BUILT THE THING. I SHOULD GET TO DRIVE IT.
I TRUST YOU WITH MY LIFE, BUT I DON'T TRUST YOU WITH MY LIFE *THAT* WAY. YOU FEEL ME?

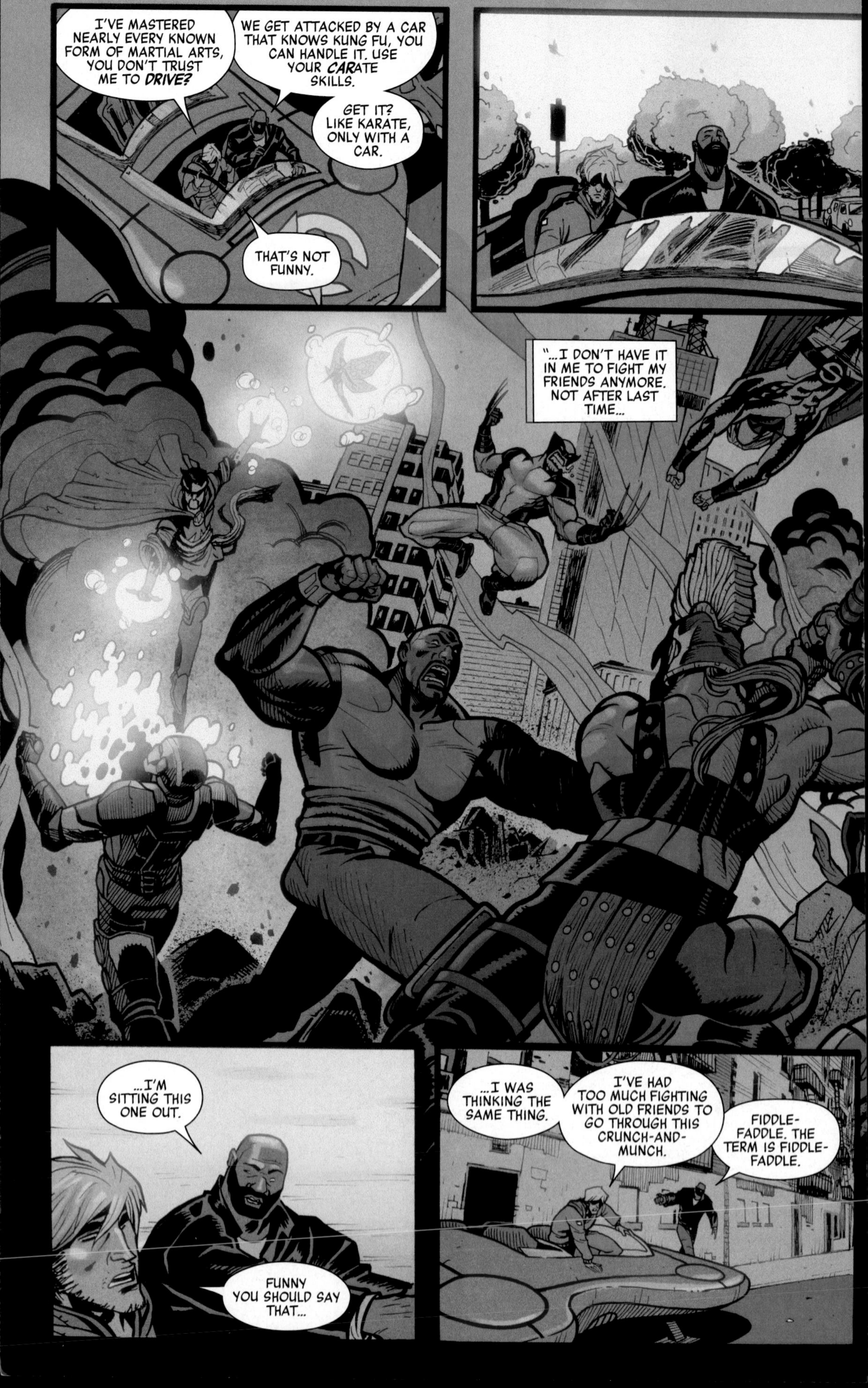
I'VE MASTERED NEARLY EVERY KNOWN FORM OF MARTIAL ARTS, YOU DON'T TRUST ME TO DRIVE?
WE GET ATTACKED BY A CAR THAT KNOWS KUNG FU, YOU CAN HANDLE IT. USE YOUR CARATE SKILLS.
GET IT? LIKE KARATE, ONLY WITH A CAR.
THAT'S NOT FUNNY.
"...I DON'T HAVE IT IN ME TO FIGHT MY FRIENDS ANYMORE. NOT AFTER LAST TIME...
...I'M SITTING THIS ONE OUT.
FUNNY YOU SHOULD SAY THAT...
...I WAS THINKING THE SAME THING.
I'VE HAD TOO MUCH FIGHTING WITH OLD FRIENDS TO GO THROUGH THIS CRUNCH-AND-MUNCH.
FIDDLE-FADDLE. THE TERM IS FIDDLE-FADDLE.

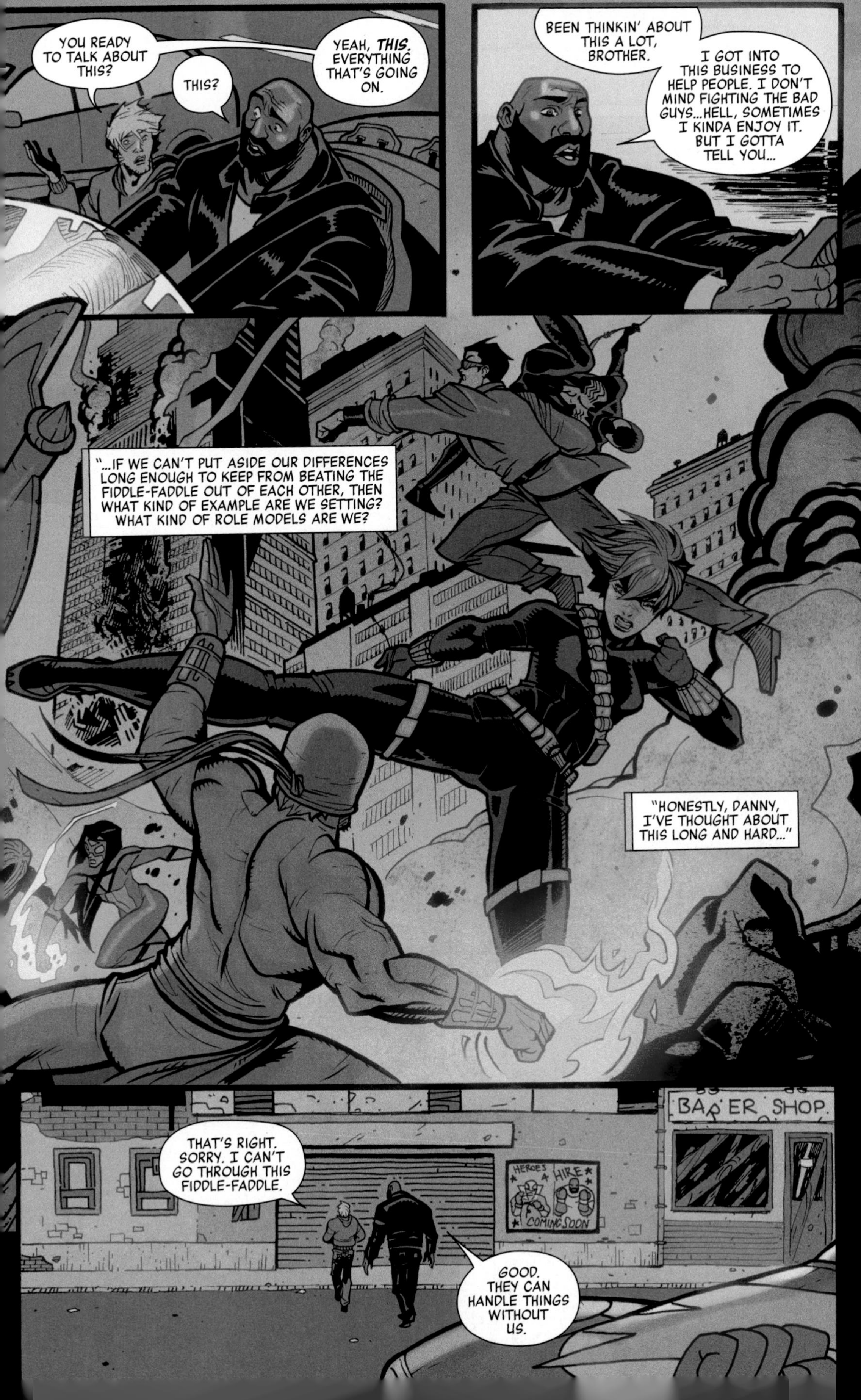
YOU READY TO TALK ABOUT THIS?
THIS?
YEAH, **THIS.** EVERYTHING THAT'S GOING ON.
BEEN THINKIN' ABOUT THIS A LOT, BROTHER.
I GOT INTO THIS BUSINESS TO HELP PEOPLE. I DON'T MIND FIGHTING THE BAD GUYS...HELL, SOMETIMES I KINDA ENJOY IT. BUT I GOTTA TELL YOU...
"...IF WE CAN'T PUT ASIDE OUR DIFFERENCES LONG ENOUGH TO KEEP FROM BEATING THE FIDDLE-FADDLE OUT OF EACH OTHER, THEN WHAT KIND OF EXAMPLE ARE WE SETTING? WHAT KIND OF ROLE MODELS ARE WE?
"HONESTLY, DANNY, I'VE THOUGHT ABOUT THIS LONG AND HARD..."
BA ER SHOP
HEROES 4 HIRE
COMING SOON
THAT'S RIGHT. SORRY. I CAN'T GO THROUGH THIS FIDDLE-FADDLE.
GOOD. THEY CAN HANDLE THINGS WITHOUT US.

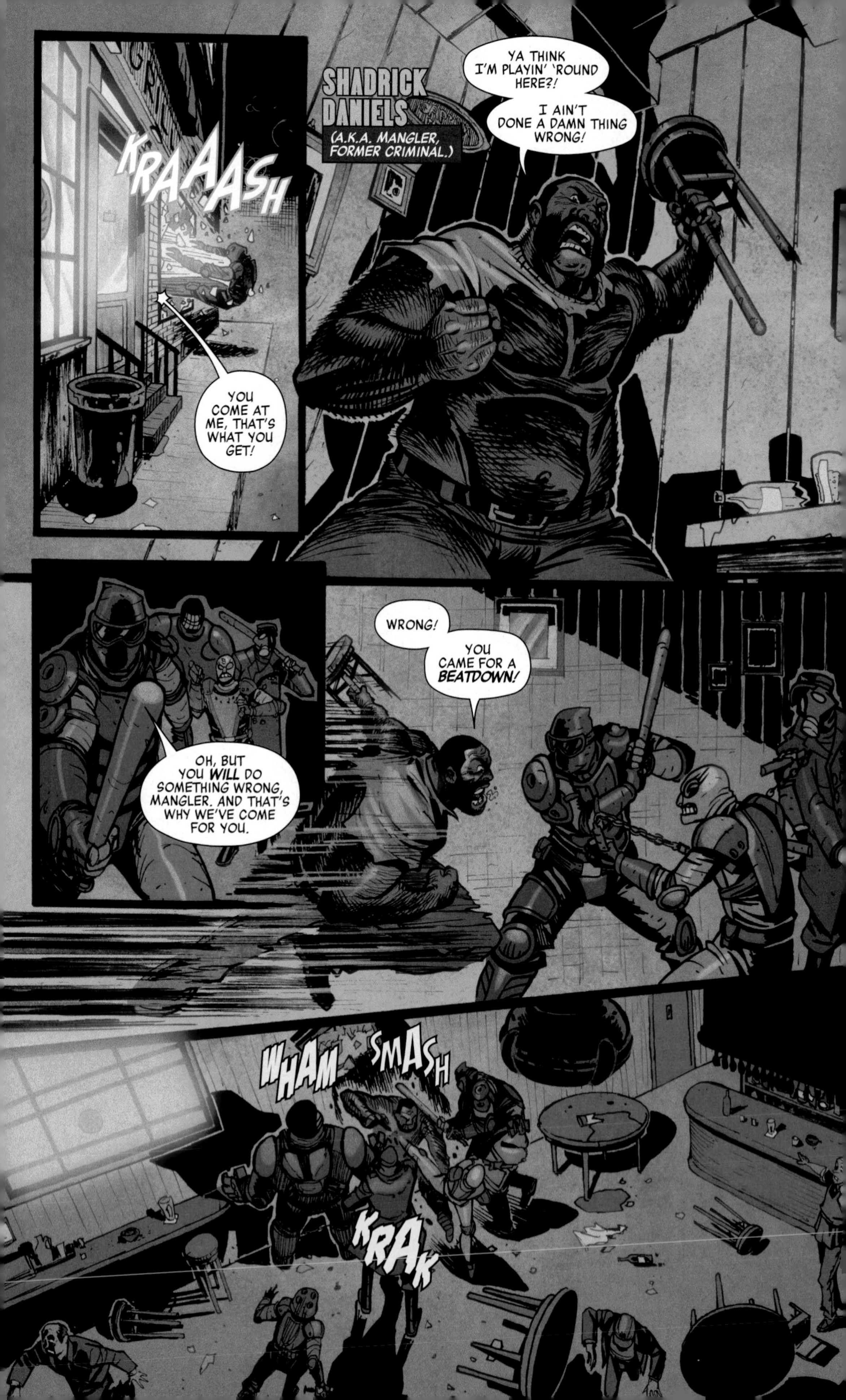
KRAAASH
YOU COME AT ME, THAT'S WHAT YOU GET!
SHADRICK DANIELS
(A.K.A. MANGLER, FORMER CRIMINAL.)
YA THINK I'M PLAYIN' 'ROUND HERE?!
I AIN'T DONE A DAMN THING WRONG!
OH, BUT YOU WILL DO SOMETHING WRONG, MANGLER. AND THAT'S WHY WE'VE COME FOR YOU.
WRONG!
YOU CAME FOR A BEATDOWN!
WHAM
SMASH
KRAK

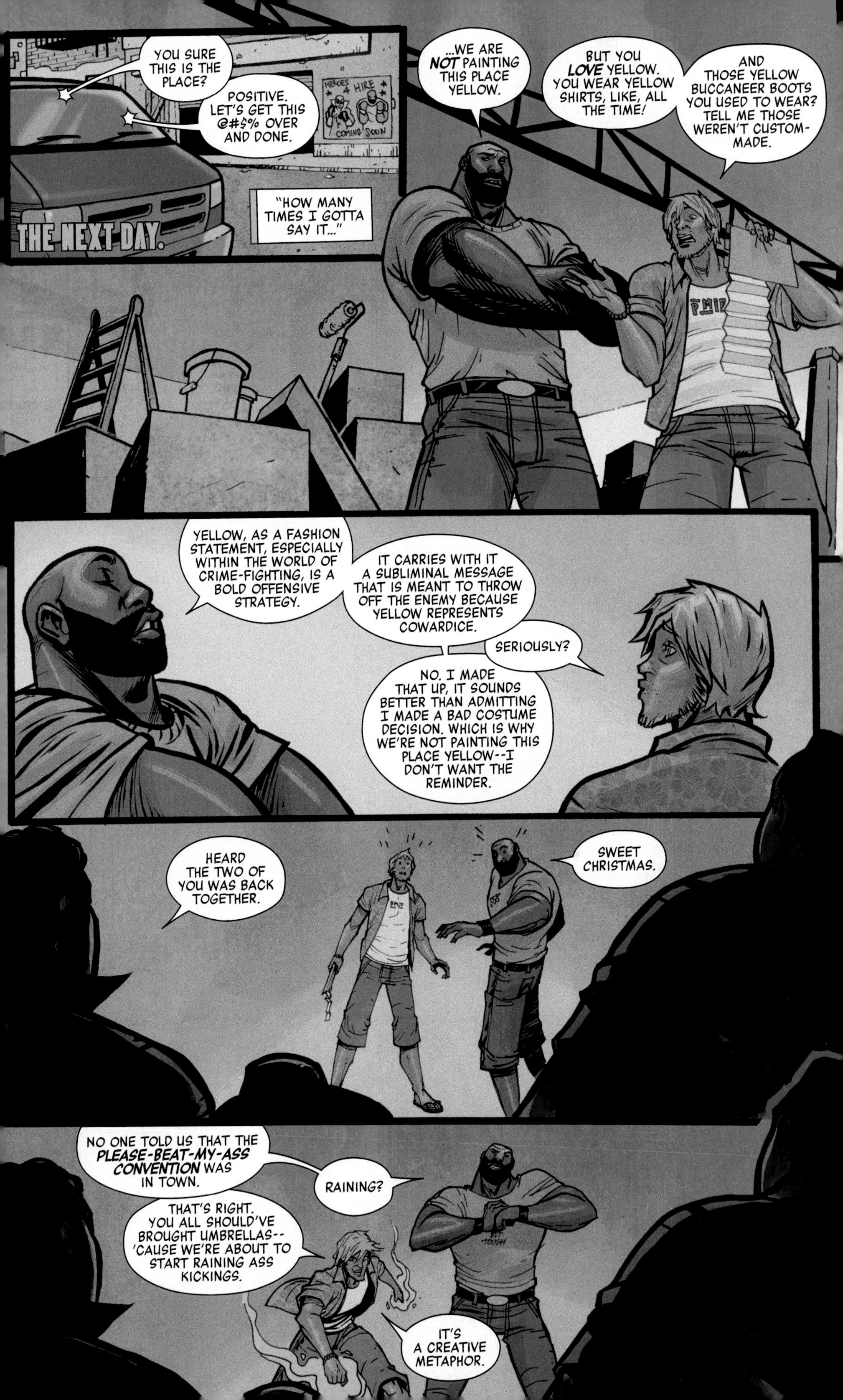

YOU SURE THIS IS THE PLACE?
POSITIVE. LET'S GET THIS @#$% OVER AND DONE.
HEROES 4 HIRE
COMING SOON
THE NEXT DAY.
"HOW MANY TIMES I GOTTA SAY IT..."
...WE ARE NOT PAINTING THIS PLACE YELLOW.
BUT YOU LOVE YELLOW. YOU WEAR YELLOW SHIRTS, LIKE, ALL THE TIME!
AND THOSE YELLOW BUCCANEER BOOTS YOU USED TO WEAR? TELL ME THOSE WEREN'T CUSTOM-MADE.
YELLOW, AS A FASHION STATEMENT, ESPECIALLY WITHIN THE WORLD OF CRIME-FIGHTING, IS A BOLD OFFENSIVE STRATEGY.
IT CARRIES WITH IT A SUBLIMINAL MESSAGE THAT IS MEANT TO THROW OFF THE ENEMY BECAUSE YELLOW REPRESENTS COWARDICE.
SERIOUSLY?
NO. I MADE THAT UP, IT SOUNDS BETTER THAN ADMITTING I MADE A BAD COSTUME DECISION. WHICH IS WHY WE'RE NOT PAINTING THIS PLACE YELLOW--I DON'T WANT THE REMINDER.
HEARD THE TWO OF YOU WAS BACK TOGETHER.
SWEET CHRISTMAS.
NO ONE TOLD US THAT THE PLEASE-BEAT-MY-ASS CONVENTION WAS IN TOWN.
RAINING?
THAT'S RIGHT. YOU ALL SHOULD'VE BROUGHT UMBRELLAS-- 'CAUSE WE'RE ABOUT TO START RAINING ASS KICKINGS.
IT'S A CREATIVE METAPHOR.

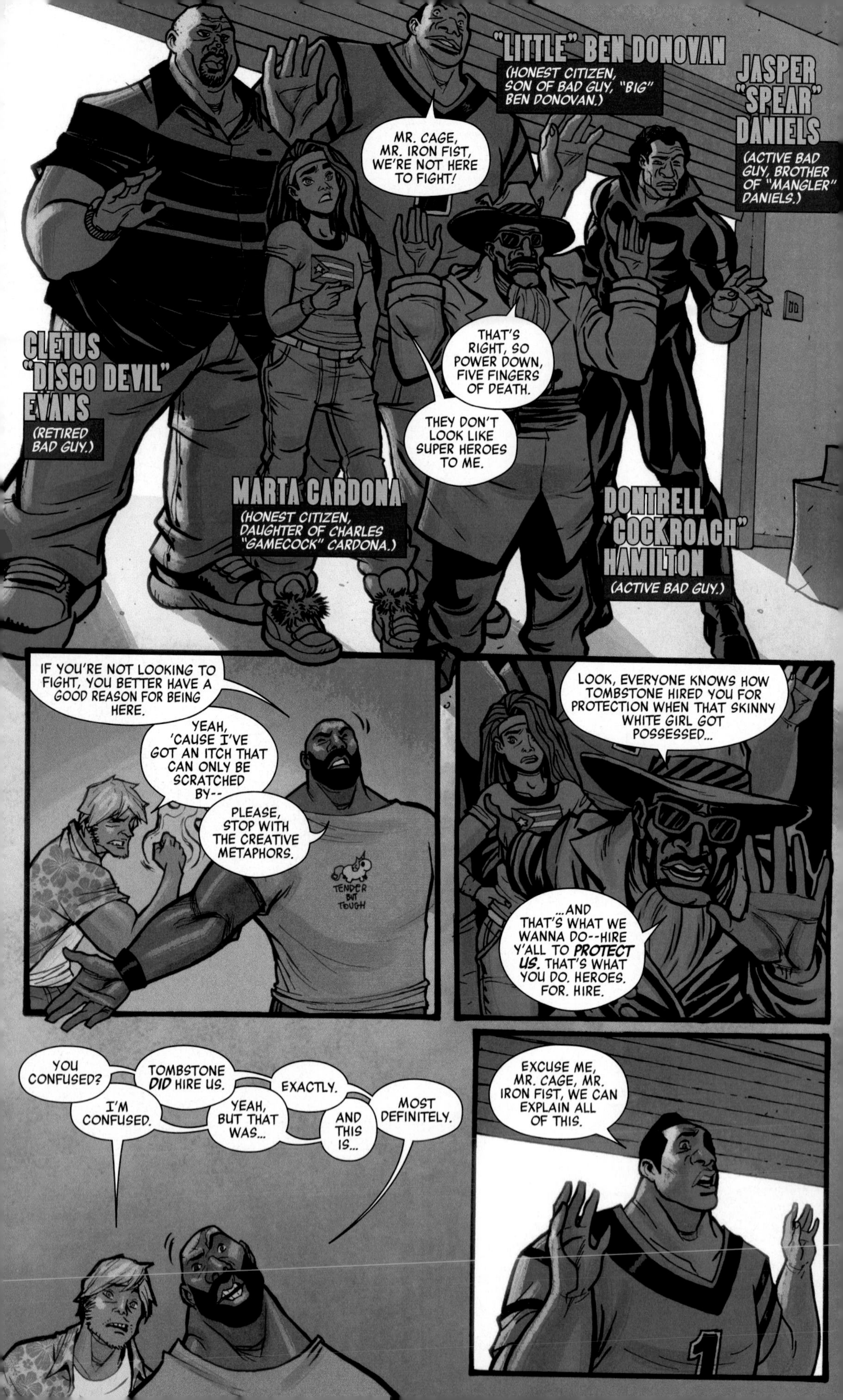
"LITTLE" BEN DONOVAN
(HONEST CITIZEN, SON OF BAD GUY, "BIG" BEN DONOVAN.)
JASPER "SPEAR" DANIELS
(ACTIVE BAD GUY, BROTHER OF "MANGLER" DANIELS.)
MR. CAGE, MR. IRON FIST, WE'RE NOT HERE TO FIGHT!
CLETUS "DISCO DEVIL" EVANS
(RETIRED BAD GUY.)
THAT'S RIGHT, SO POWER DOWN, FIVE FINGERS OF DEATH.
THEY DON'T LOOK LIKE SUPER HEROES TO ME.
MARTA CARDONA
(HONEST CITIZEN, DAUGHTER OF CHARLES "GAMECOCK" CARDONA.)
DONTRELL "COCKROACH" HAMILTON
(ACTIVE BAD GUY.)
IF YOU'RE NOT LOOKING TO FIGHT, YOU BETTER HAVE A GOOD REASON FOR BEING HERE.
YEAH, 'CAUSE I'VE GOT AN ITCH THAT CAN ONLY BE SCRATCHED BY--
PLEASE, STOP WITH THE CREATIVE METAPHORS.
TENDER BUT TOUGH
LOOK, EVERYONE KNOWS HOW TOMBSTONE HIRED YOU FOR PROTECTION WHEN THAT SKINNY WHITE GIRL GOT POSSESSED...
...AND THAT'S WHAT WE WANNA DO--HIRE Y'ALL TO PROTECT US. THAT'S WHAT YOU DO. HEROES. FOR. HIRE.
YOU CONFUSED?
I'M CONFUSED.
TOMBSTONE DID HIRE US.
YEAH, BUT THAT WAS...
EXACTLY.
AND THIS IS...
MOST DEFINITELY.
EXCUSE ME, MR. CAGE, MR. IRON FIST, WE CAN EXPLAIN ALL OF THIS.

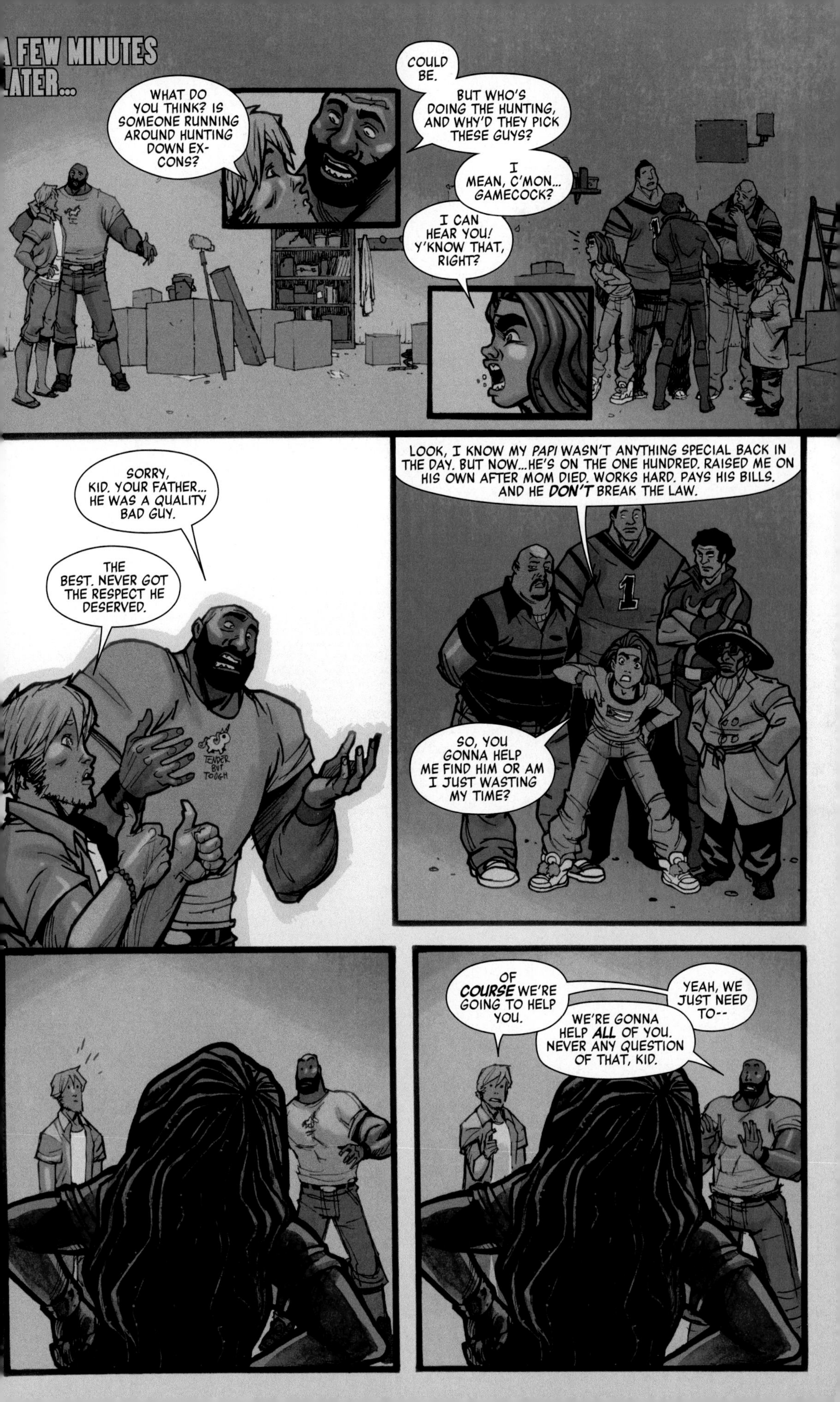
A FEW MINUTES LATER...
WHAT DO YOU THINK? IS SOMEONE RUNNING AROUND HUNTING DOWN EX-CONS?
COULD BE.
BUT WHO'S DOING THE HUNTING, AND WHY'D THEY PICK THESE GUYS?
I MEAN, C'MON... GAMECOCK?
I CAN HEAR YOU! Y'KNOW THAT, RIGHT?
SORRY, KID. YOUR FATHER... HE WAS A QUALITY BAD GUY.
THE BEST. NEVER GOT THE RESPECT HE DESERVED.
TENDER BUT TOUGH
LOOK, I KNOW MY PAPI WASN'T ANYTHING SPECIAL BACK IN THE DAY. BUT NOW...HE'S ON THE ONE HUNDRED. RAISED ME ON HIS OWN AFTER MOM DIED. WORKS HARD. PAYS HIS BILLS. AND HE DON'T BREAK THE LAW.
SO, YOU GONNA HELP ME FIND HIM OR AM I JUST WASTING MY TIME?
OF COURSE WE'RE GOING TO HELP YOU.
YEAH, WE JUST NEED TO--
WE'RE GONNA HELP ALL OF YOU. NEVER ANY QUESTION OF THAT, KID.

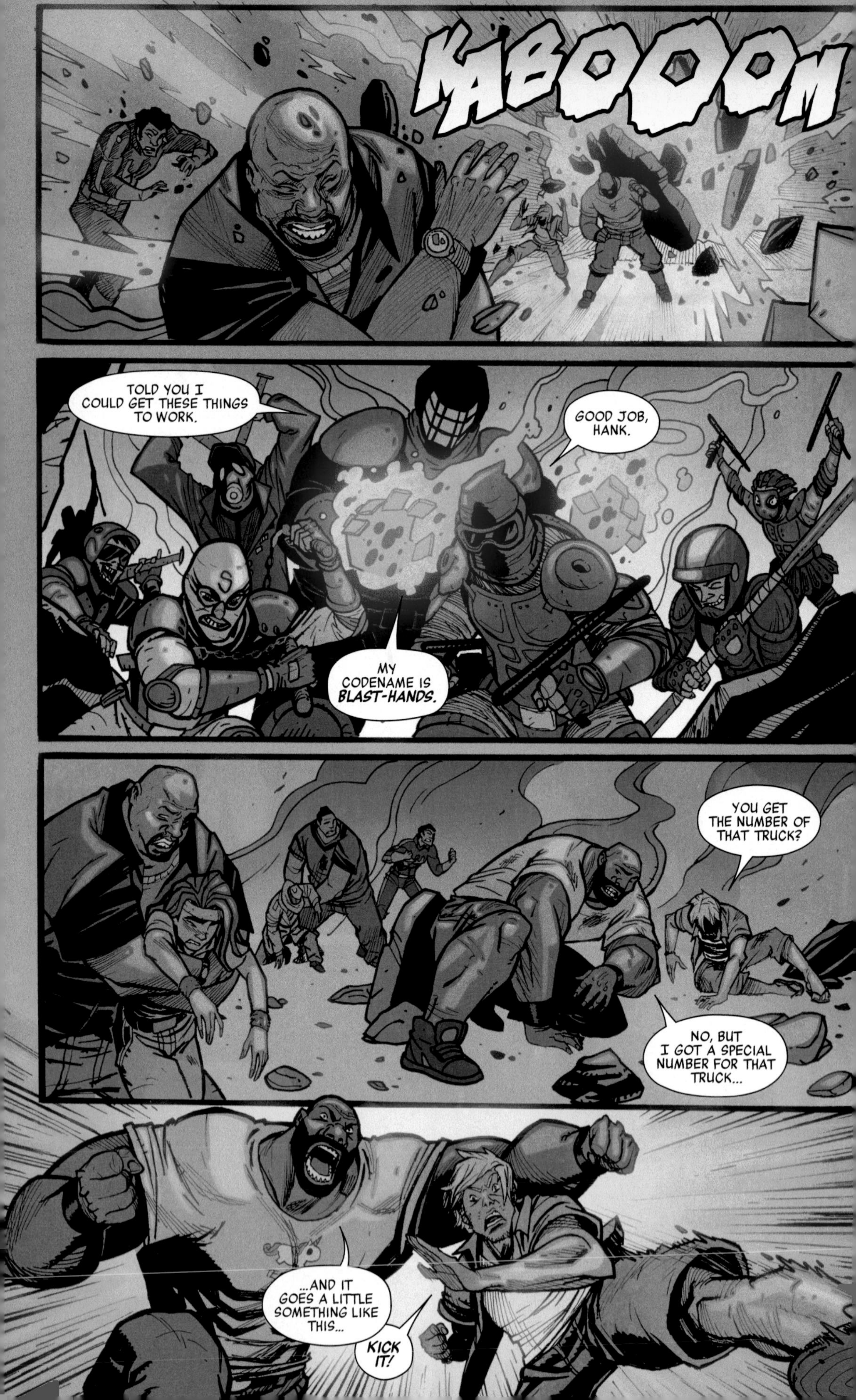
KABOOOM
TOLD YOU I COULD GET THESE THINGS TO WORK.
GOOD JOB, HANK.
MY CODENAME IS BLAST-HANDS.
YOU GET THE NUMBER OF THAT TRUCK?
NO, BUT I GOT A SPECIAL NUMBER FOR THAT TRUCK...
...AND IT GOES A LITTLE SOMETHING LIKE THIS...
KICK IT!

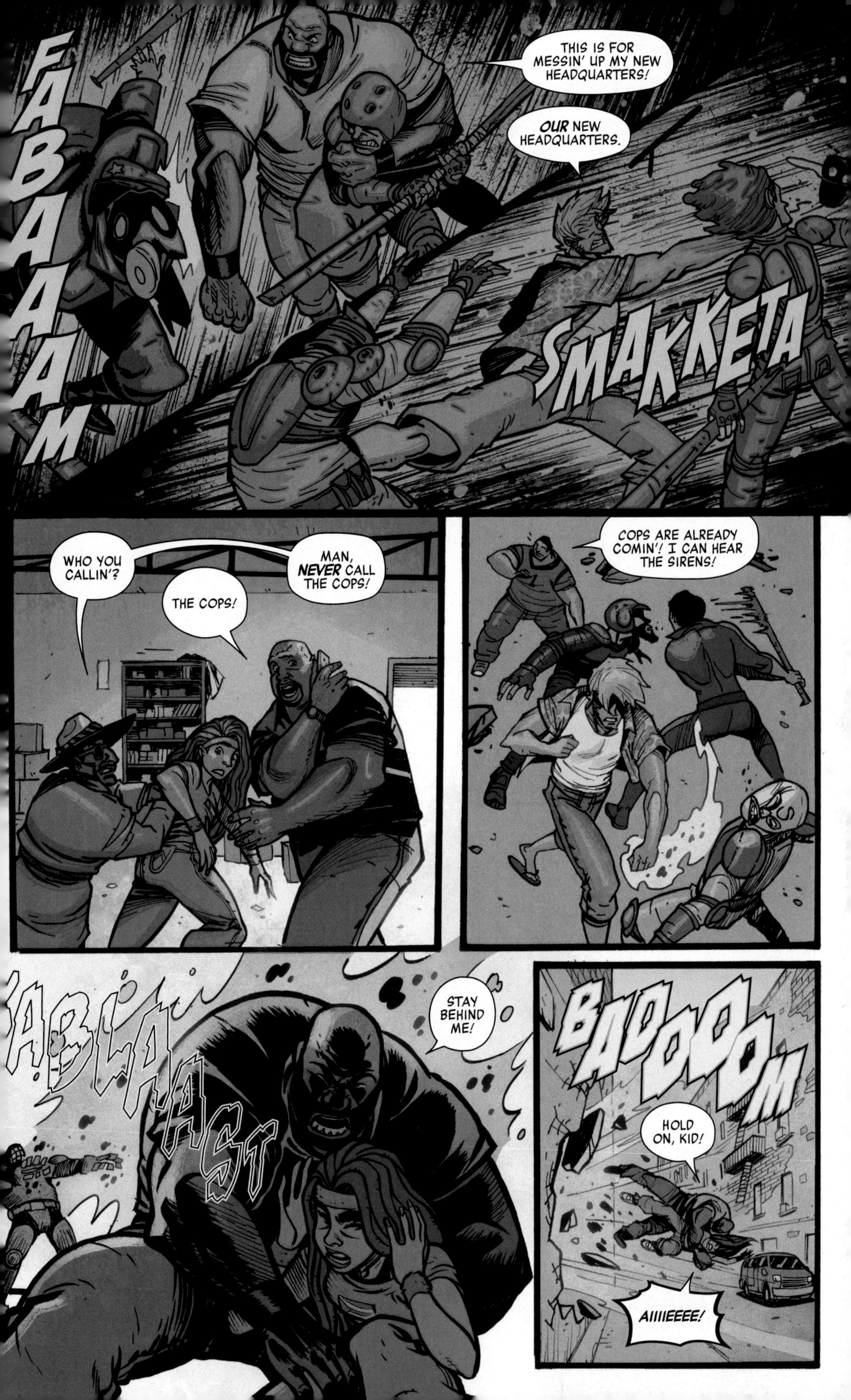
FABAAAAM
THIS IS FOR MESSIN' UP MY NEW HEADQUARTERS!
OUR NEW HEADQUARTERS.
SMAKKETA
WHO YOU CALLIN'?
THE COPS!
MAN, NEVER CALL THE COPS!
COPS ARE ALREADY COMIN'! I CAN HEAR THE SIRENS!
ABLAAAST
STAY BEHIND ME!
BADOOOM
HOLD ON, KID!
AIIIIEEEE!

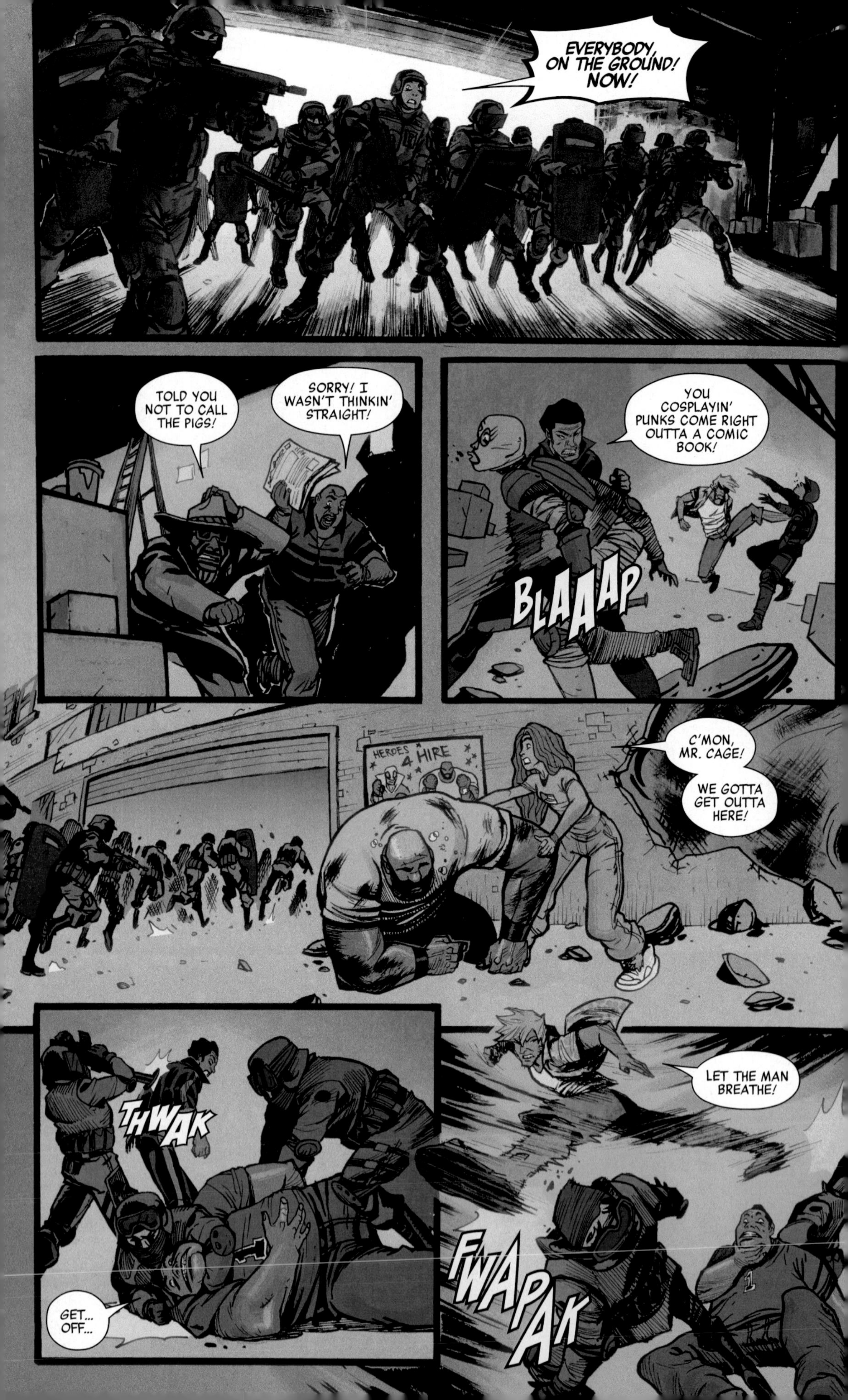
EVERYBODY, ON THE GROUND! NOW!
TOLD YOU NOT TO CALL THE PIGS!
SORRY! I WASN'T THINKIN' STRAIGHT!
YOU COSPLAYIN' PUNKS COME RIGHT OUTTA A COMIC BOOK!
BLAAAP
HEROES 4 HIRE
C'MON, MR. CAGE!
WE GOTTA GET OUTTA HERE!
THWAK
GET... OFF...
LET THE MAN BREATHE!
FWAPAK

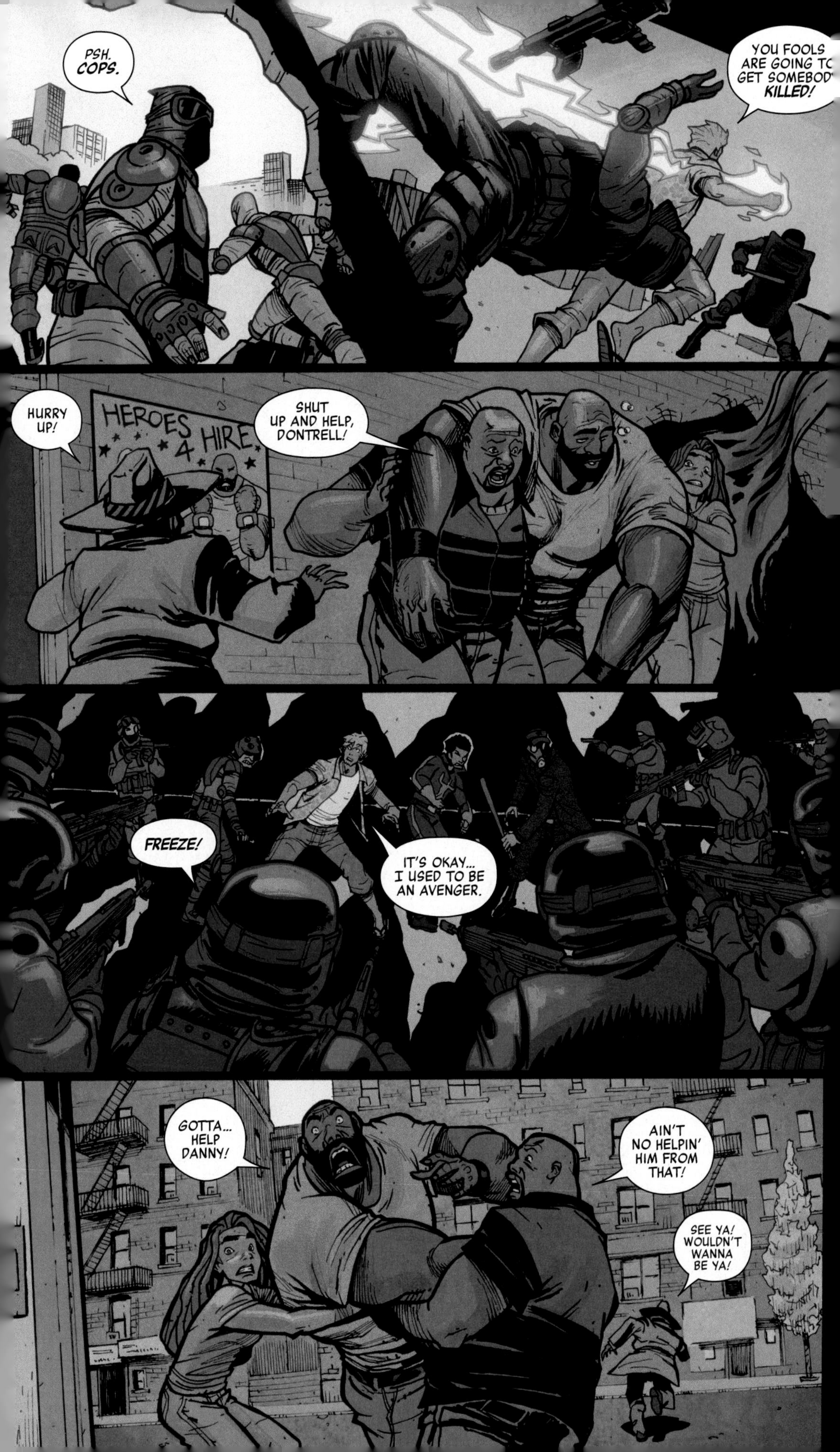
PSH. COPS.
YOU FOOLS ARE GOING TO GET SOMEBODY KILLED!
HURRY UP!
HEROES 4 HIRE
SHUT UP AND HELP, DONTRELL!
FREEZE!
IT'S OKAY... I USED TO BE AN AVENGER.
GOTTA... HELP DANNY!
AIN'T NO HELPIN' HIM FROM THAT!
SEE YA! WOULDN'T WANNA BE YA!

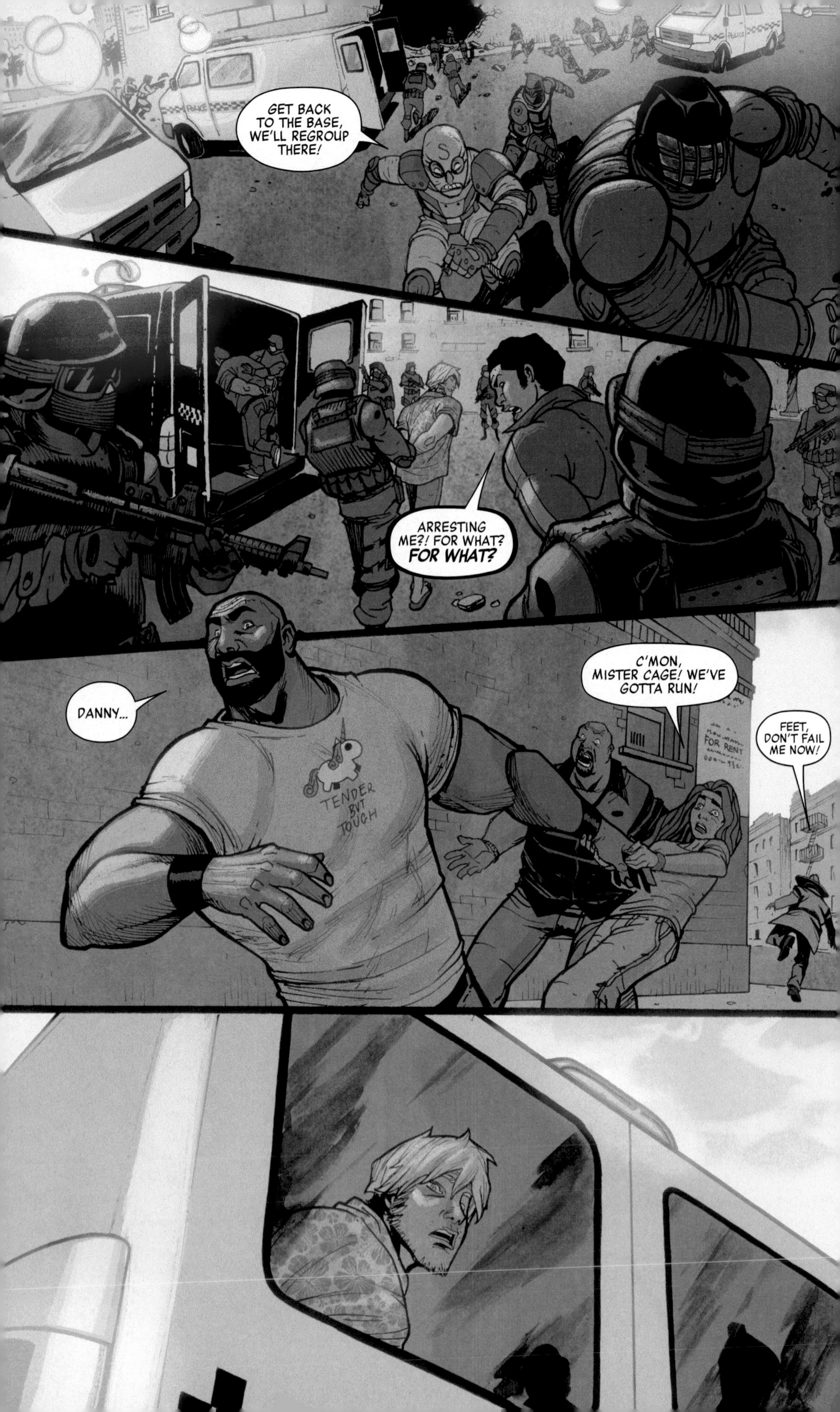
GET BACK TO THE BASE, WE'LL REGROUP THERE!
ARRESTING ME?! FOR WHAT? FOR WHAT?
DANNY...
C'MON, MISTER CAGE! WE'VE GOTTA RUN!
FEET, DON'T FAIL ME NOW!
TENDER BUT TOUGH
FOR RENT

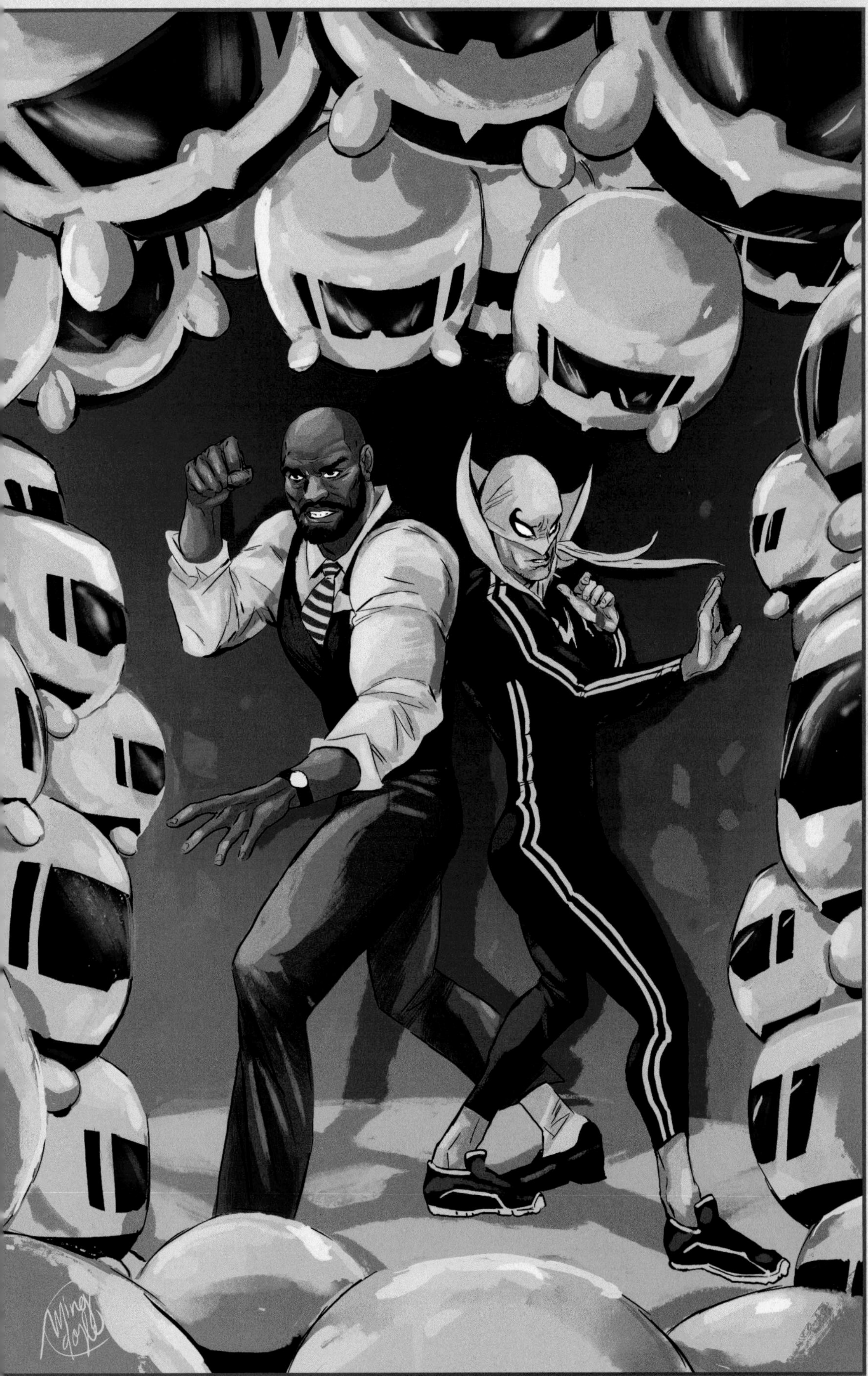
ming doyle

MING DOYLE
7 MARVEL TSUM TSUM TAKEOVER VARIANT

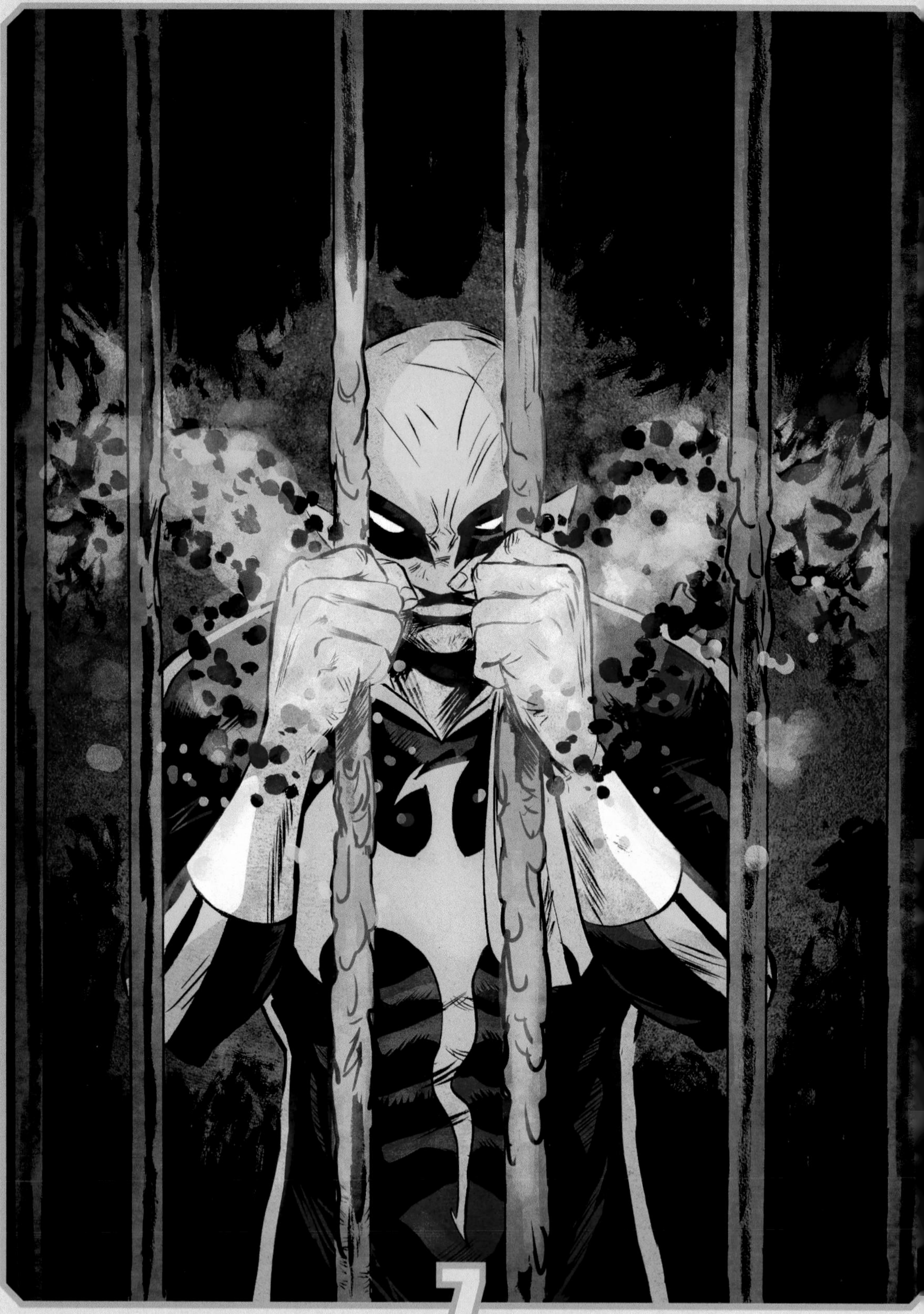

7

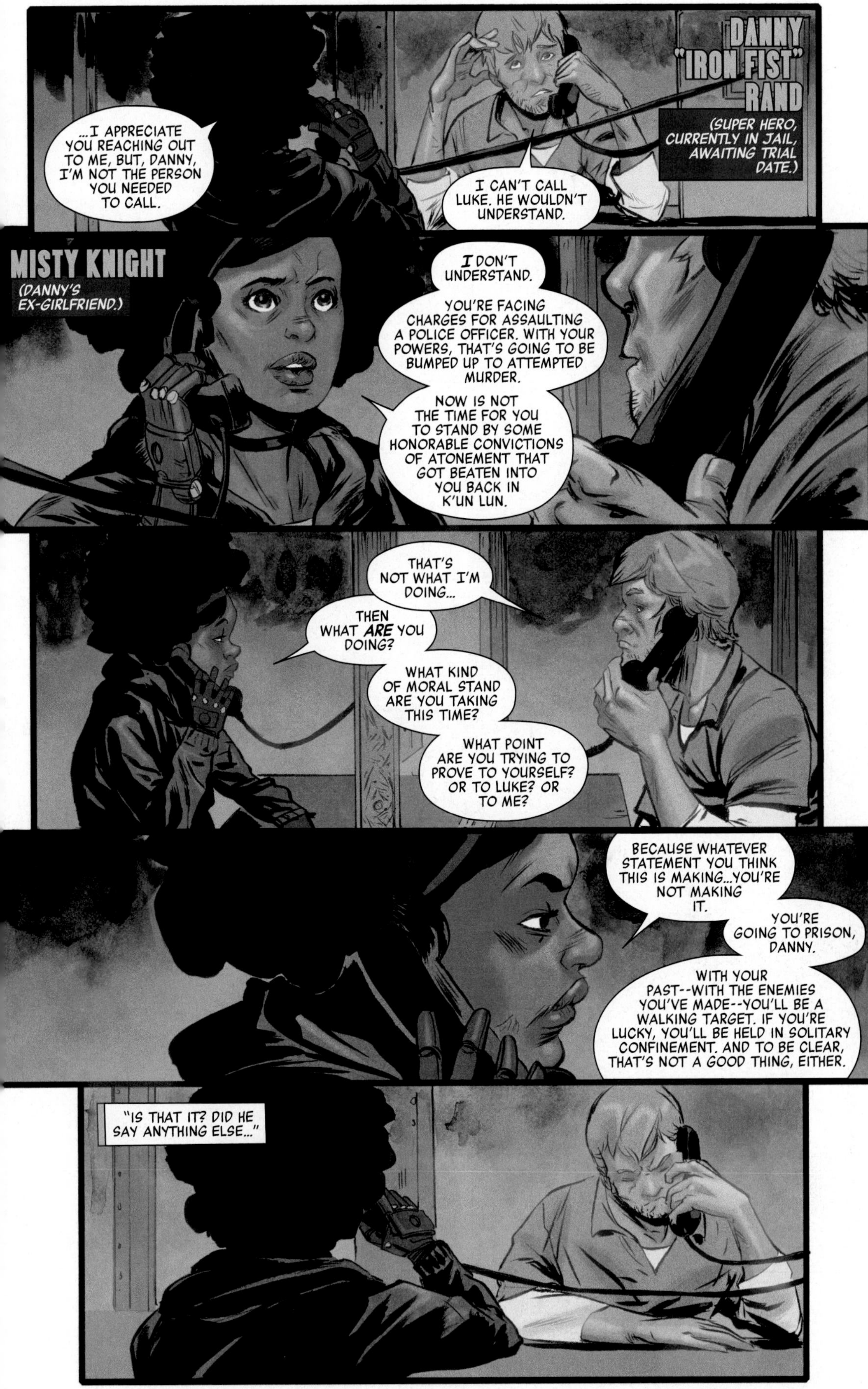
DANNY "IRON FIST" RAND
(SUPER HERO, CURRENTLY IN JAIL, AWAITING TRIAL DATE.)
...I APPRECIATE YOU REACHING OUT TO ME, BUT, DANNY, I'M NOT THE PERSON YOU NEEDED TO CALL.
I CAN'T CALL LUKE. HE WOULDN'T UNDERSTAND.
MISTY KNIGHT
(DANNY'S EX-GIRLFRIEND.)
I DON'T UNDERSTAND.
YOU'RE FACING CHARGES FOR ASSAULTING A POLICE OFFICER. WITH YOUR POWERS, THAT'S GOING TO BE BUMPED UP TO ATTEMPTED MURDER.
NOW IS NOT THE TIME FOR YOU TO STAND BY SOME HONORABLE CONVICTIONS OF ATONEMENT THAT GOT BEATEN INTO YOU BACK IN K'UN LUN.
THAT'S NOT WHAT I'M DOING...
THEN WHAT ARE YOU DOING?
WHAT KIND OF MORAL STAND ARE YOU TAKING THIS TIME?
WHAT POINT ARE YOU TRYING TO PROVE TO YOURSELF? OR TO LUKE? OR TO ME?
BECAUSE WHATEVER STATEMENT YOU THINK THIS IS MAKING...YOU'RE NOT MAKING IT.
YOU'RE GOING TO PRISON, DANNY.
WITH YOUR PAST--WITH THE ENEMIES YOU'VE MADE--YOU'LL BE A WALKING TARGET. IF YOU'RE LUCKY, YOU'LL BE HELD IN SOLITARY CONFINEMENT. AND TO BE CLEAR, THAT'S NOT A GOOD THING, EITHER.
"IS THAT IT? DID HE SAY ANYTHING ELSE..."

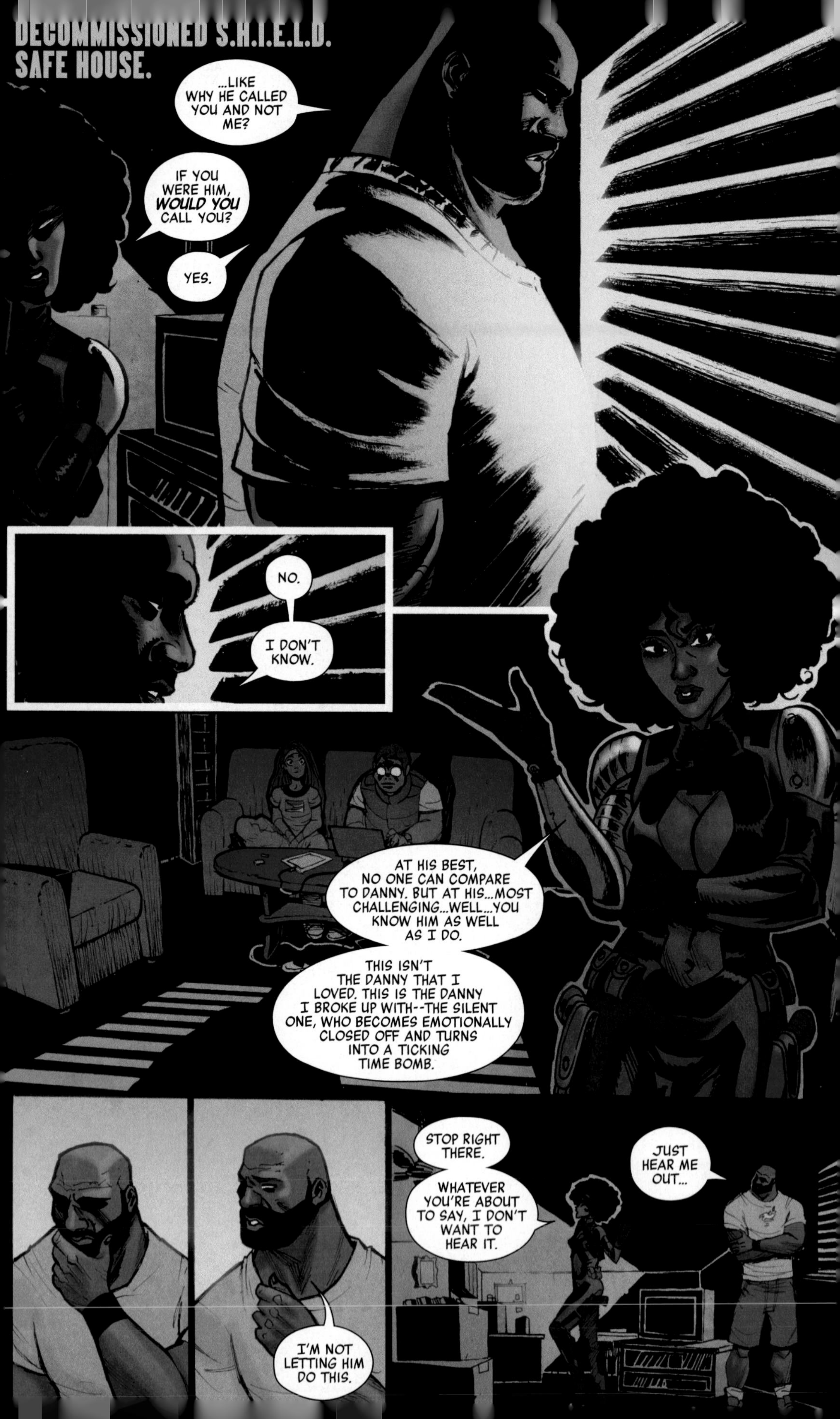

DECOMMISSIONED S.H.I.E.L.D. SAFE HOUSE.
...LIKE WHY HE CALLED YOU AND NOT ME?
IF YOU WERE HIM, WOULD YOU CALL YOU?
YES.
NO.
I DON'T KNOW.
AT HIS BEST, NO ONE CAN COMPARE TO DANNY. BUT AT HIS...MOST CHALLENGING...WELL...YOU KNOW HIM AS WELL AS I DO.
THIS ISN'T THE DANNY THAT I LOVED. THIS IS THE DANNY I BROKE UP WITH--THE SILENT ONE, WHO BECOMES EMOTIONALLY CLOSED OFF AND TURNS INTO A TICKING TIME BOMB.
I'M NOT LETTING HIM DO THIS.
STOP RIGHT THERE.
WHATEVER YOU'RE ABOUT TO SAY, I DON'T WANT TO HEAR IT.
JUST HEAR ME OUT...

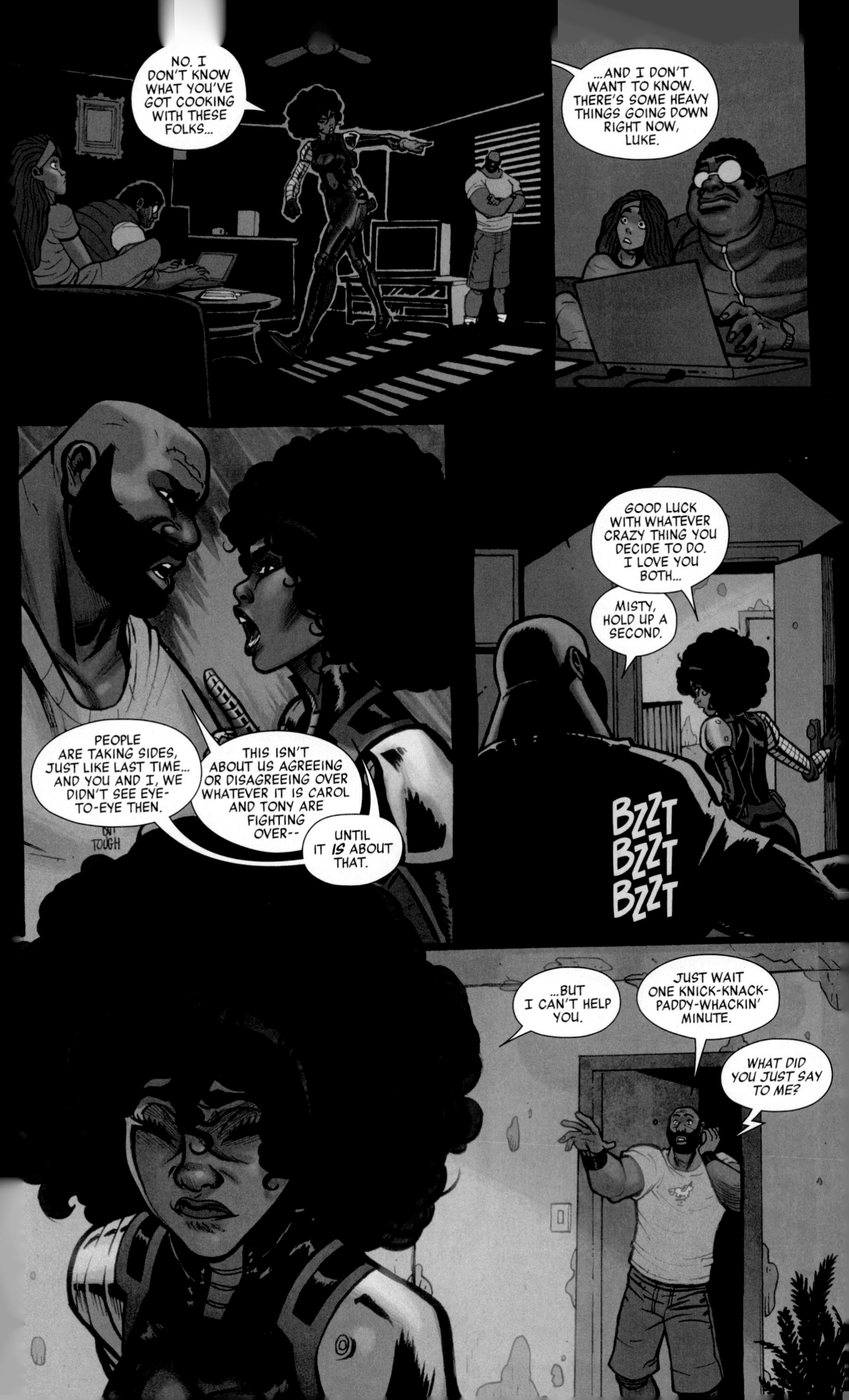
NO. I DON'T KNOW WHAT YOU'VE GOT COOKING WITH THESE FOLKS...
...AND I DON'T WANT TO KNOW. THERE'S SOME HEAVY THINGS GOING DOWN RIGHT NOW, LUKE.
PEOPLE ARE TAKING SIDES, JUST LIKE LAST TIME... AND YOU AND I, WE DIDN'T SEE EYE-TO-EYE THEN.
THIS ISN'T ABOUT US AGREEING OR DISAGREEING OVER WHATEVER IT IS CAROL AND TONY ARE FIGHTING OVER--
UNTIL IT *IS* ABOUT THAT.
GOOD LUCK WITH WHATEVER CRAZY THING YOU DECIDE TO DO. I LOVE YOU BOTH...
MISTY, HOLD UP A SECOND.
BZZT BZZT BZZT
...BUT I CAN'T HELP YOU.
JUST WAIT ONE KNICK-KNACK-PADDY-WHACKIN' MINUTE.
WHAT DID YOU JUST SAY TO ME?

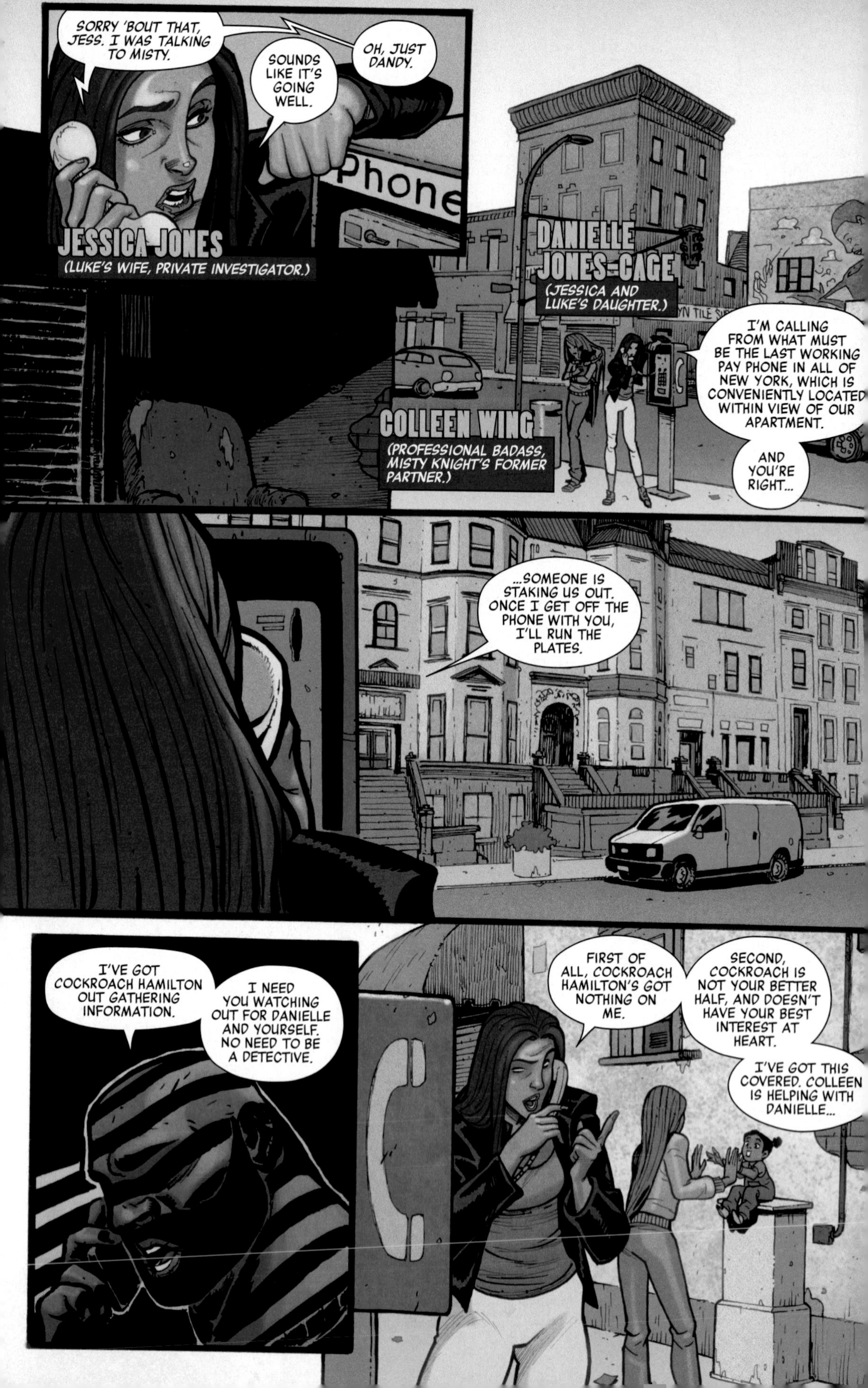
SORRY 'BOUT THAT, JESS. I WAS TALKING TO MISTY.
SOUNDS LIKE IT'S GOING WELL.
OH, JUST DANDY.
JESSICA JONES
(LUKE'S WIFE, PRIVATE INVESTIGATOR.)
DANIELLE JONES-CAGE
(JESSICA AND LUKE'S DAUGHTER.)
COLLEEN WING
(PROFESSIONAL BADASS, MISTY KNIGHT'S FORMER PARTNER.)
I'M CALLING FROM WHAT MUST BE THE LAST WORKING PAY PHONE IN ALL OF NEW YORK, WHICH IS CONVENIENTLY LOCATED WITHIN VIEW OF OUR APARTMENT.
AND YOU'RE RIGHT...
...SOMEONE IS STAKING US OUT. ONCE I GET OFF THE PHONE WITH YOU, I'LL RUN THE PLATES.
I'VE GOT COCKROACH HAMILTON OUT GATHERING INFORMATION.
I NEED YOU WATCHING OUT FOR DANIELLE AND YOURSELF. NO NEED TO BE A DETECTIVE.
FIRST OF ALL, COCKROACH HAMILTON'S GOT NOTHING ON ME.
SECOND, COCKROACH IS NOT YOUR BETTER HALF, AND DOESN'T HAVE YOUR BEST INTEREST AT HEART.
I'VE GOT THIS COVERED. COLLEEN IS HELPING WITH DANIELLE...

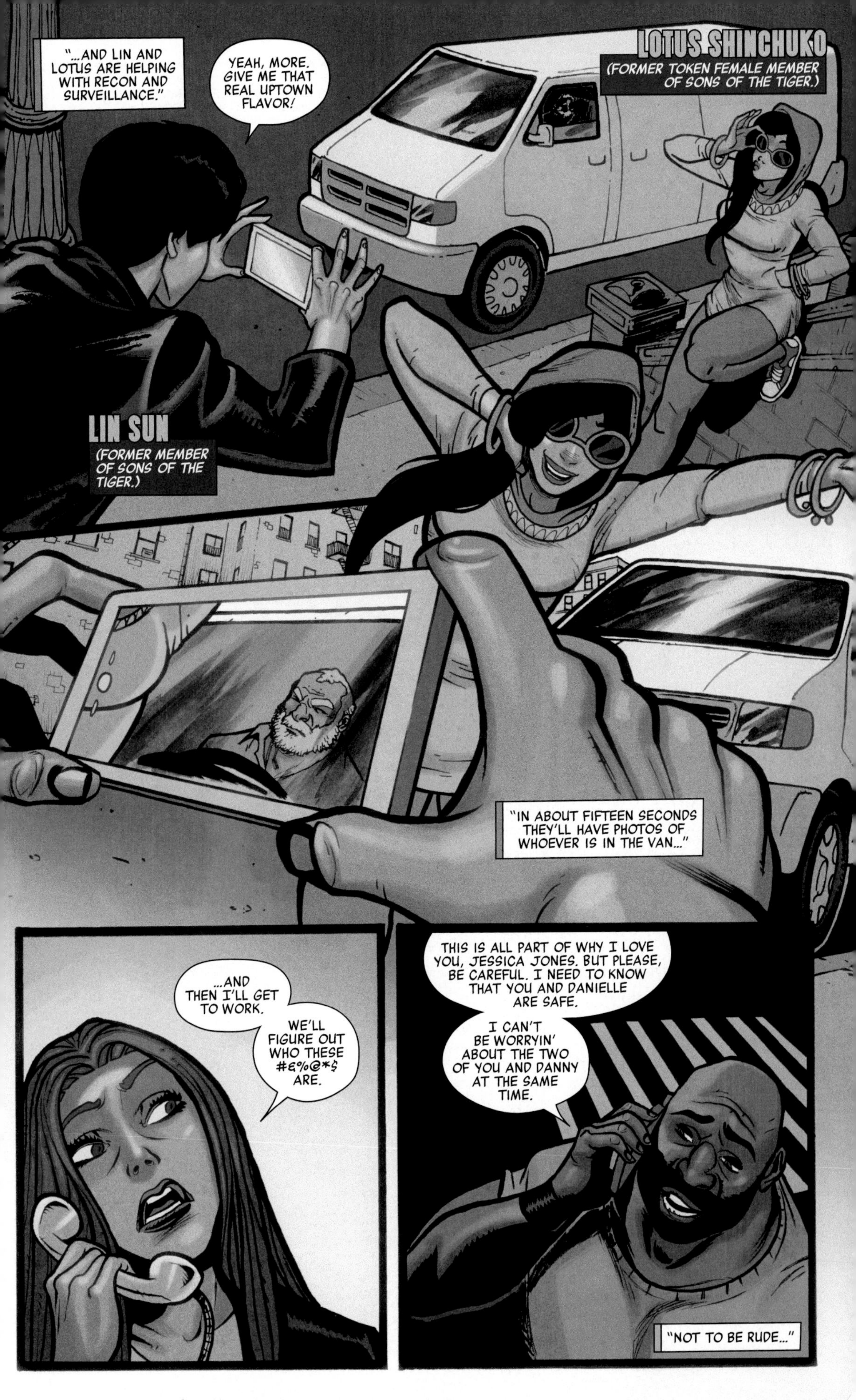
"...AND LIN AND LOTUS ARE HELPING WITH RECON AND SURVEILLANCE."
YEAH, MORE. GIVE ME THAT REAL UPTOWN FLAVOR!
LOTUS SHINCHUKO
(FORMER TOKEN FEMALE MEMBER OF SONS OF THE TIGER.)
LIN SUN
(FORMER MEMBER OF SONS OF THE TIGER.)
"IN ABOUT FIFTEEN SECONDS THEY'LL HAVE PHOTOS OF WHOEVER IS IN THE VAN..."
...AND THEN I'LL GET TO WORK.
WE'LL FIGURE OUT WHO THESE #&%@*$ ARE.
THIS IS ALL PART OF WHY I LOVE YOU, JESSICA JONES. BUT PLEASE, BE CAREFUL. I NEED TO KNOW THAT YOU AND DANIELLE ARE SAFE.
I CAN'T BE WORRYIN' ABOUT THE TWO OF YOU AND DANNY AT THE SAME TIME.
"NOT TO BE RUDE..."

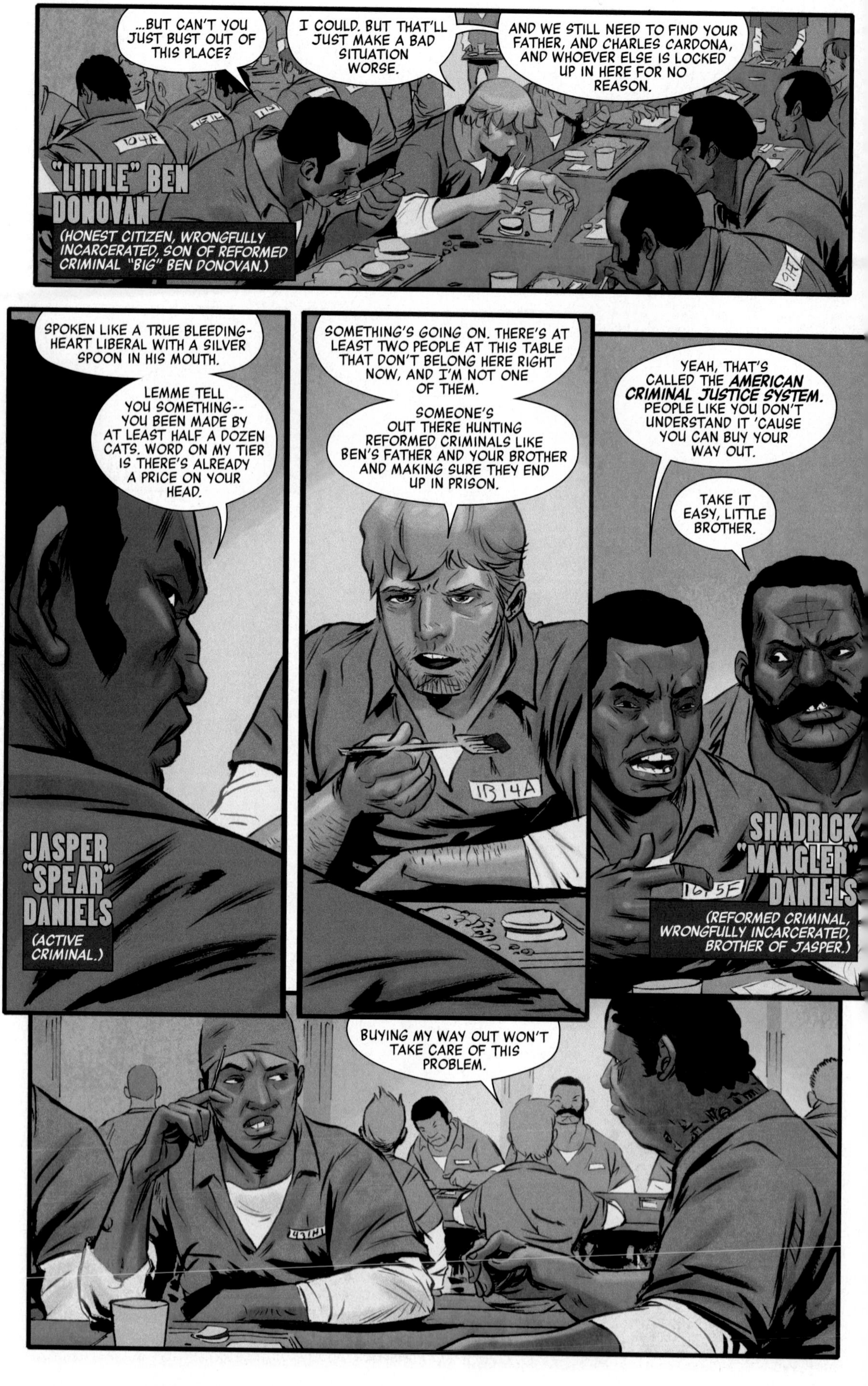
...BUT CAN'T YOU JUST BUST OUT OF THIS PLACE?
I COULD. BUT THAT'LL JUST MAKE A BAD SITUATION WORSE.
AND WE STILL NEED TO FIND YOUR FATHER, AND CHARLES CARDONA, AND WHOEVER ELSE IS LOCKED UP IN HERE FOR NO REASON.
"LITTLE" BEN DONOVAN
(HONEST CITIZEN, WRONGFULLY INCARCERATED, SON OF REFORMED CRIMINAL "BIG" BEN DONOVAN.)
SPOKEN LIKE A TRUE BLEEDING-HEART LIBERAL WITH A SILVER SPOON IN HIS MOUTH.
LEMME TELL YOU SOMETHING-- YOU BEEN MADE BY AT LEAST HALF A DOZEN CATS. WORD ON MY TIER IS THERE'S ALREADY A PRICE ON YOUR HEAD.
JASPER "SPEAR" DANIELS
(ACTIVE CRIMINAL.)
SOMETHING'S GOING ON. THERE'S AT LEAST TWO PEOPLE AT THIS TABLE THAT DON'T BELONG HERE RIGHT NOW, AND I'M NOT ONE OF THEM.
SOMEONE'S OUT THERE HUNTING REFORMED CRIMINALS LIKE BEN'S FATHER AND YOUR BROTHER AND MAKING SURE THEY END UP IN PRISON.
1B14A
YEAH, THAT'S CALLED THE AMERICAN CRIMINAL JUSTICE SYSTEM. PEOPLE LIKE YOU DON'T UNDERSTAND IT 'CAUSE YOU CAN BUY YOUR WAY OUT.
TAKE IT EASY, LITTLE BROTHER.
SHADRICK "MANGLER" DANIELS
(REFORMED CRIMINAL, WRONGFULLY INCARCERATED, BROTHER OF JASPER.)
BUYING MY WAY OUT WON'T TAKE CARE OF THIS PROBLEM.

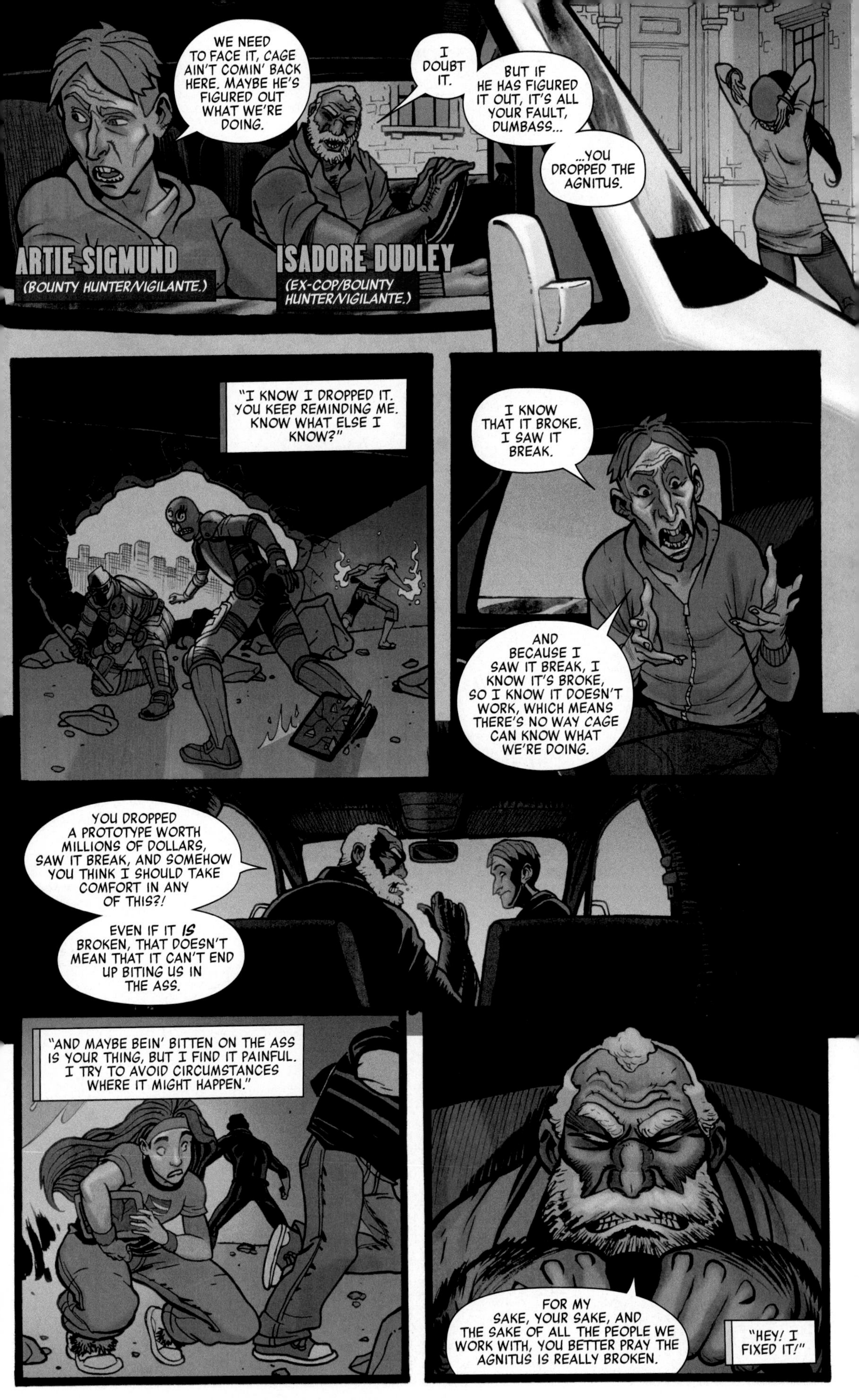
WE NEED TO FACE IT, CAGE AIN'T COMIN' BACK HERE. MAYBE HE'S FIGURED OUT WHAT WE'RE DOING.
I DOUBT IT.
BUT IF HE HAS FIGURED IT OUT, IT'S ALL YOUR FAULT, DUMBASS...
...YOU DROPPED THE AGNITUS.
ARTIE SIGMUND
(BOUNTY HUNTER/VIGILANTE.)
ISADORE DUDLEY
(EX-COP/BOUNTY HUNTER/VIGILANTE.)
"I KNOW I DROPPED IT. YOU KEEP REMINDING ME. KNOW WHAT ELSE I KNOW?"
I KNOW THAT IT BROKE. I SAW IT BREAK.
AND BECAUSE I SAW IT BREAK, I KNOW IT'S BROKE, SO I KNOW IT DOESN'T WORK, WHICH MEANS THERE'S NO WAY CAGE CAN KNOW WHAT WE'RE DOING.
YOU DROPPED A PROTOTYPE WORTH MILLIONS OF DOLLARS, SAW IT BREAK, AND SOMEHOW YOU THINK I SHOULD TAKE COMFORT IN ANY OF THIS?!
EVEN IF IT IS BROKEN, THAT DOESN'T MEAN THAT IT CAN'T END UP BITING US IN THE ASS.
"AND MAYBE BEIN' BITTEN ON THE ASS IS YOUR THING, BUT I FIND IT PAINFUL. I TRY TO AVOID CIRCUMSTANCES WHERE IT MIGHT HAPPEN."
FOR MY SAKE, YOUR SAKE, AND THE SAKE OF ALL THE PEOPLE WE WORK WITH, YOU BETTER PRAY THE AGNITUS IS REALLY BROKEN.
"HEY! I FIXED IT!"

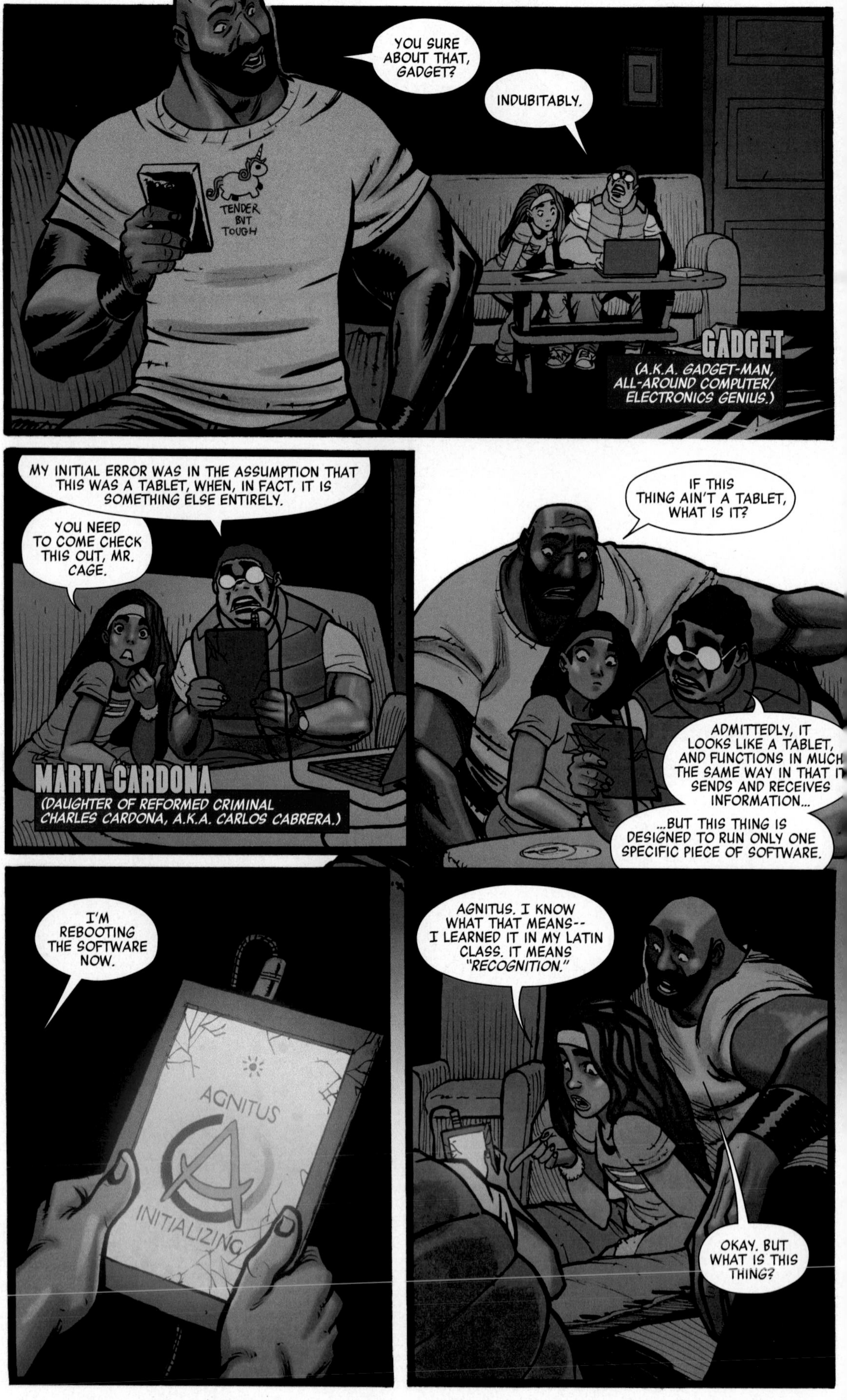
YOU SURE ABOUT THAT, GADGET?
INDUBITABLY.
TENDER BUT TOUGH
GADGET
(A.K.A. GADGET-MAN, ALL-AROUND COMPUTER/ ELECTRONICS GENIUS.)
MY INITIAL ERROR WAS IN THE ASSUMPTION THAT THIS WAS A TABLET, WHEN, IN FACT, IT IS SOMETHING ELSE ENTIRELY.
YOU NEED TO COME CHECK THIS OUT, MR. CAGE.
MARTA CARDONA
(DAUGHTER OF REFORMED CRIMINAL CHARLES CARDONA, A.K.A. CARLOS CABRERA.)
IF THIS THING AIN'T A TABLET, WHAT IS IT?
ADMITTEDLY, IT LOOKS LIKE A TABLET, AND FUNCTIONS IN MUCH THE SAME WAY IN THAT IT SENDS AND RECEIVES INFORMATION...
...BUT THIS THING IS DESIGNED TO RUN ONLY ONE SPECIFIC PIECE OF SOFTWARE.
I'M REBOOTING THE SOFTWARE NOW.
AGNITUS
INITIALIZING
AGNITUS. I KNOW WHAT THAT MEANS-- I LEARNED IT IN MY LATIN CLASS. IT MEANS "RECOGNITION."
OKAY. BUT WHAT IS THIS THING?

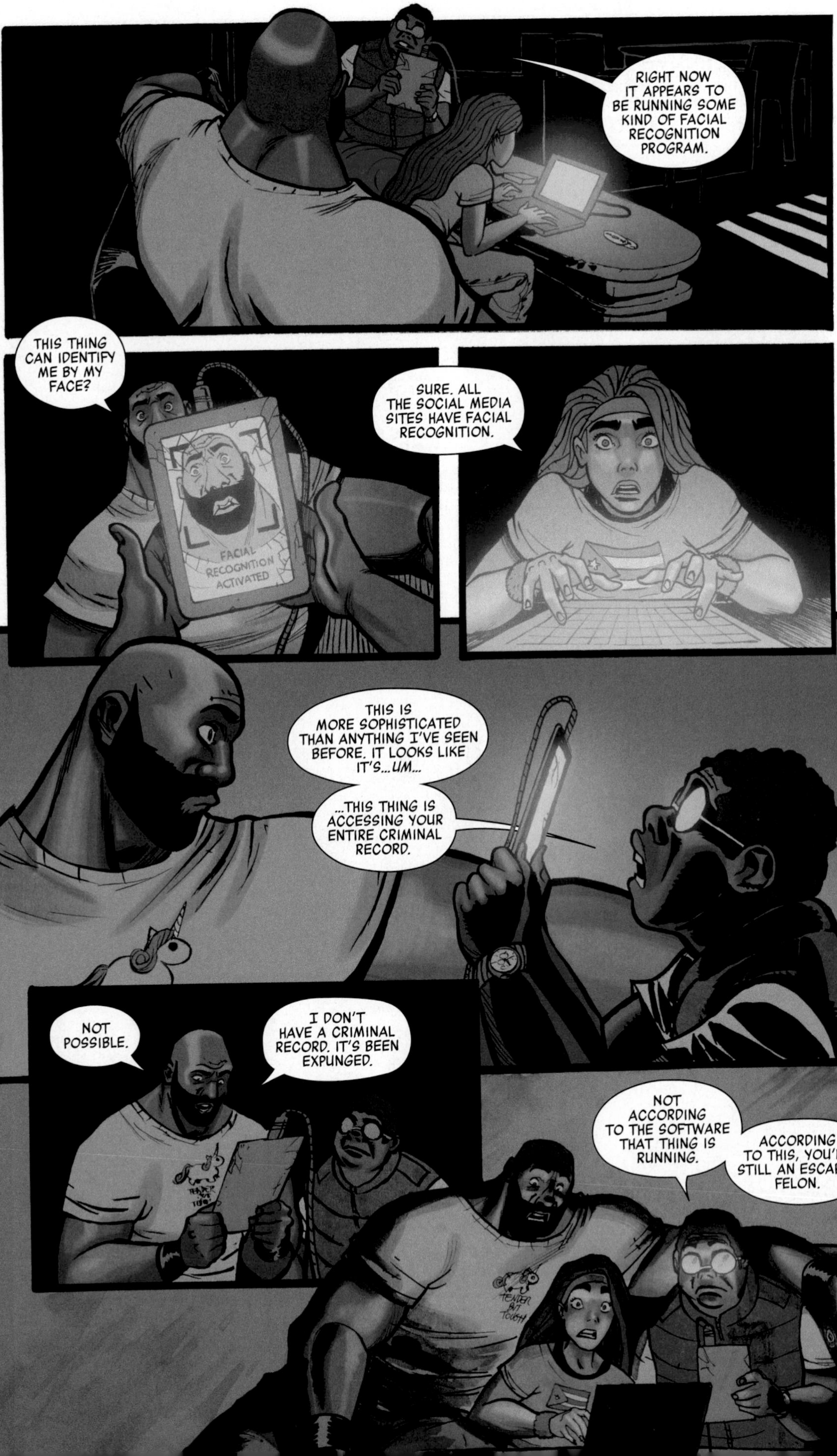
RIGHT NOW IT APPEARS TO BE RUNNING SOME KIND OF FACIAL RECOGNITION PROGRAM.
THIS THING CAN IDENTIFY ME BY MY FACE?
FACIAL RECOGNITION ACTIVATED
SURE. ALL THE SOCIAL MEDIA SITES HAVE FACIAL RECOGNITION.
THIS IS MORE SOPHISTICATED THAN ANYTHING I'VE SEEN BEFORE. IT LOOKS LIKE IT'S...UM...
...THIS THING IS ACCESSING YOUR ENTIRE CRIMINAL RECORD.
NOT POSSIBLE.
I DON'T HAVE A CRIMINAL RECORD. IT'S BEEN EXPUNGED.
NOT ACCORDING TO THE SOFTWARE THAT THING IS RUNNING.
ACCORDING TO THIS, YOU'RE STILL AN ESCAPED FELON.

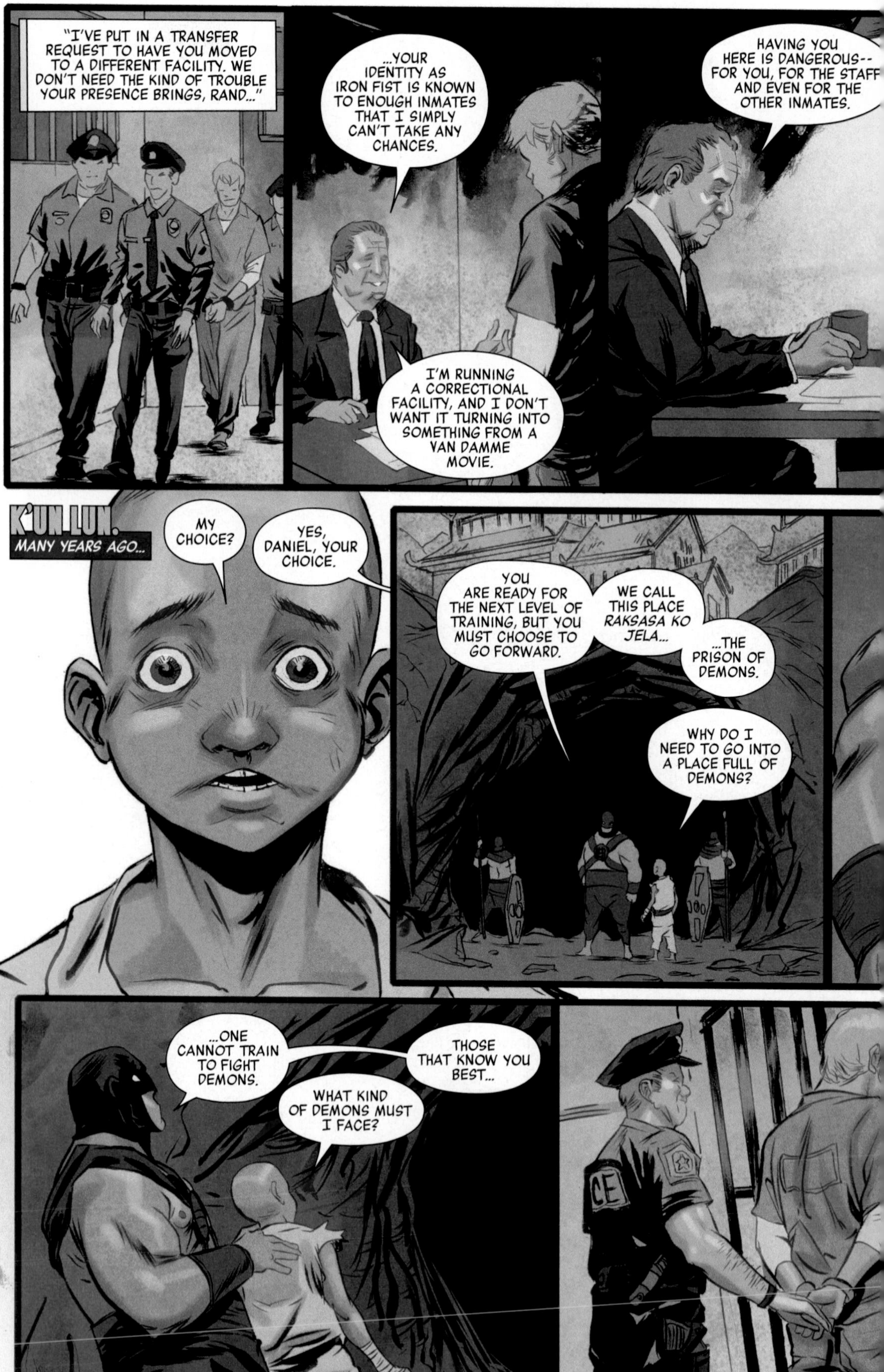
"I'VE PUT IN A TRANSFER REQUEST TO HAVE YOU MOVED TO A DIFFERENT FACILITY. WE DON'T NEED THE KIND OF TROUBLE YOUR PRESENCE BRINGS, RAND..."
...YOUR IDENTITY AS IRON FIST IS KNOWN TO ENOUGH INMATES THAT I SIMPLY CAN'T TAKE ANY CHANCES.
I'M RUNNING A CORRECTIONAL FACILITY, AND I DON'T WANT IT TURNING INTO SOMETHING FROM A VAN DAMME MOVIE.
HAVING YOU HERE IS DANGEROUS--FOR YOU, FOR THE STAFF AND EVEN FOR THE OTHER INMATES.
K'UN LUN.
MANY YEARS AGO...
MY CHOICE?
YES, DANIEL, YOUR CHOICE.
YOU ARE READY FOR THE NEXT LEVEL OF TRAINING, BUT YOU MUST CHOOSE TO GO FORWARD.
WE CALL THIS PLACE RAKSASA KO JELA...
...THE PRISON OF DEMONS.
WHY DO I NEED TO GO INTO A PLACE FULL OF DEMONS?
...ONE CANNOT TRAIN TO FIGHT DEMONS.
THOSE THAT KNOW YOU BEST...
WHAT KIND OF DEMONS MUST I FACE?
CE

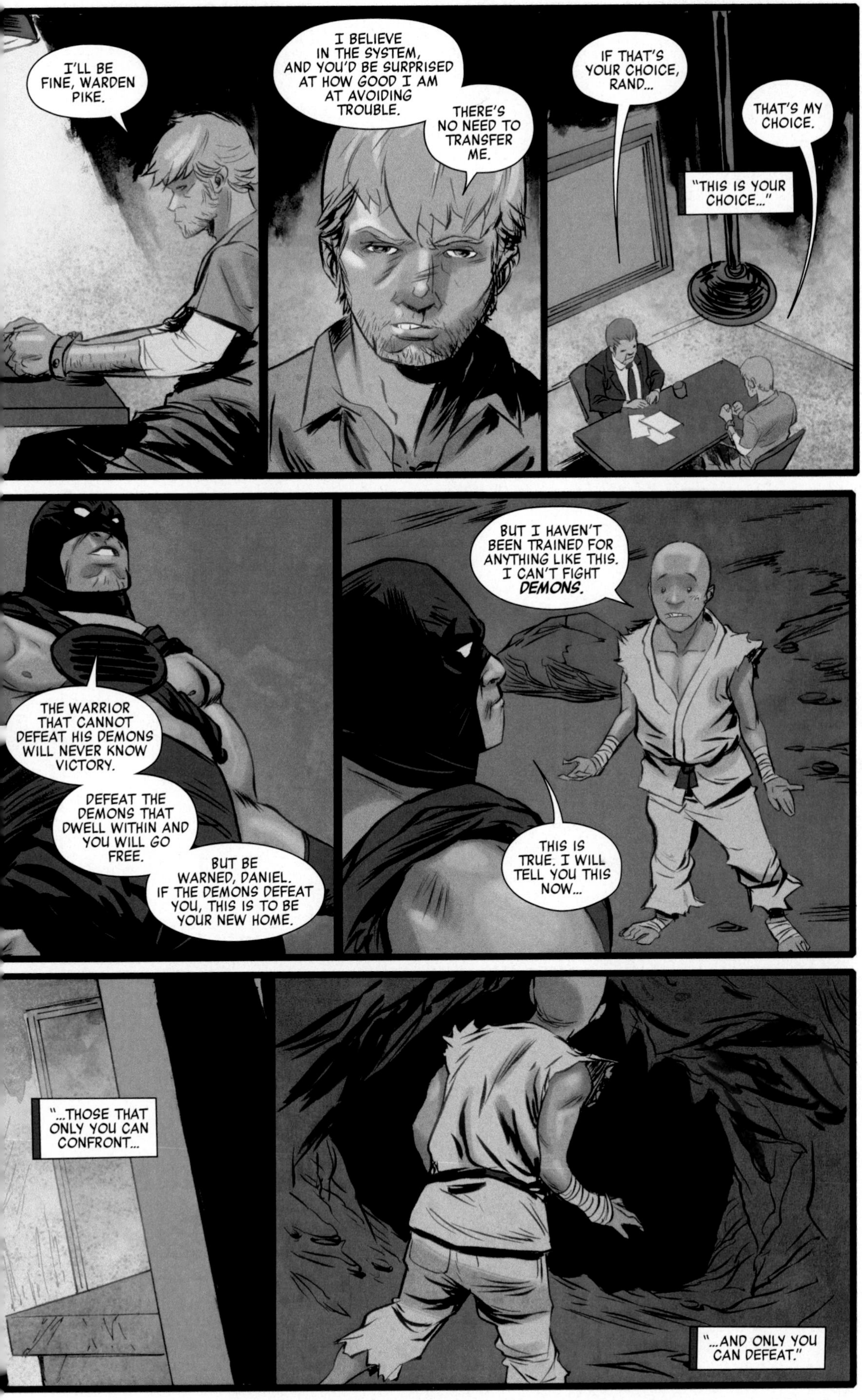
I'LL BE FINE, WARDEN PIKE.
I BELIEVE IN THE SYSTEM, AND YOU'D BE SURPRISED AT HOW GOOD I AM AT AVOIDING TROUBLE.
THERE'S NO NEED TO TRANSFER ME.
IF THAT'S YOUR CHOICE, RAND...
THAT'S MY CHOICE.
"THIS IS YOUR CHOICE..."
THE WARRIOR THAT CANNOT DEFEAT HIS DEMONS WILL NEVER KNOW VICTORY.
DEFEAT THE DEMONS THAT DWELL WITHIN AND YOU WILL GO FREE.
BUT BE WARNED, DANIEL. IF THE DEMONS DEFEAT YOU, THIS IS TO BE YOUR NEW HOME.
BUT I HAVEN'T BEEN TRAINED FOR ANYTHING LIKE THIS. I CAN'T FIGHT DEMONS.
THIS IS TRUE. I WILL TELL YOU THIS NOW...
"...THOSE THAT ONLY YOU CAN CONFRONT...
"...AND ONLY YOU CAN DEFEAT."

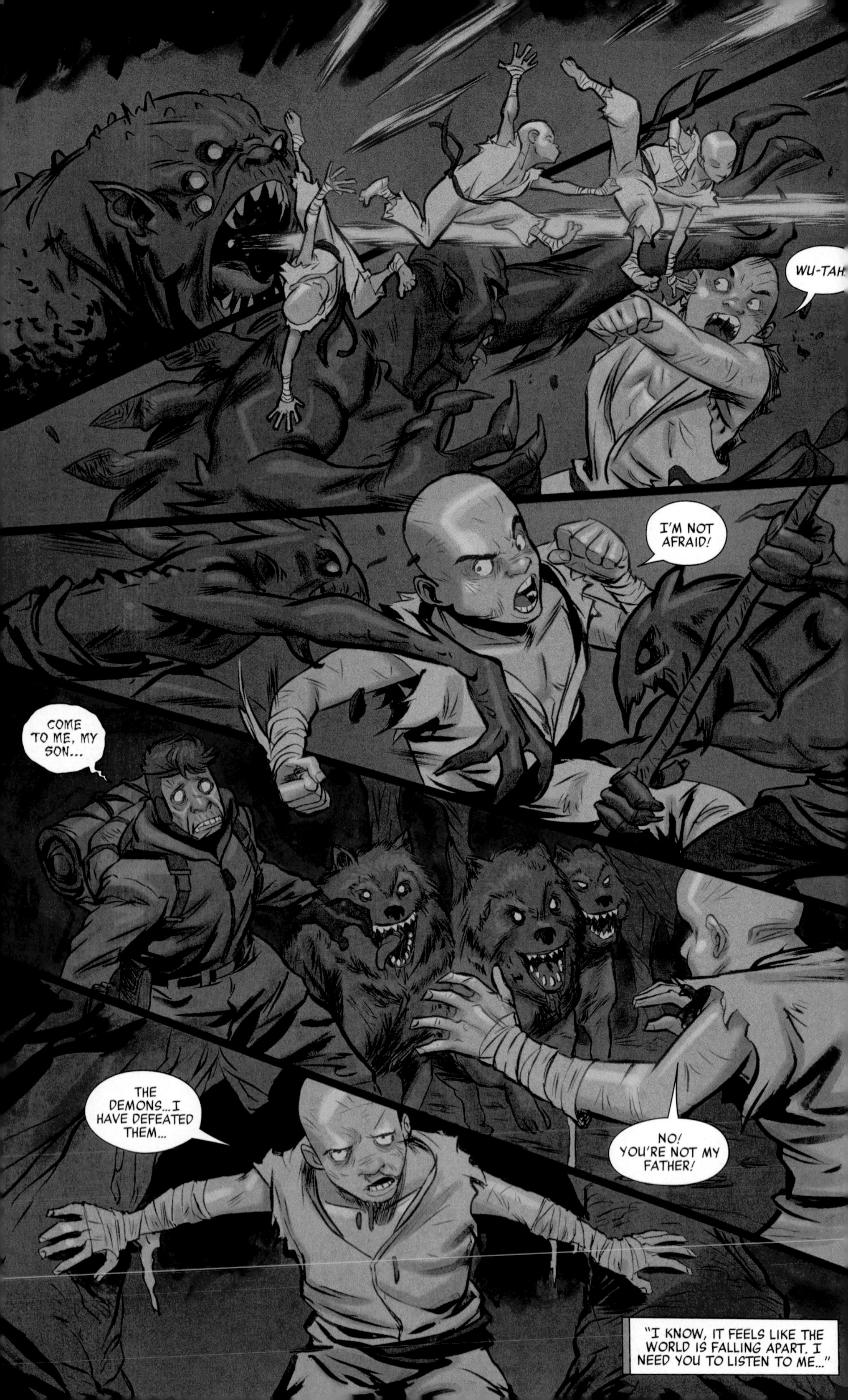
WU-TAH!
I'M NOT AFRAID!
COME TO ME, MY SON...
NO! YOU'RE NOT MY FATHER!
THE DEMONS...I HAVE DEFEATED THEM...
"I KNOW, IT FEELS LIKE THE WORLD IS FALLING APART. I NEED YOU TO LISTEN TO ME..."

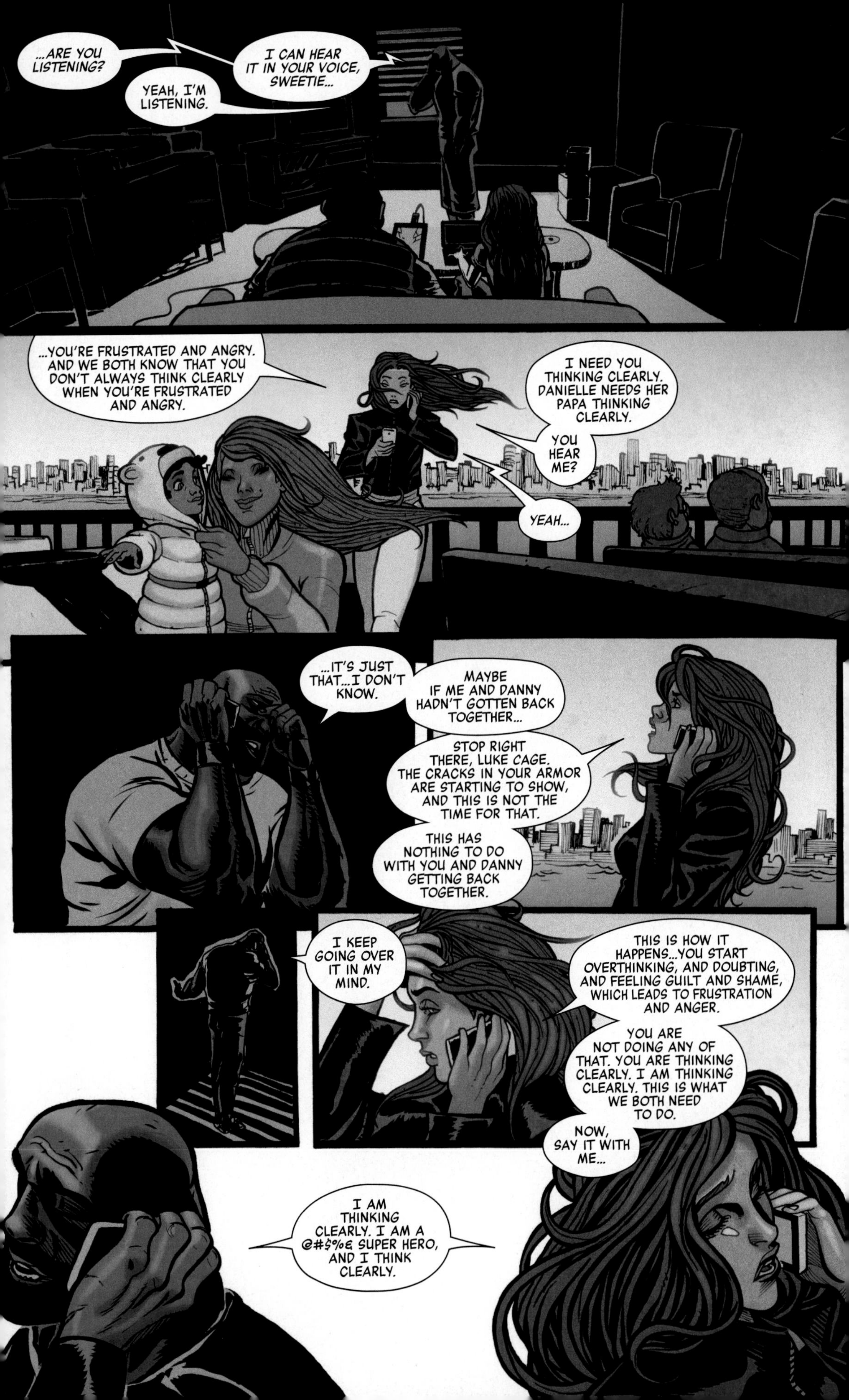
...ARE YOU LISTENING?
I CAN HEAR IT IN YOUR VOICE, SWEETIE...
YEAH, I'M LISTENING.
...YOU'RE FRUSTRATED AND ANGRY. AND WE BOTH KNOW THAT YOU DON'T ALWAYS THINK CLEARLY WHEN YOU'RE FRUSTRATED AND ANGRY.
I NEED YOU THINKING CLEARLY. DANIELLE NEEDS HER PAPA THINKING CLEARLY.
YOU HEAR ME?
YEAH...
...IT'S JUST THAT...I DON'T KNOW.
MAYBE IF ME AND DANNY HADN'T GOTTEN BACK TOGETHER...
STOP RIGHT THERE, LUKE CAGE. THE CRACKS IN YOUR ARMOR ARE STARTING TO SHOW, AND THIS IS NOT THE TIME FOR THAT.
THIS HAS NOTHING TO DO WITH YOU AND DANNY GETTING BACK TOGETHER.
I KEEP GOING OVER IT IN MY MIND.
THIS IS HOW IT HAPPENS...YOU START OVERTHINKING, AND DOUBTING, AND FEELING GUILT AND SHAME, WHICH LEADS TO FRUSTRATION AND ANGER.
YOU ARE NOT DOING ANY OF THAT. YOU ARE THINKING CLEARLY. I AM THINKING CLEARLY. THIS IS WHAT WE BOTH NEED TO DO.
NOW, SAY IT WITH ME...
I AM THINKING CLEARLY. I AM A @#$%& SUPER HERO, AND I THINK CLEARLY.

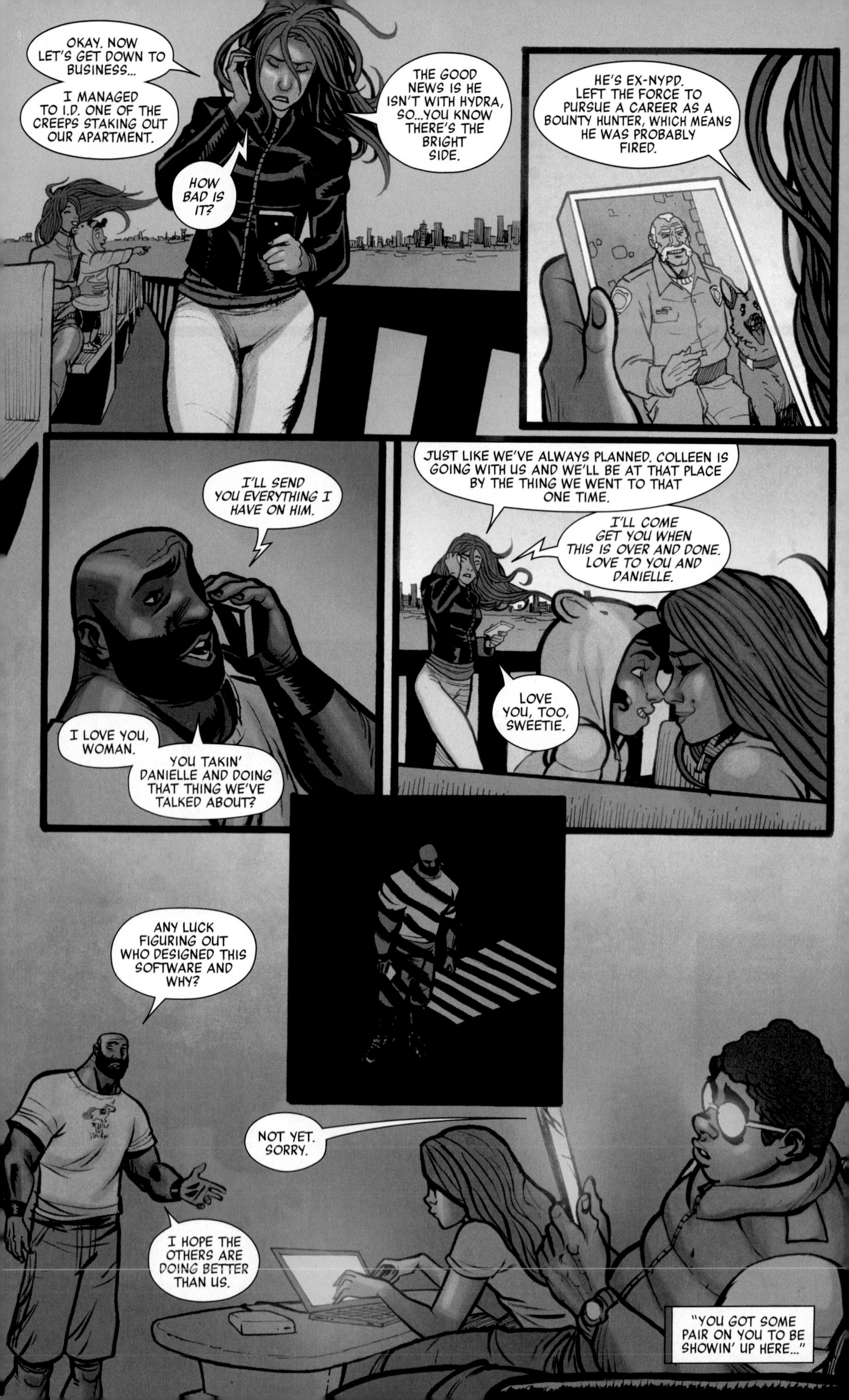

OKAY. NOW LET'S GET DOWN TO BUSINESS...
I MANAGED TO I.D. ONE OF THE CREEPS STAKING OUT OUR APARTMENT.
HOW BAD IS IT?
THE GOOD NEWS IS HE ISN'T WITH HYDRA, SO...YOU KNOW THERE'S THE BRIGHT SIDE.
HE'S EX-NYPD. LEFT THE FORCE TO PURSUE A CAREER AS A BOUNTY HUNTER, WHICH MEANS HE WAS PROBABLY FIRED.
I'LL SEND YOU EVERYTHING I HAVE ON HIM.
I LOVE YOU, WOMAN.
YOU TAKIN' DANIELLE AND DOING THAT THING WE'VE TALKED ABOUT?
JUST LIKE WE'VE ALWAYS PLANNED. COLLEEN IS GOING WITH US AND WE'LL BE AT THAT PLACE BY THE THING WE WENT TO THAT ONE TIME.
I'LL COME GET YOU WHEN THIS IS OVER AND DONE. LOVE TO YOU AND DANIELLE.
LOVE YOU, TOO, SWEETIE.
ANY LUCK FIGURING OUT WHO DESIGNED THIS SOFTWARE AND WHY?
NOT YET. SORRY.
I HOPE THE OTHERS ARE DOING BETTER THAN US.
"YOU GOT SOME PAIR ON YOU TO BE SHOWIN' UP HERE..."

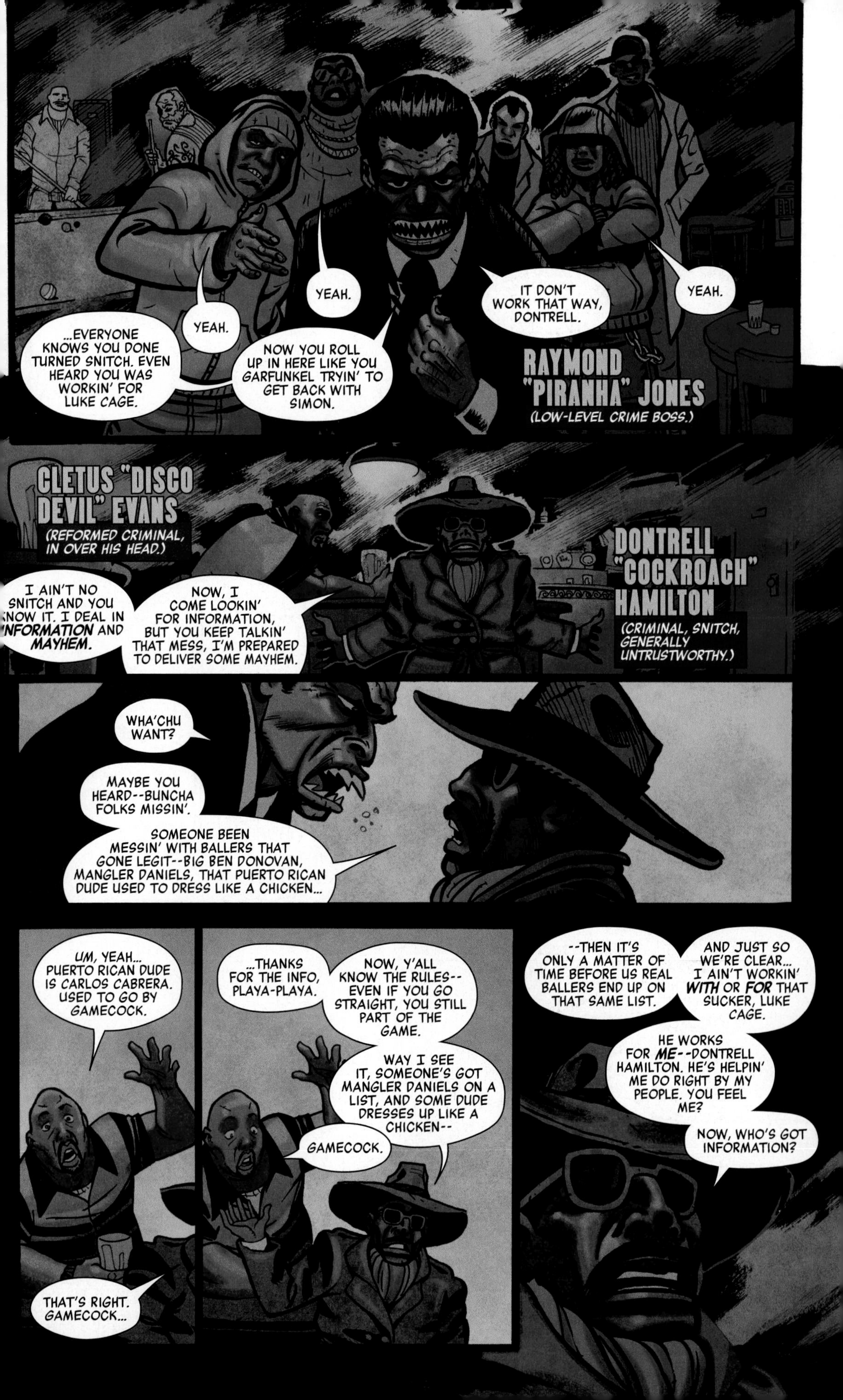
...EVERYONE KNOWS YOU DONE TURNED SNITCH. EVEN HEARD YOU WAS WORKIN' FOR LUKE CAGE.
YEAH.
YEAH.
NOW YOU ROLL UP IN HERE LIKE YOU GARFUNKEL TRYIN' TO GET BACK WITH SIMON.
IT DON'T WORK THAT WAY, DONTRELL.
YEAH.
RAYMOND "PIRANHA" JONES
(LOW-LEVEL CRIME BOSS.)
CLETUS "DISCO DEVIL" EVANS
(REFORMED CRIMINAL, IN OVER HIS HEAD.)
DONTRELL "COCKROACH" HAMILTON
(CRIMINAL, SNITCH, GENERALLY UNTRUSTWORTHY.)
I AIN'T NO SNITCH AND YOU KNOW IT. I DEAL IN *INFORMATION* AND *MAYHEM.*
NOW, I COME LOOKIN' FOR INFORMATION, BUT YOU KEEP TALKIN' THAT MESS, I'M PREPARED TO DELIVER SOME MAYHEM.
WHA'CHU WANT?
MAYBE YOU HEARD--BUNCHA FOLKS MISSIN'.
SOMEONE BEEN MESSIN' WITH BALLERS THAT GONE LEGIT--BIG BEN DONOVAN, MANGLER DANIELS, THAT PUERTO RICAN DUDE USED TO DRESS LIKE A CHICKEN...
UM, YEAH... PUERTO RICAN DUDE IS CARLOS CABRERA. USED TO GO BY GAMECOCK.
THAT'S RIGHT. GAMECOCK...
...THANKS FOR THE INFO, PLAYA-PLAYA.
NOW, Y'ALL KNOW THE RULES-- EVEN IF YOU GO STRAIGHT, YOU STILL PART OF THE GAME.
WAY I SEE IT, SOMEONE'S GOT MANGLER DANIELS ON A LIST, AND SOME DUDE DRESSES UP LIKE A CHICKEN--
GAMECOCK.
--THEN IT'S ONLY A MATTER OF TIME BEFORE US REAL BALLERS END UP ON THAT SAME LIST.
AND JUST SO WE'RE CLEAR... I AIN'T WORKIN' *WITH* OR *FOR* THAT SUCKER, LUKE CAGE.
HE WORKS FOR *ME*--DONTRELL HAMILTON. HE'S HELPIN' ME DO RIGHT BY MY PEOPLE. YOU FEEL ME?
NOW, WHO'S GOT INFORMATION?

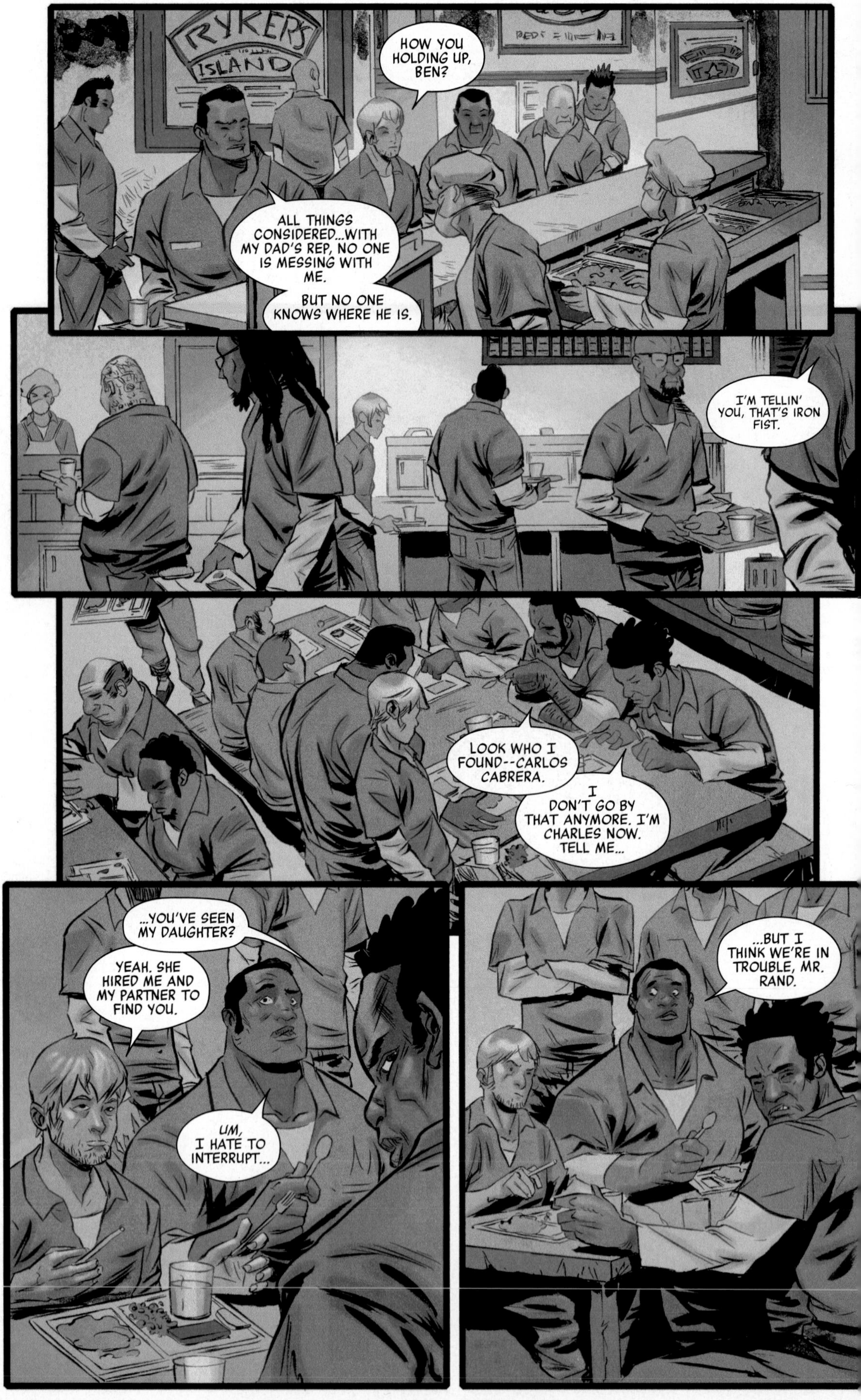
RYKER'S ISLAND
HOW YOU HOLDING UP, BEN?
ALL THINGS CONSIDERED...WITH MY DAD'S REP, NO ONE IS MESSING WITH ME.
BUT NO ONE KNOWS WHERE HE IS.
I'M TELLIN' YOU, THAT'S IRON FIST.
LOOK WHO I FOUND--CARLOS CABRERA.
I DON'T GO BY THAT ANYMORE. I'M CHARLES NOW. TELL ME...
...YOU'VE SEEN MY DAUGHTER?
YEAH. SHE HIRED ME AND MY PARTNER TO FIND YOU.
UM, I HATE TO INTERRUPT...
...BUT I THINK WE'RE IN TROUBLE, MR. RAND.

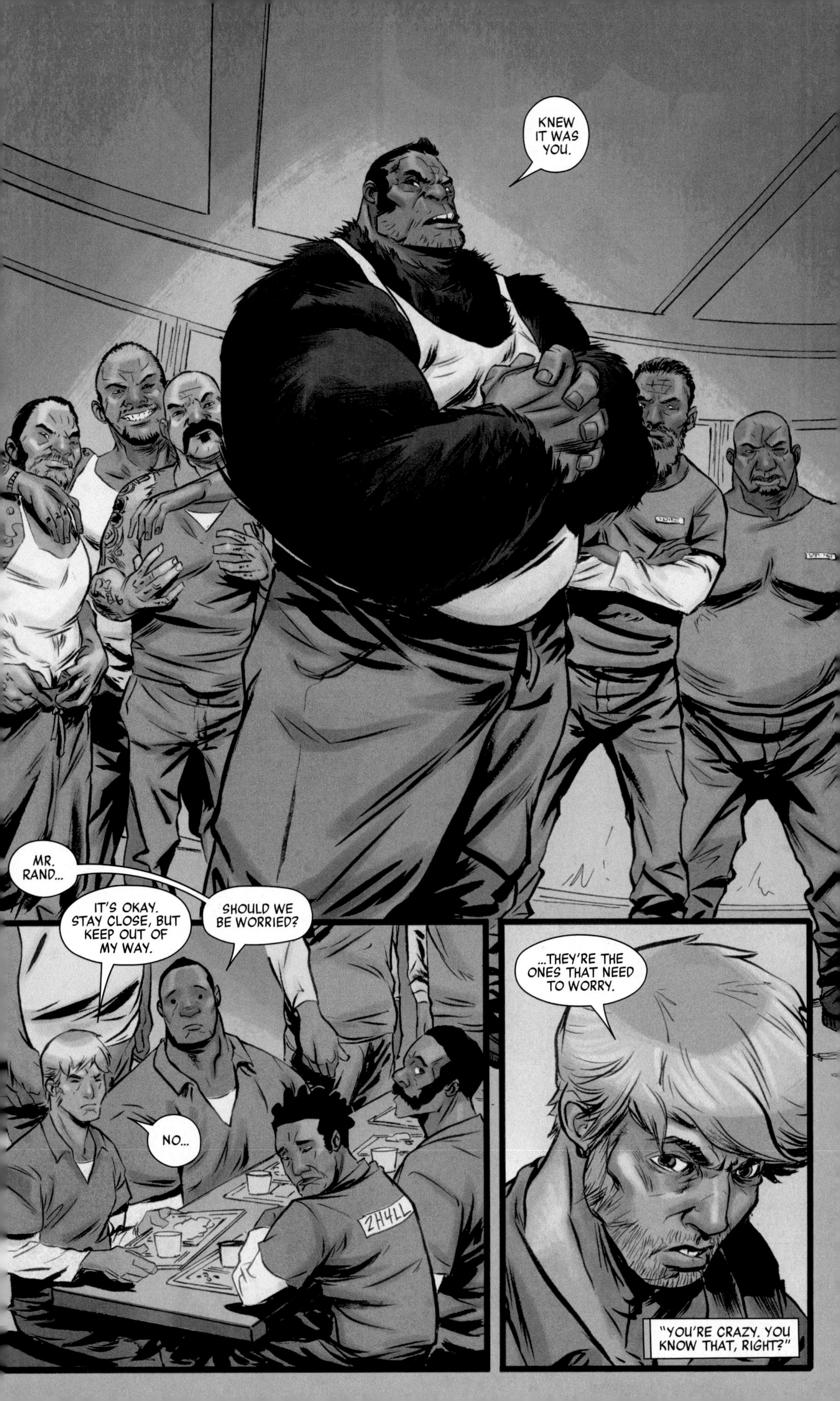
KNEW IT WAS YOU.
MR. RAND...
SHOULD WE BE WORRIED?
IT'S OKAY. STAY CLOSE, BUT KEEP OUT OF MY WAY.
NO...
...THEY'RE THE ONES THAT NEED TO WORRY.
"YOU'RE CRAZY. YOU KNOW THAT, RIGHT?"

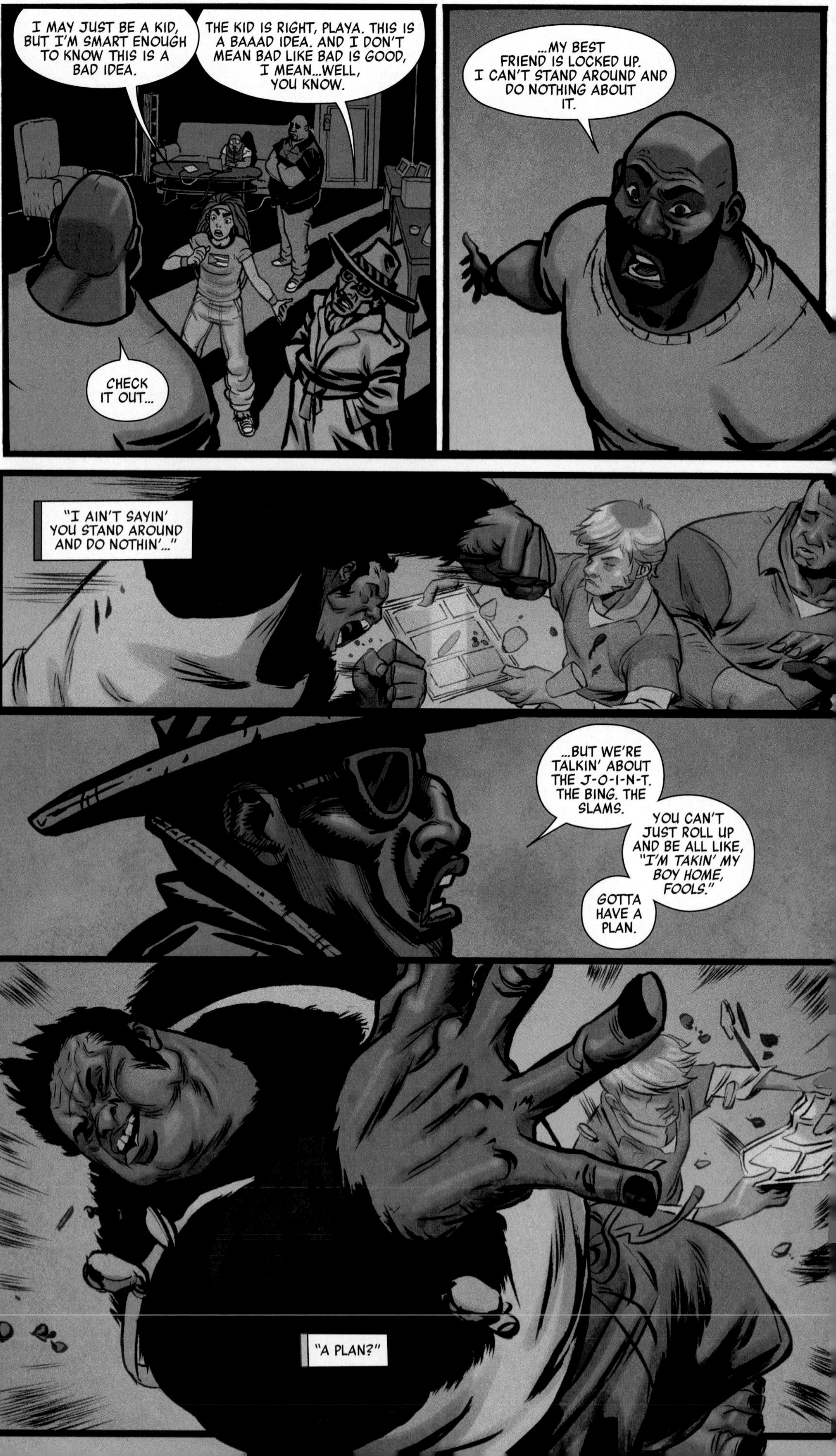
I MAY JUST BE A KID, BUT I'M SMART ENOUGH TO KNOW THIS IS A BAD IDEA.
THE KID IS RIGHT, PLAYA. THIS IS A BAAAD IDEA. AND I DON'T MEAN BAD LIKE BAD IS GOOD, I MEAN...WELL, YOU KNOW.
CHECK IT OUT...
...MY BEST FRIEND IS LOCKED UP. I CAN'T STAND AROUND AND DO NOTHING ABOUT IT.
"I AIN'T SAYIN' YOU STAND AROUND AND DO NOTHIN'..."
...BUT WE'RE TALKIN' ABOUT THE J-O-I-N-T. THE BING. THE SLAMS.
YOU CAN'T JUST ROLL UP AND BE ALL LIKE, "I'M TAKIN' MY BOY HOME, FOOLS."
GOTTA HAVE A PLAN.
"A PLAN?"

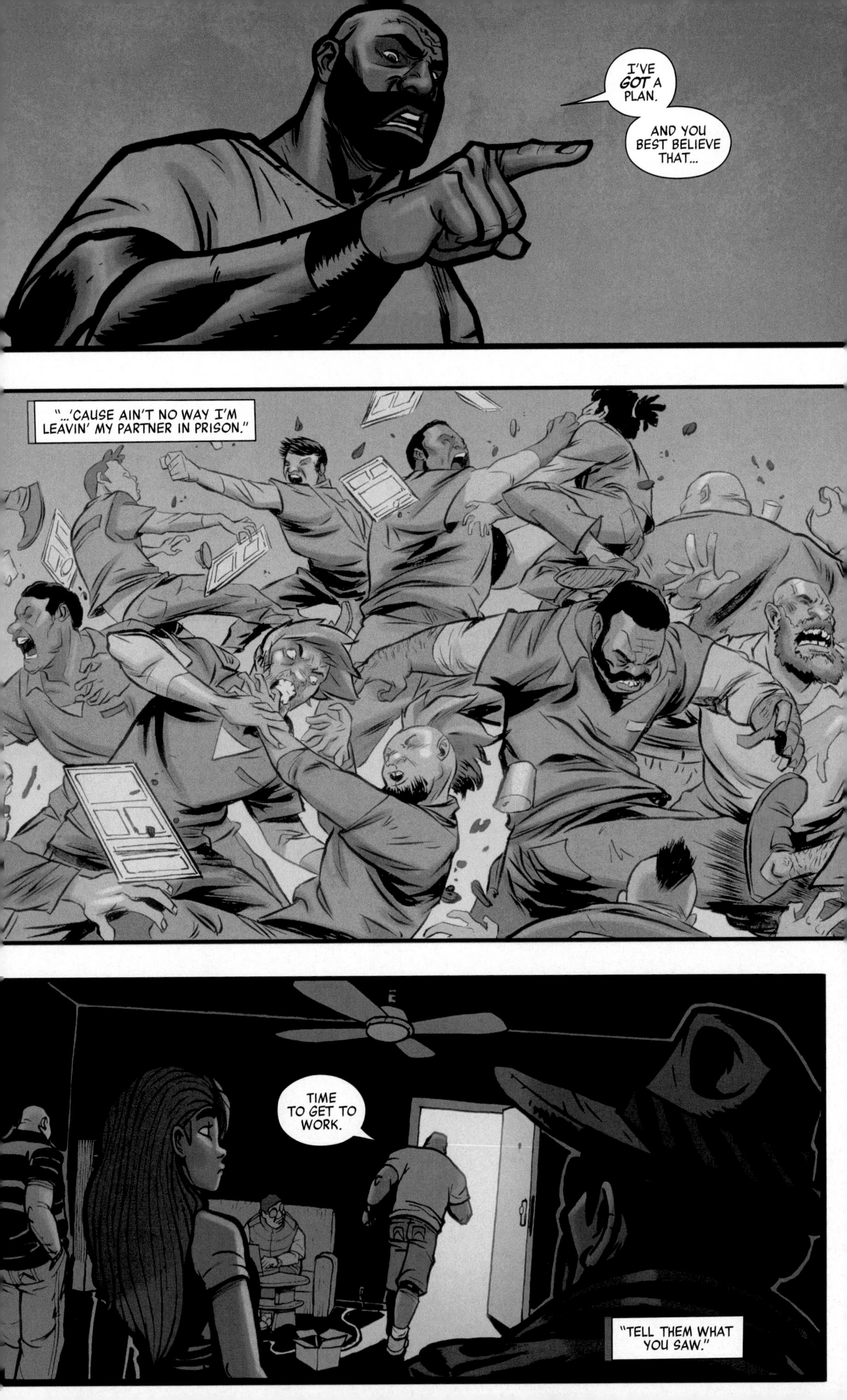
I'VE GOT A PLAN.
AND YOU BEST BELIEVE THAT...
"...'CAUSE AIN'T NO WAY I'M LEAVIN' MY PARTNER IN PRISON."
TIME TO GET TO WORK.
"TELL THEM WHAT YOU SAW."

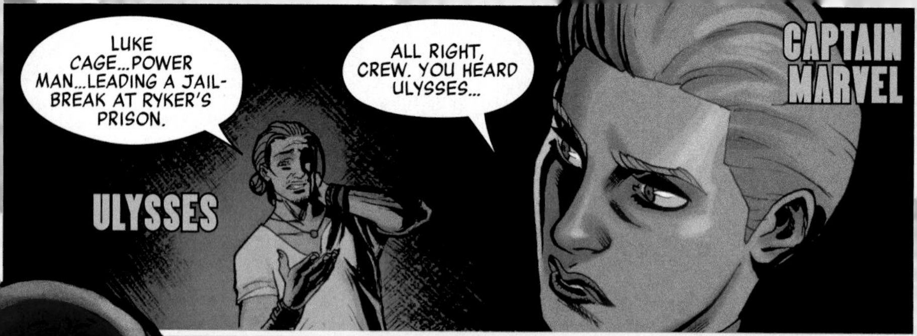
LUKE CAGE...POWER MAN...LEADING A JAIL-BREAK AT RYKER'S PRISON.
ULYSSES
ALL RIGHT, CREW. YOU HEARD ULYSSES...
CAPTAIN MARVEL

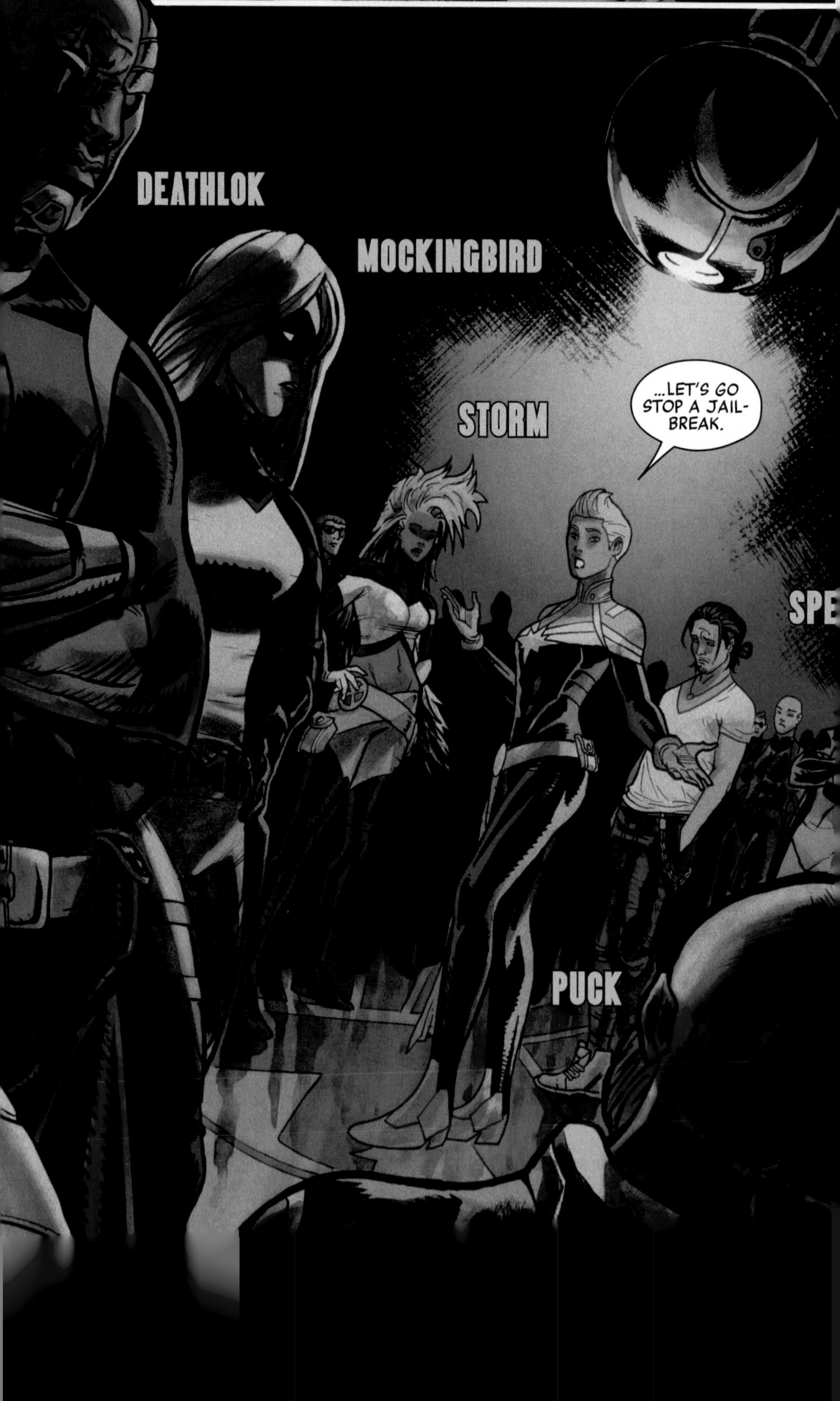
DEATHLOK
MOCKINGBIRD
STORM
...LET'S GO STOP A JAIL-BREAK.
SPE
PUCK

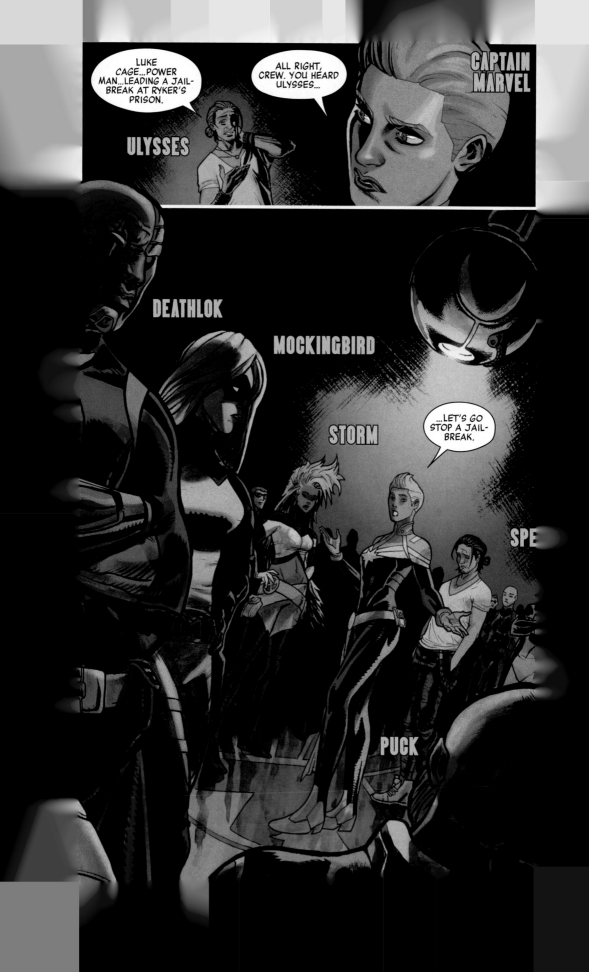

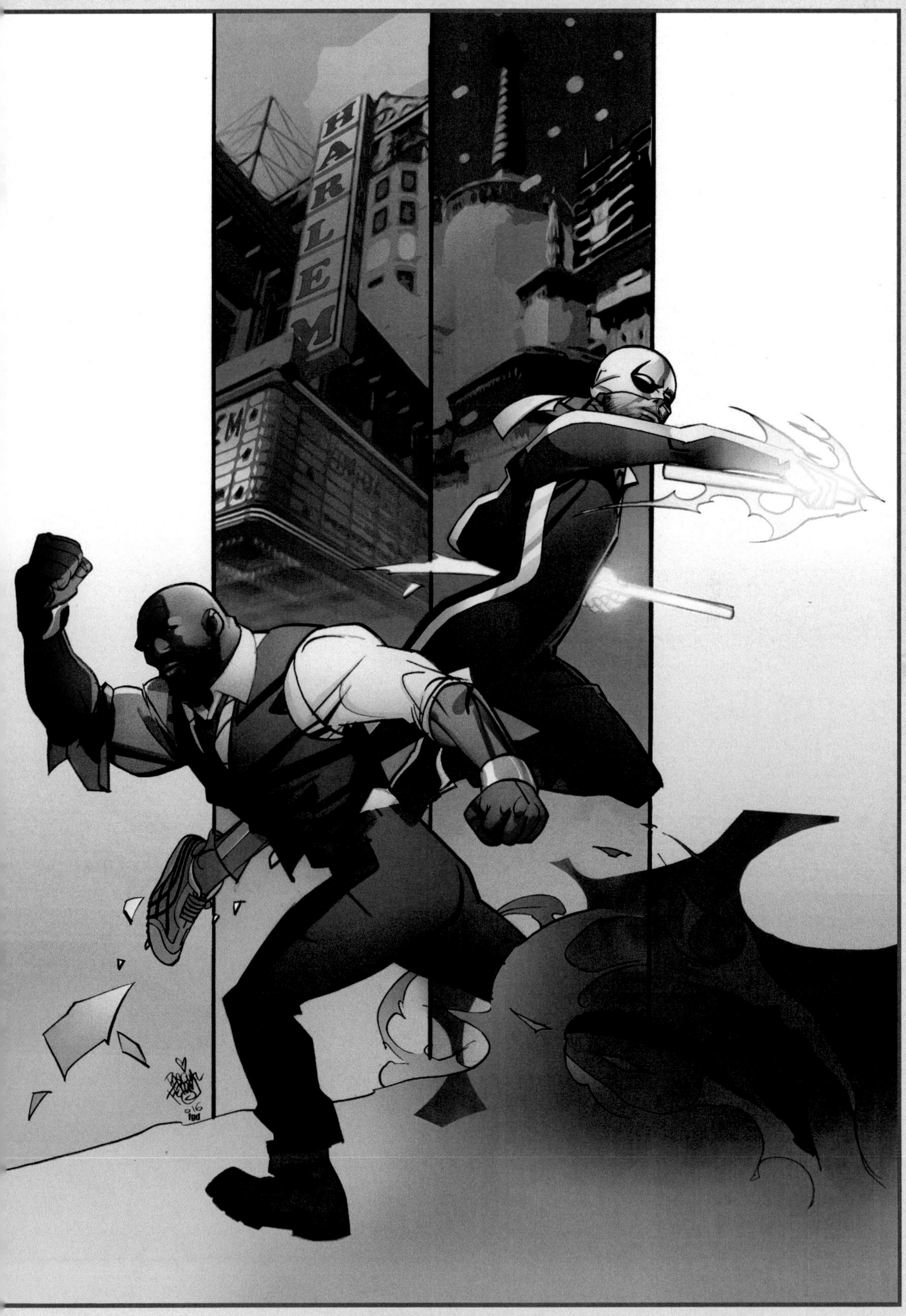
HARLEM

PASQUAL FERRY
8 DEFENDERS VARIANT

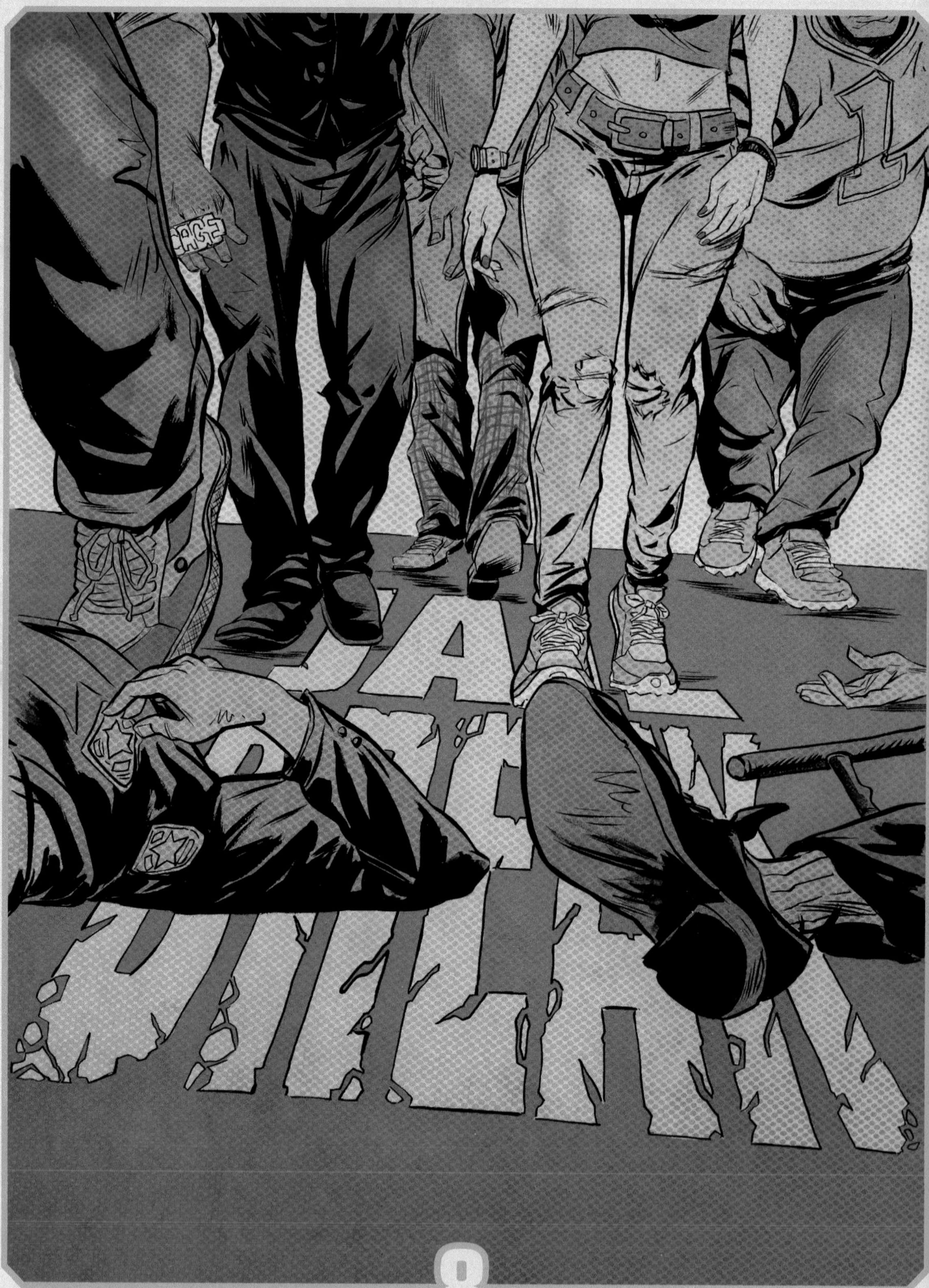
CAGE

8

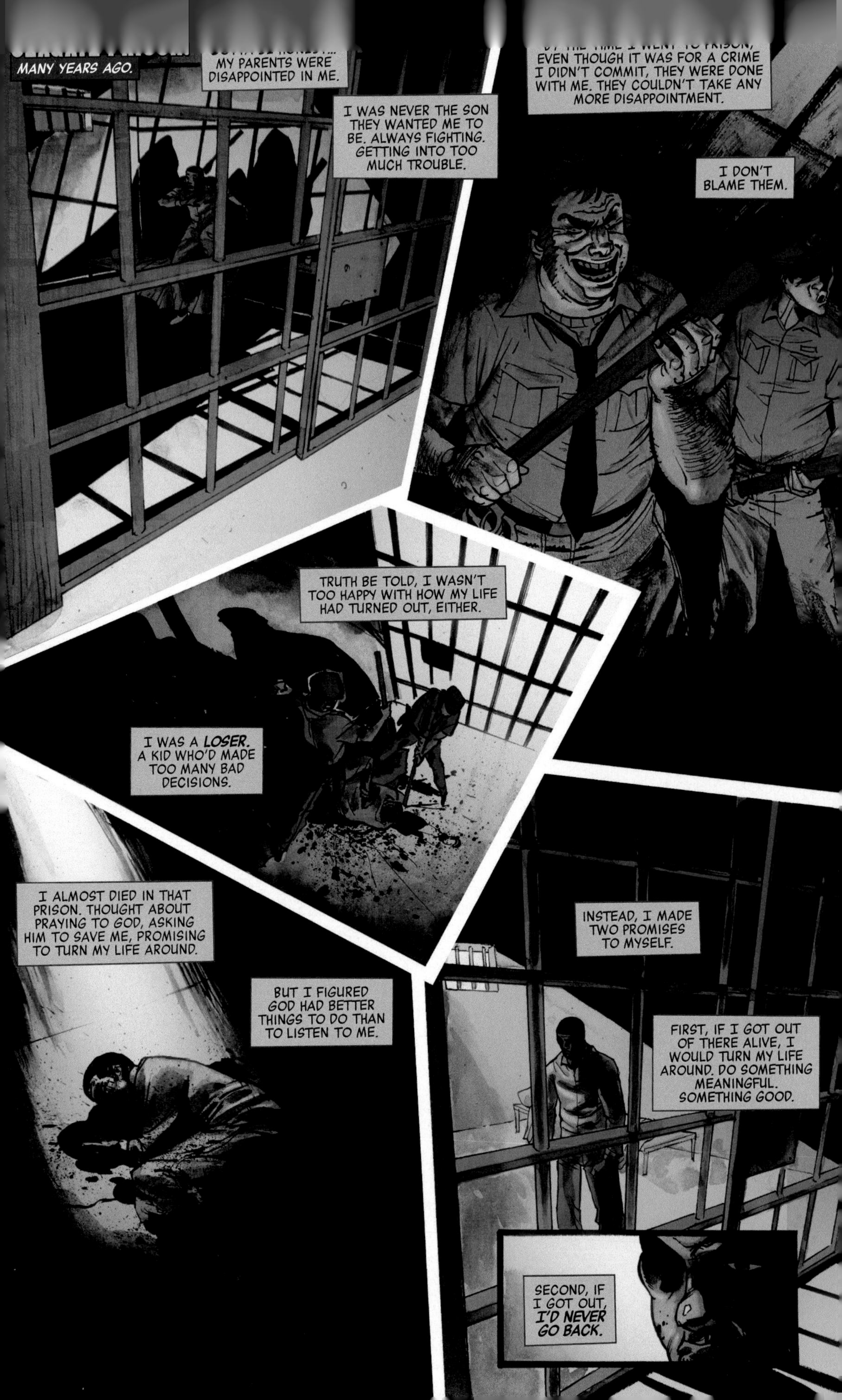

MANY YEARS AGO.
MY PARENTS WERE DISAPPOINTED IN ME.
I WAS NEVER THE SON THEY WANTED ME TO BE. ALWAYS FIGHTING. GETTING INTO TOO MUCH TROUBLE.
EVEN THOUGH IT WAS FOR A CRIME I DIDN'T COMMIT, THEY WERE DONE WITH ME. THEY COULDN'T TAKE ANY MORE DISAPPOINTMENT.
I DON'T BLAME THEM.
TRUTH BE TOLD, I WASN'T TOO HAPPY WITH HOW MY LIFE HAD TURNED OUT, EITHER.
I WAS A *LOSER.* A KID WHO'D MADE TOO MANY BAD DECISIONS.
I ALMOST DIED IN THAT PRISON. THOUGHT ABOUT PRAYING TO GOD, ASKING HIM TO SAVE ME, PROMISING TO TURN MY LIFE AROUND.
BUT I FIGURED GOD HAD BETTER THINGS TO DO THAN TO LISTEN TO ME.
INSTEAD, I MADE TWO PROMISES TO MYSELF.
FIRST, IF I GOT OUT OF THERE ALIVE, I WOULD TURN MY LIFE AROUND. DO SOMETHING MEANINGFUL. SOMETHING GOOD.
SECOND, IF I GOT OUT, *I'D NEVER GO BACK.*

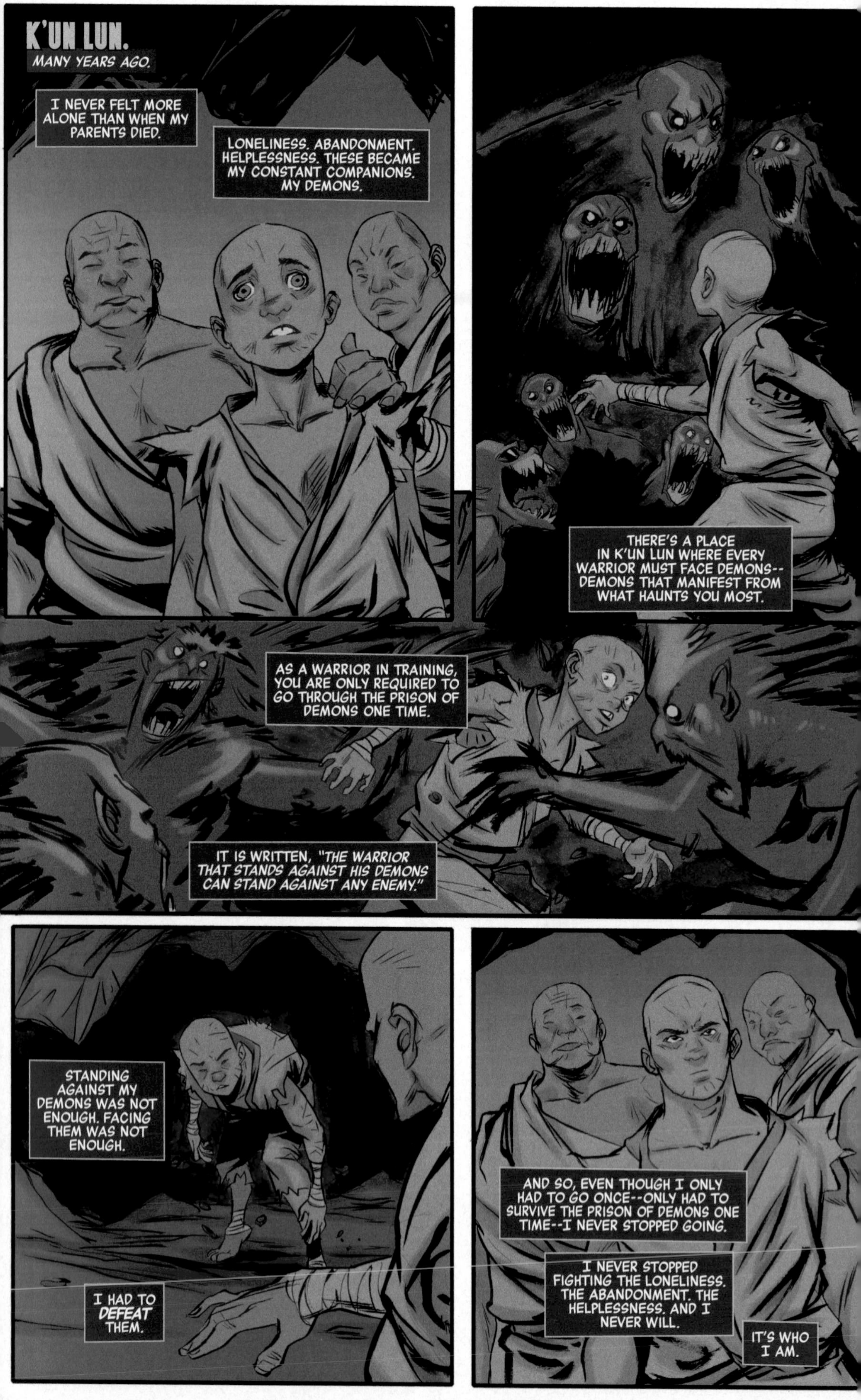
K'UN LUN.
MANY YEARS AGO.
I NEVER FELT MORE ALONE THAN WHEN MY PARENTS DIED.
LONELINESS. ABANDONMENT. HELPLESSNESS. THESE BECAME MY CONSTANT COMPANIONS. MY DEMONS.
THERE'S A PLACE IN K'UN LUN WHERE EVERY WARRIOR MUST FACE DEMONS-- DEMONS THAT MANIFEST FROM WHAT HAUNTS YOU MOST.
AS A WARRIOR IN TRAINING, YOU ARE ONLY REQUIRED TO GO THROUGH THE PRISON OF DEMONS ONE TIME.
IT IS WRITTEN, "THE WARRIOR THAT STANDS AGAINST HIS DEMONS CAN STAND AGAINST ANY ENEMY."
STANDING AGAINST MY DEMONS WAS NOT ENOUGH. FACING THEM WAS NOT ENOUGH.
I HAD TO DEFEAT THEM.
AND SO, EVEN THOUGH I ONLY HAD TO GO ONCE--ONLY HAD TO SURVIVE THE PRISON OF DEMONS ONE TIME--I NEVER STOPPED GOING.
I NEVER STOPPED FIGHTING THE LONELINESS. THE ABANDONMENT. THE HELPLESSNESS. AND I NEVER WILL.
IT'S WHO I AM.

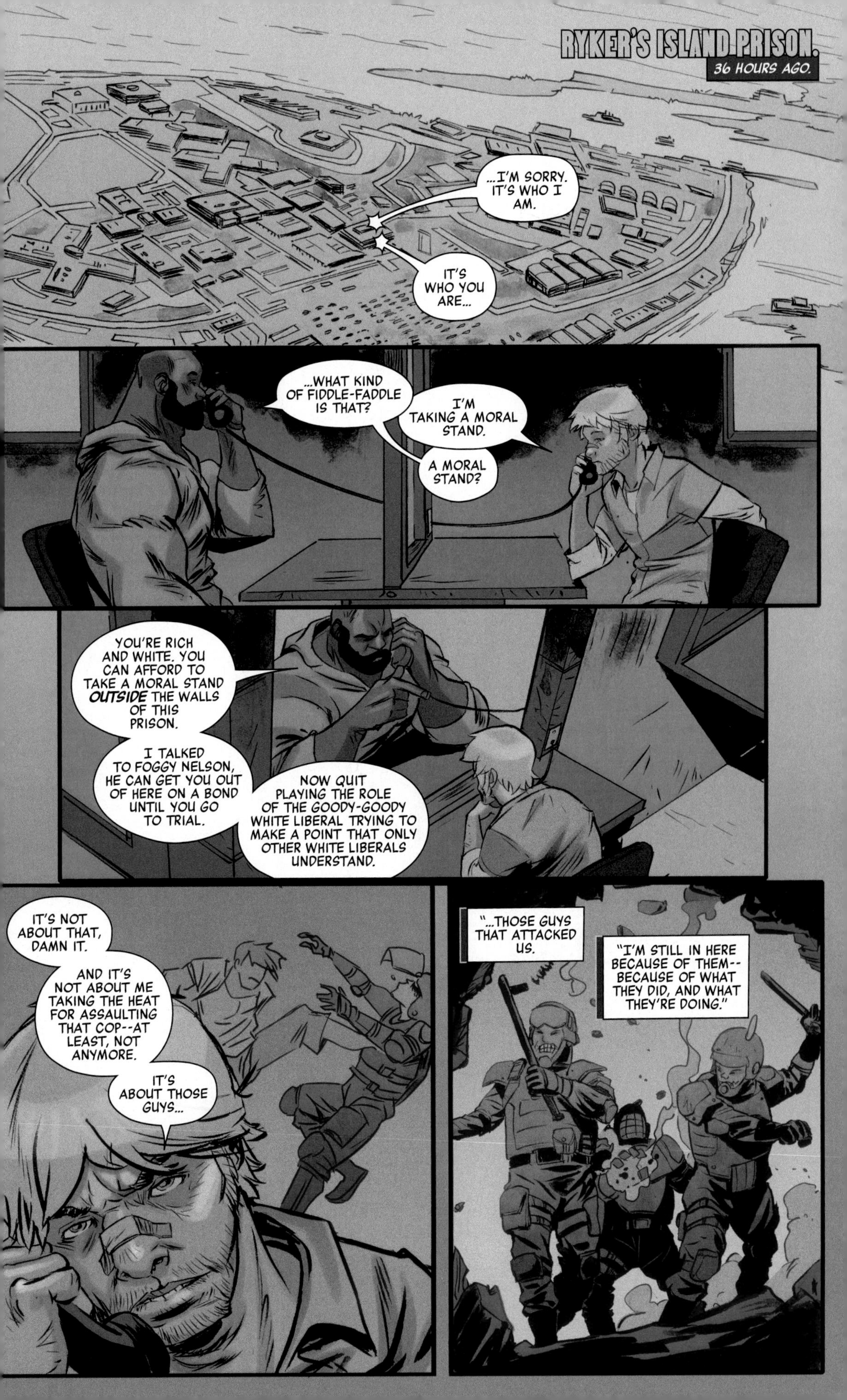
RYKER'S ISLAND PRISON.
36 HOURS AGO.
...I'M SORRY. IT'S WHO I AM.
IT'S WHO YOU ARE...
...WHAT KIND OF FIDDLE-FADDLE IS THAT?
I'M TAKING A MORAL STAND.
A MORAL STAND?
YOU'RE RICH AND WHITE. YOU CAN AFFORD TO TAKE A MORAL STAND OUTSIDE THE WALLS OF THIS PRISON.
I TALKED TO FOGGY NELSON, HE CAN GET YOU OUT OF HERE ON A BOND UNTIL YOU GO TO TRIAL.
NOW QUIT PLAYING THE ROLE OF THE GOODY-GOODY WHITE LIBERAL TRYING TO MAKE A POINT THAT ONLY OTHER WHITE LIBERALS UNDERSTAND.
IT'S NOT ABOUT THAT, DAMN IT.
AND IT'S NOT ABOUT ME TAKING THE HEAT FOR ASSAULTING THAT COP--AT LEAST, NOT ANYMORE.
IT'S ABOUT THOSE GUYS...
"...THOSE GUYS THAT ATTACKED US.
"I'M STILL IN HERE BECAUSE OF THEM--BECAUSE OF WHAT THEY DID, AND WHAT THEY'RE DOING."

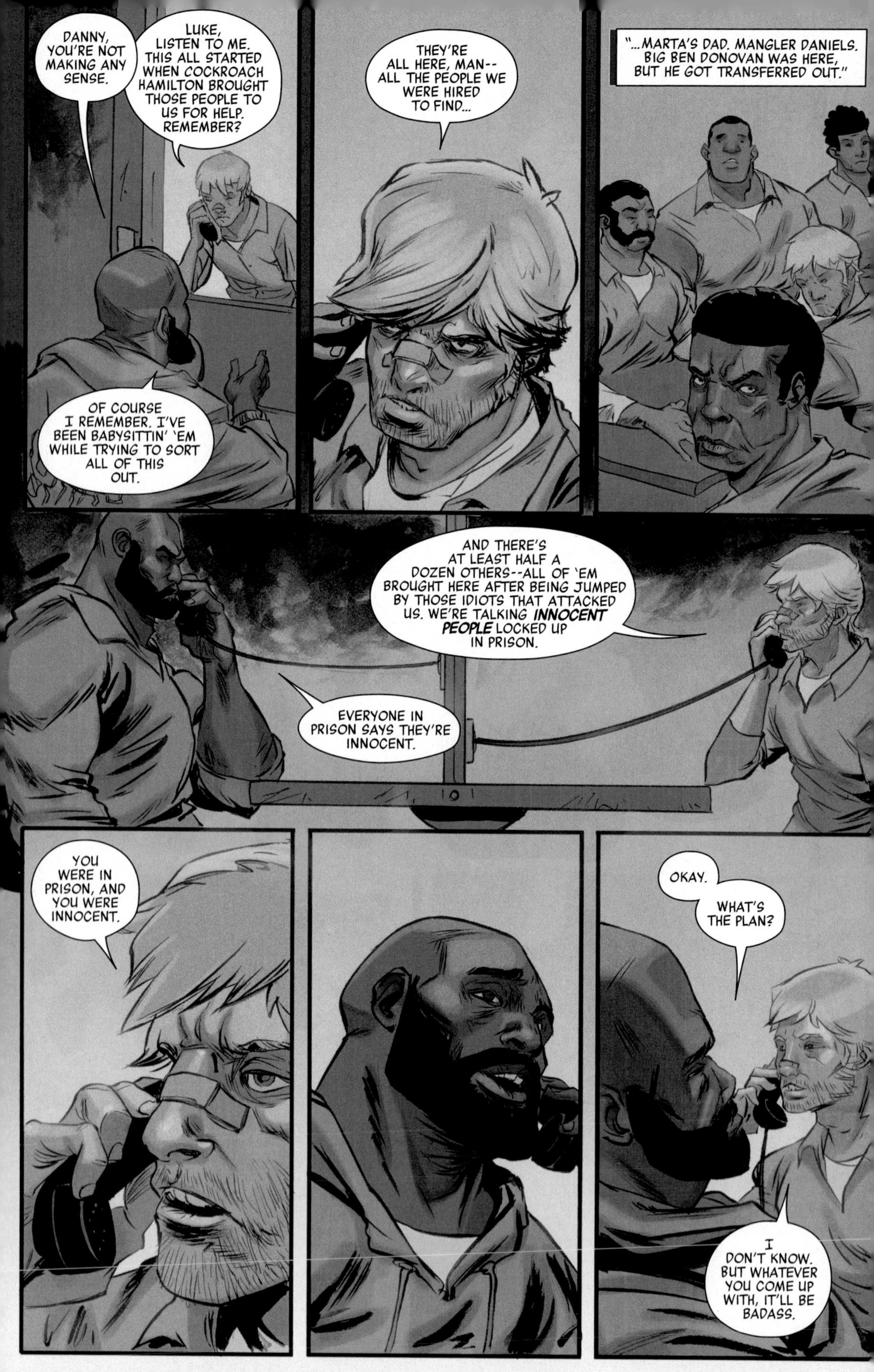
DANNY, YOU'RE NOT MAKING ANY SENSE.
LUKE, LISTEN TO ME. THIS ALL STARTED WHEN COCKROACH HAMILTON BROUGHT THOSE PEOPLE TO US FOR HELP. REMEMBER?
OF COURSE I REMEMBER. I'VE BEEN BABYSITTIN' 'EM WHILE TRYING TO SORT ALL OF THIS OUT.
THEY'RE ALL HERE, MAN-- ALL THE PEOPLE WE WERE HIRED TO FIND...
"...MARTA'S DAD. MANGLER DANIELS. BIG BEN DONOVAN WAS HERE, BUT HE GOT TRANSFERRED OUT."
AND THERE'S AT LEAST HALF A DOZEN OTHERS--ALL OF 'EM BROUGHT HERE AFTER BEING JUMPED BY THOSE IDIOTS THAT ATTACKED US. WE'RE TALKING INNOCENT PEOPLE LOCKED UP IN PRISON.
EVERYONE IN PRISON SAYS THEY'RE INNOCENT.
YOU WERE IN PRISON, AND YOU WERE INNOCENT.
OKAY.
WHAT'S THE PLAN?
I DON'T KNOW. BUT WHATEVER YOU COME UP WITH, IT'LL BE BADASS.

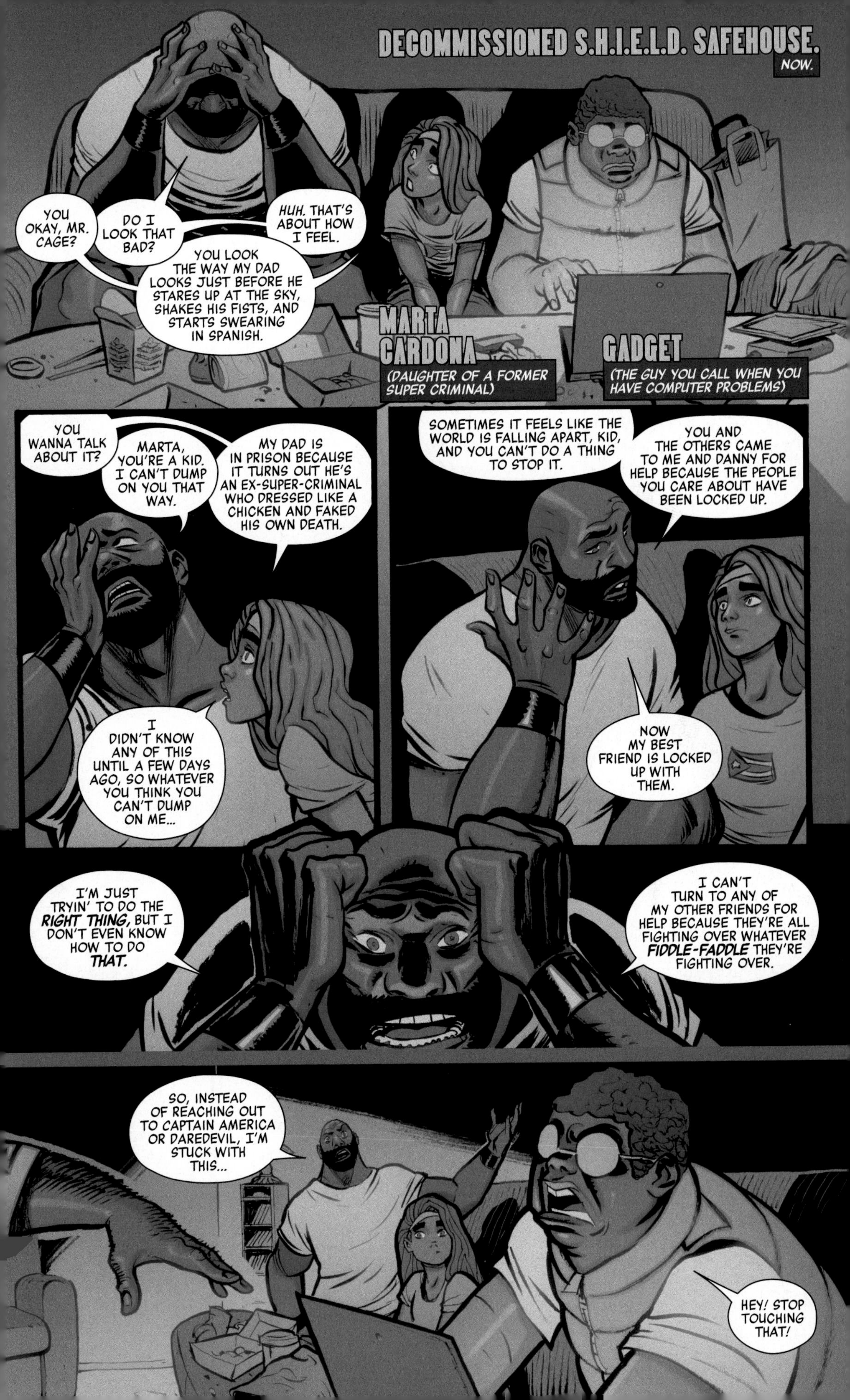

DECOMMISSIONED S.H.I.E.L.D. SAFEHOUSE.
NOW.
YOU OKAY, MR. CAGE?
DO I LOOK THAT BAD?
HUH. THAT'S ABOUT HOW I FEEL.
YOU LOOK THE WAY MY DAD LOOKS JUST BEFORE HE STARES UP AT THE SKY, SHAKES HIS FISTS, AND STARTS SWEARING IN SPANISH.
MARTA CARDONA
(DAUGHTER OF A FORMER SUPER CRIMINAL)
GADGET
(THE GUY YOU CALL WHEN YOU HAVE COMPUTER PROBLEMS)
YOU WANNA TALK ABOUT IT?
MARTA, YOU'RE A KID. I CAN'T DUMP ON YOU THAT WAY.
MY DAD IS IN PRISON BECAUSE IT TURNS OUT HE'S AN EX-SUPER-CRIMINAL WHO DRESSED LIKE A CHICKEN AND FAKED HIS OWN DEATH.
I DIDN'T KNOW ANY OF THIS UNTIL A FEW DAYS AGO, SO WHATEVER YOU THINK YOU CAN'T DUMP ON ME...
SOMETIMES IT FEELS LIKE THE WORLD IS FALLING APART, KID, AND YOU CAN'T DO A THING TO STOP IT.
YOU AND THE OTHERS CAME TO ME AND DANNY FOR HELP BECAUSE THE PEOPLE YOU CARE ABOUT HAVE BEEN LOCKED UP.
NOW MY BEST FRIEND IS LOCKED UP WITH THEM.
I'M JUST TRYIN' TO DO THE RIGHT THING, BUT I DON'T EVEN KNOW HOW TO DO THAT.
I CAN'T TURN TO ANY OF MY OTHER FRIENDS FOR HELP BECAUSE THEY'RE ALL FIGHTING OVER WHATEVER FIDDLE-FADDLE THEY'RE FIGHTING OVER.
SO, INSTEAD OF REACHING OUT TO CAPTAIN AMERICA OR DAREDEVIL, I'M STUCK WITH THIS...
HEY! STOP TOUCHING THAT!

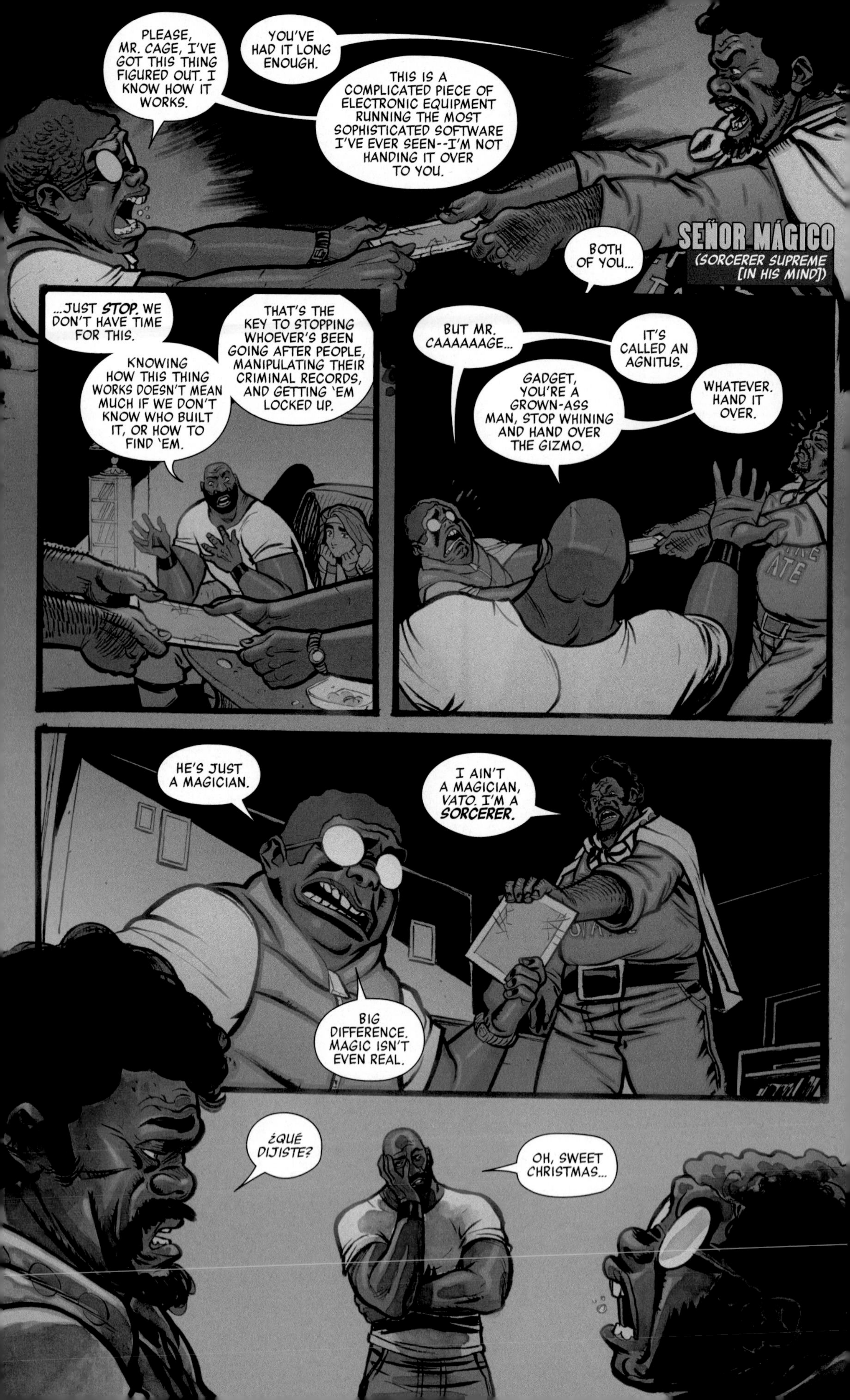
PLEASE, MR. CAGE, I'VE GOT THIS THING FIGURED OUT. I KNOW HOW IT WORKS.
YOU'VE HAD IT LONG ENOUGH.
THIS IS A COMPLICATED PIECE OF ELECTRONIC EQUIPMENT RUNNING THE MOST SOPHISTICATED SOFTWARE I'VE EVER SEEN--I'M NOT HANDING IT OVER TO YOU.
SEÑOR MÁGICO
(SORCERER SUPREME [IN HIS MIND])
BOTH OF YOU...
...JUST STOP. WE DON'T HAVE TIME FOR THIS.
KNOWING HOW THIS THING WORKS DOESN'T MEAN MUCH IF WE DON'T KNOW WHO BUILT IT, OR HOW TO FIND 'EM.
THAT'S THE KEY TO STOPPING WHOEVER'S BEEN GOING AFTER PEOPLE, MANIPULATING THEIR CRIMINAL RECORDS, AND GETTING 'EM LOCKED UP.
BUT MR. CAAAAAAGE...
IT'S CALLED AN AGNITUS.
GADGET, YOU'RE A GROWN-ASS MAN, STOP WHINING AND HAND OVER THE GIZMO.
WHATEVER. HAND IT OVER.
HE'S JUST A MAGICIAN.
I AIN'T A MAGICIAN, VATO. I'M A SORCERER.
BIG DIFFERENCE. MAGIC ISN'T EVEN REAL.
¿QUÉ DIJISTE?
OH, SWEET CHRISTMAS...

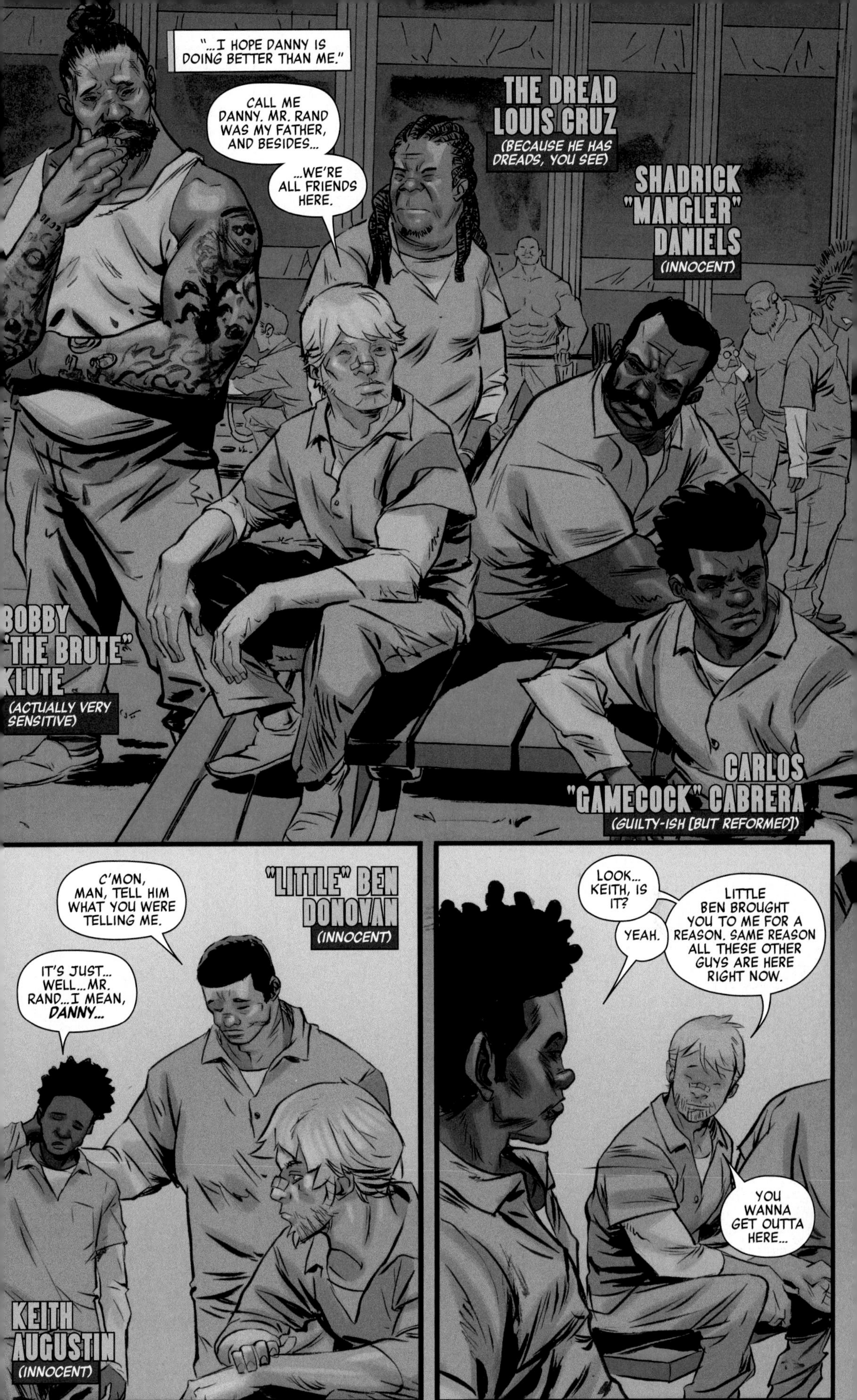
"...I HOPE DANNY IS DOING BETTER THAN ME."
CALL ME DANNY. MR. RAND WAS MY FATHER, AND BESIDES...
...WE'RE ALL FRIENDS HERE.
THE DREAD LOUIS CRUZ
(BECAUSE HE HAS DREADS, YOU SEE)
SHADRICK "MANGLER" DANIELS
(INNOCENT)
BOBBY "THE BRUTE" KLUTE
(ACTUALLY VERY SENSITIVE)
CARLOS "GAMECOCK" CABRERA
(GUILTY-ISH [BUT REFORMED])
C'MON, MAN, TELL HIM WHAT YOU WERE TELLING ME.
"LITTLE" BEN DONOVAN
(INNOCENT)
IT'S JUST... WELL...MR. RAND...I MEAN, DANNY...
KEITH AUGUSTIN
(INNOCENT)
LOOK... KEITH, IS IT?
YEAH.
LITTLE BEN BROUGHT YOU TO ME FOR A REASON. SAME REASON ALL THESE OTHER GUYS ARE HERE RIGHT NOW.
YOU WANNA GET OUTTA HERE...

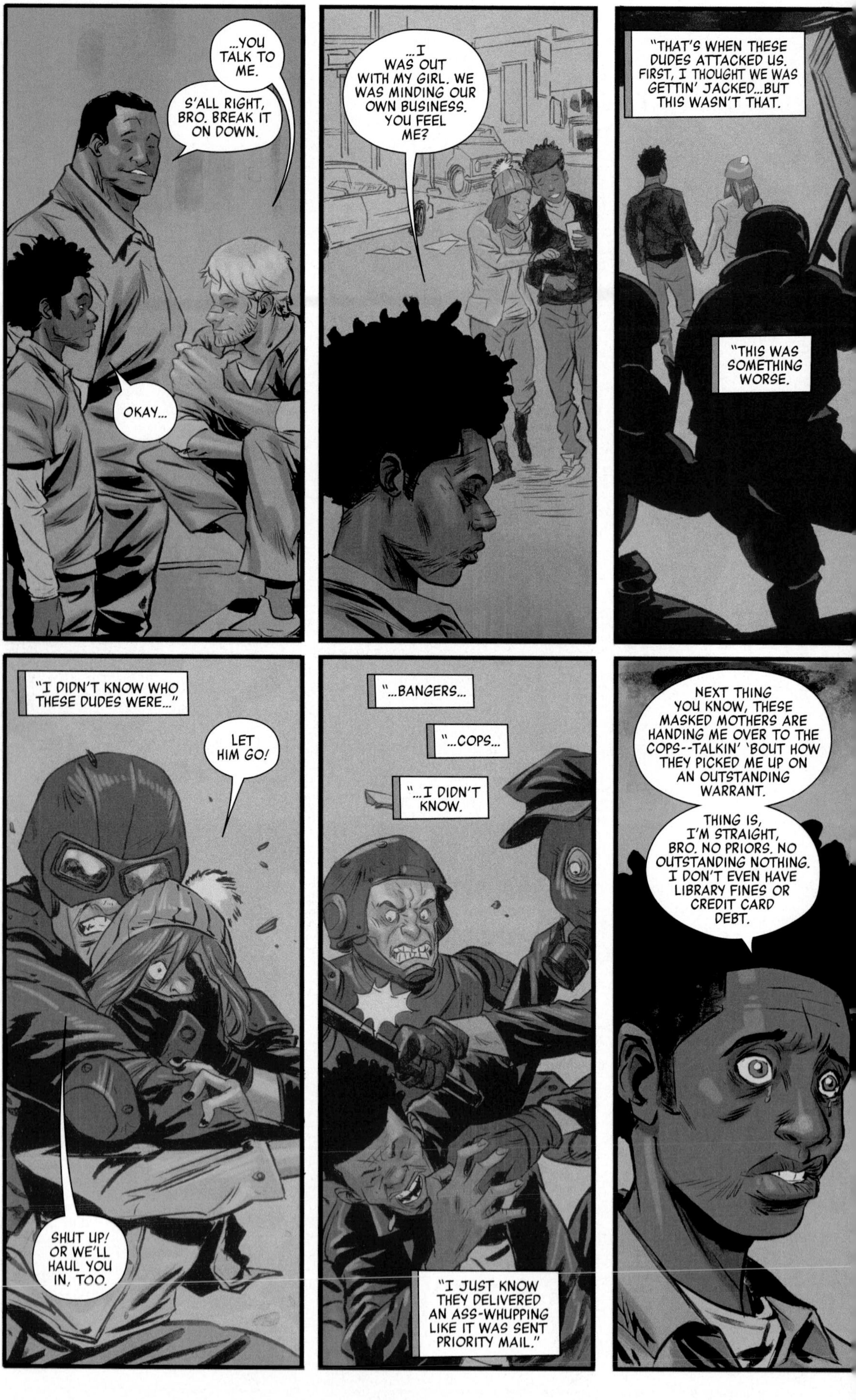
...YOU TALK TO ME.
S'ALL RIGHT, BRO. BREAK IT ON DOWN.
OKAY...
...I WAS OUT WITH MY GIRL. WE WAS MINDING OUR OWN BUSINESS. YOU FEEL ME?
"THAT'S WHEN THESE DUDES ATTACKED US. FIRST, I THOUGHT WE WAS GETTIN' JACKED...BUT THIS WASN'T THAT.
"THIS WAS SOMETHING WORSE.
"I DIDN'T KNOW WHO THESE DUDES WERE..."
LET HIM GO!
SHUT UP! OR WE'LL HAUL YOU IN, TOO.
"...BANGERS...
"...COPS...
"...I DIDN'T KNOW.
"I JUST KNOW THEY DELIVERED AN ASS-WHUPPING LIKE IT WAS SENT PRIORITY MAIL."
NEXT THING YOU KNOW, THESE MASKED MOTHERS ARE HANDING ME OVER TO THE COPS--TALKIN' 'BOUT HOW THEY PICKED ME UP ON AN OUTSTANDING WARRANT.
THING IS, I'M STRAIGHT, BRO. NO PRIORS. NO OUTSTANDING NOTHING. I DON'T EVEN HAVE LIBRARY FINES OR CREDIT CARD DEBT.

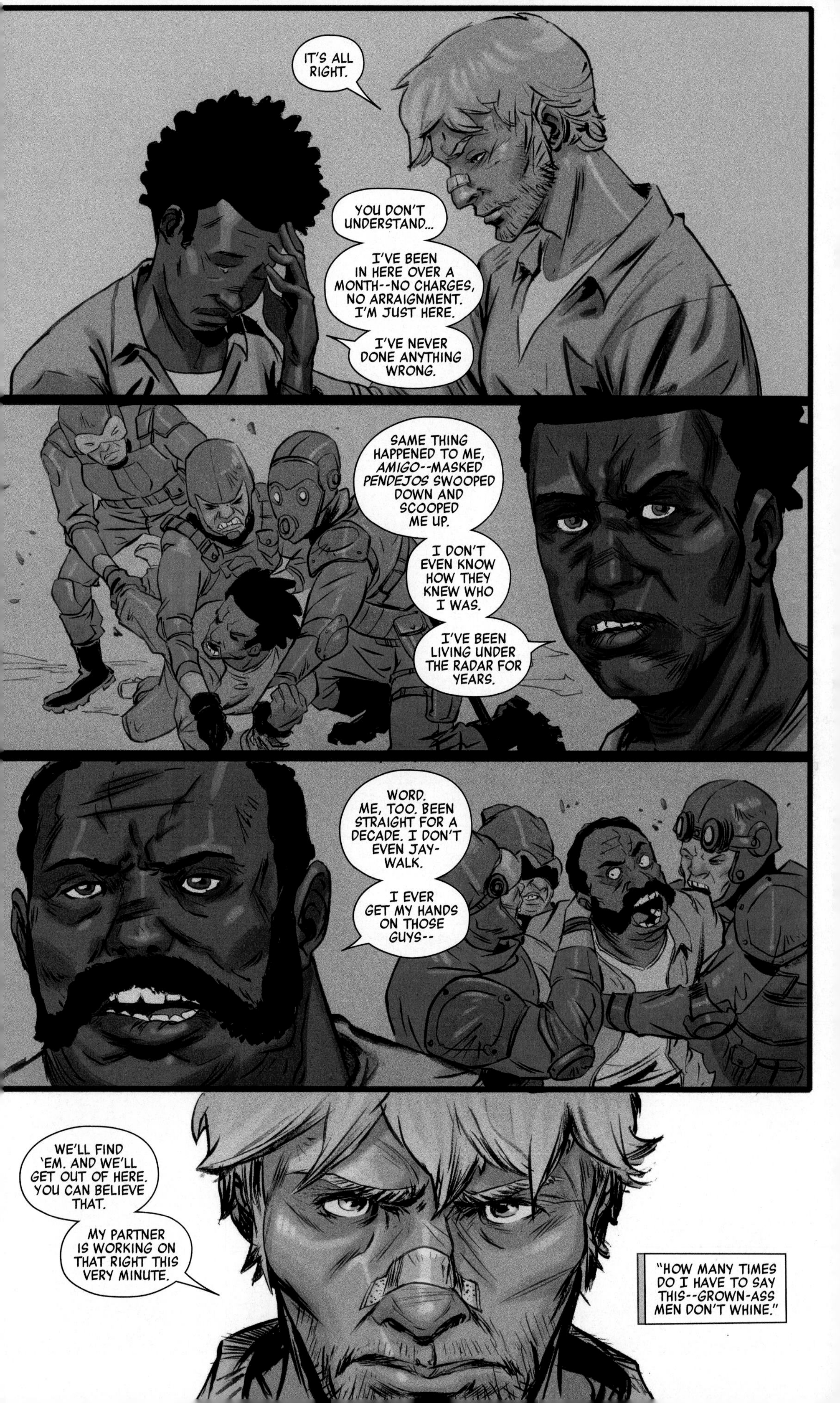
IT'S ALL RIGHT.
YOU DON'T UNDERSTAND...
I'VE BEEN IN HERE OVER A MONTH--NO CHARGES, NO ARRAIGNMENT. I'M JUST HERE.
I'VE NEVER DONE ANYTHING WRONG.
SAME THING HAPPENED TO ME, AMIGO--MASKED PENDEJOS SWOOPED DOWN AND SCOOPED ME UP.
I DON'T EVEN KNOW HOW THEY KNEW WHO I WAS.
I'VE BEEN LIVING UNDER THE RADAR FOR YEARS.
WORD. ME, TOO. BEEN STRAIGHT FOR A DECADE. I DON'T EVEN JAY-WALK.
I EVER GET MY HANDS ON THOSE GUYS--
WE'LL FIND 'EM. AND WE'LL GET OUT OF HERE. YOU CAN BELIEVE THAT.
MY PARTNER IS WORKING ON THAT RIGHT THIS VERY MINUTE.
"HOW MANY TIMES DO I HAVE TO SAY THIS--GROWN-ASS MEN DON'T WHINE."

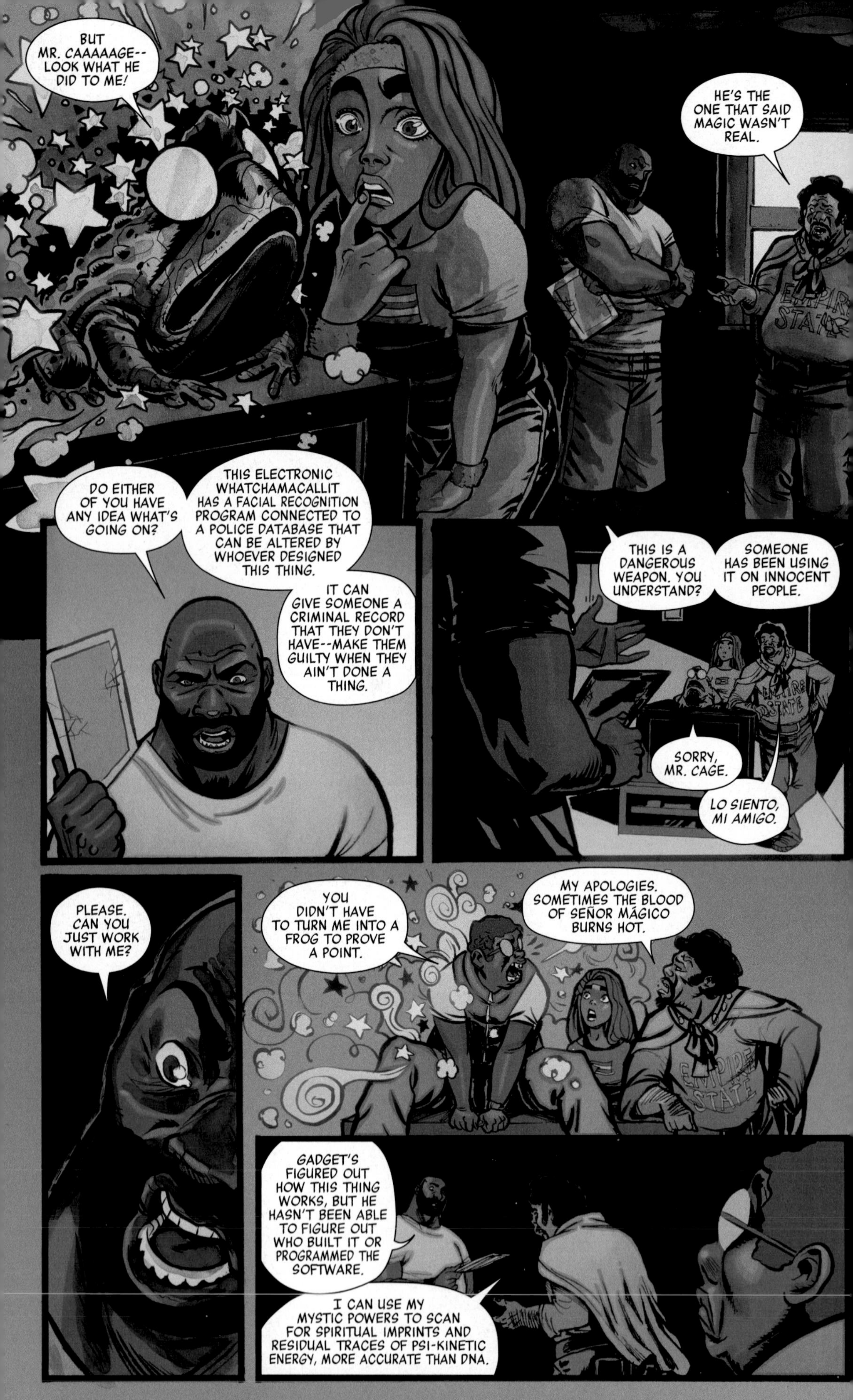
BUT MR. CAAAAAGE--LOOK WHAT HE DID TO ME!
HE'S THE ONE THAT SAID MAGIC WASN'T REAL.
DO EITHER OF YOU HAVE ANY IDEA WHAT'S GOING ON?
THIS ELECTRONIC WHATCHAMACALLIT HAS A FACIAL RECOGNITION PROGRAM CONNECTED TO A POLICE DATABASE THAT CAN BE ALTERED BY WHOEVER DESIGNED THIS THING.
IT CAN GIVE SOMEONE A CRIMINAL RECORD THAT THEY DON'T HAVE--MAKE THEM GUILTY WHEN THEY AIN'T DONE A THING.
THIS IS A DANGEROUS WEAPON. YOU UNDERSTAND?
SOMEONE HAS BEEN USING IT ON INNOCENT PEOPLE.
SORRY, MR. CAGE.
LO SIENTO, MI AMIGO.
PLEASE. CAN YOU JUST WORK WITH ME?
YOU DIDN'T HAVE TO TURN ME INTO A FROG TO PROVE A POINT.
MY APOLOGIES. SOMETIMES THE BLOOD OF SEÑOR MÁGICO BURNS HOT.
GADGET'S FIGURED OUT HOW THIS THING WORKS, BUT HE HASN'T BEEN ABLE TO FIGURE OUT WHO BUILT IT OR PROGRAMMED THE SOFTWARE.
I CAN USE MY MYSTIC POWERS TO SCAN FOR SPIRITUAL IMPRINTS AND RESIDUAL TRACES OF PSI-KINETIC ENERGY, MORE ACCURATE THAN DNA.
EMPIRE STATE

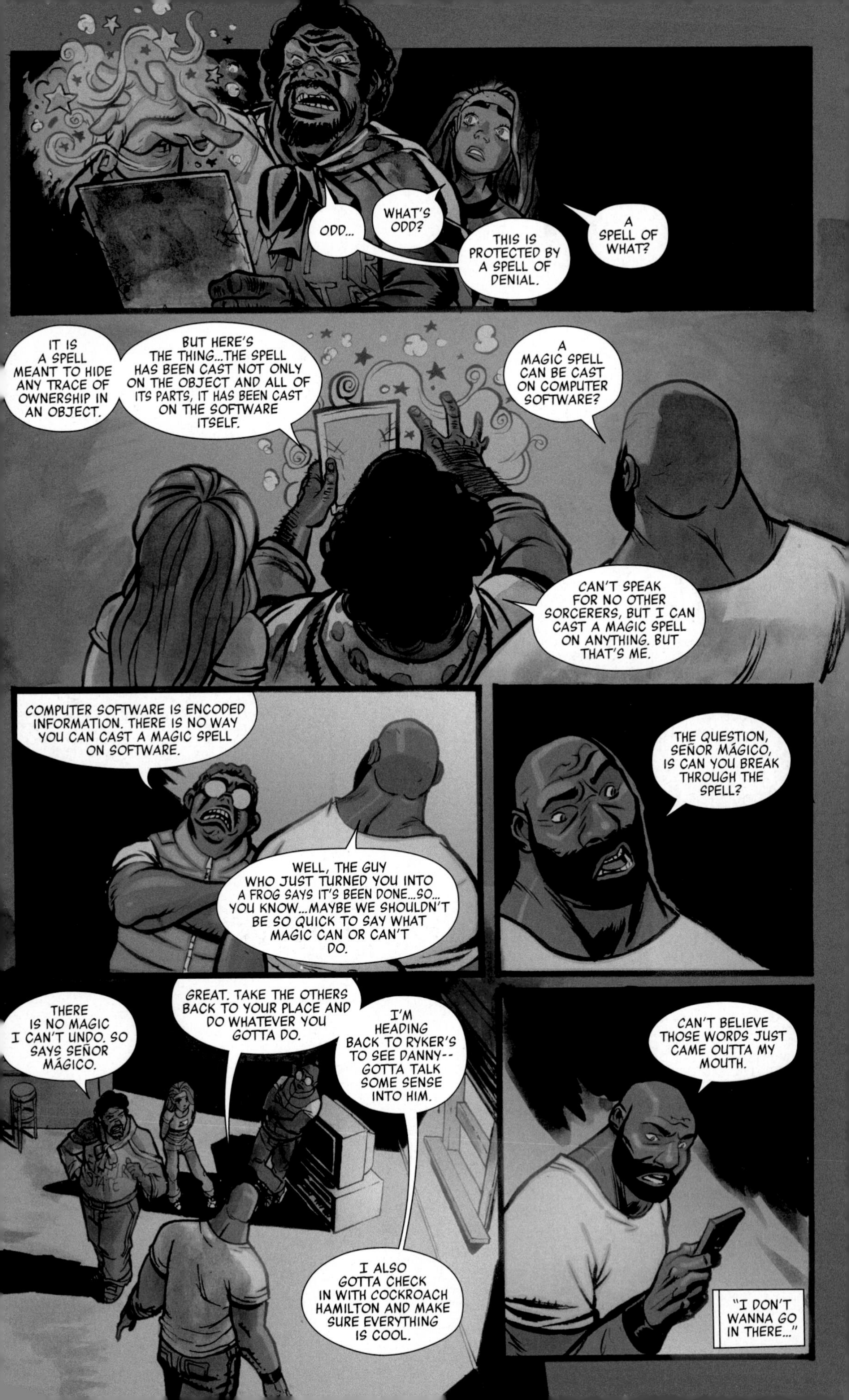
ODD...
WHAT'S ODD?
THIS IS PROTECTED BY A SPELL OF DENIAL.
A SPELL OF WHAT?
IT IS A SPELL MEANT TO HIDE ANY TRACE OF OWNERSHIP IN AN OBJECT.
BUT HERE'S THE THING...THE SPELL HAS BEEN CAST NOT ONLY ON THE OBJECT AND ALL OF ITS PARTS, IT HAS BEEN CAST ON THE SOFTWARE ITSELF.
A MAGIC SPELL CAN BE CAST ON COMPUTER SOFTWARE?
CAN'T SPEAK FOR NO OTHER SORCERERS, BUT I CAN CAST A MAGIC SPELL ON ANYTHING. BUT THAT'S ME.
COMPUTER SOFTWARE IS ENCODED INFORMATION. THERE IS NO WAY YOU CAN CAST A MAGIC SPELL ON SOFTWARE.
WELL, THE GUY WHO JUST TURNED YOU INTO A FROG SAYS IT'S BEEN DONE...SO... YOU KNOW...MAYBE WE SHOULDN'T BE SO QUICK TO SAY WHAT MAGIC CAN OR CAN'T DO.
THE QUESTION, SEÑOR MÁGICO, IS CAN YOU BREAK THROUGH THE SPELL?
THERE IS NO MAGIC I CAN'T UNDO. SO SAYS SEÑOR MÁGICO.
GREAT. TAKE THE OTHERS BACK TO YOUR PLACE AND DO WHATEVER YOU GOTTA DO.
I'M HEADING BACK TO RYKER'S TO SEE DANNY-- GOTTA TALK SOME SENSE INTO HIM.
I ALSO GOTTA CHECK IN WITH COCKROACH HAMILTON AND MAKE SURE EVERYTHING IS COOL.
CAN'T BELIEVE THOSE WORDS JUST CAME OUTTA MY MOUTH.
"I DON'T WANNA GO IN THERE..."

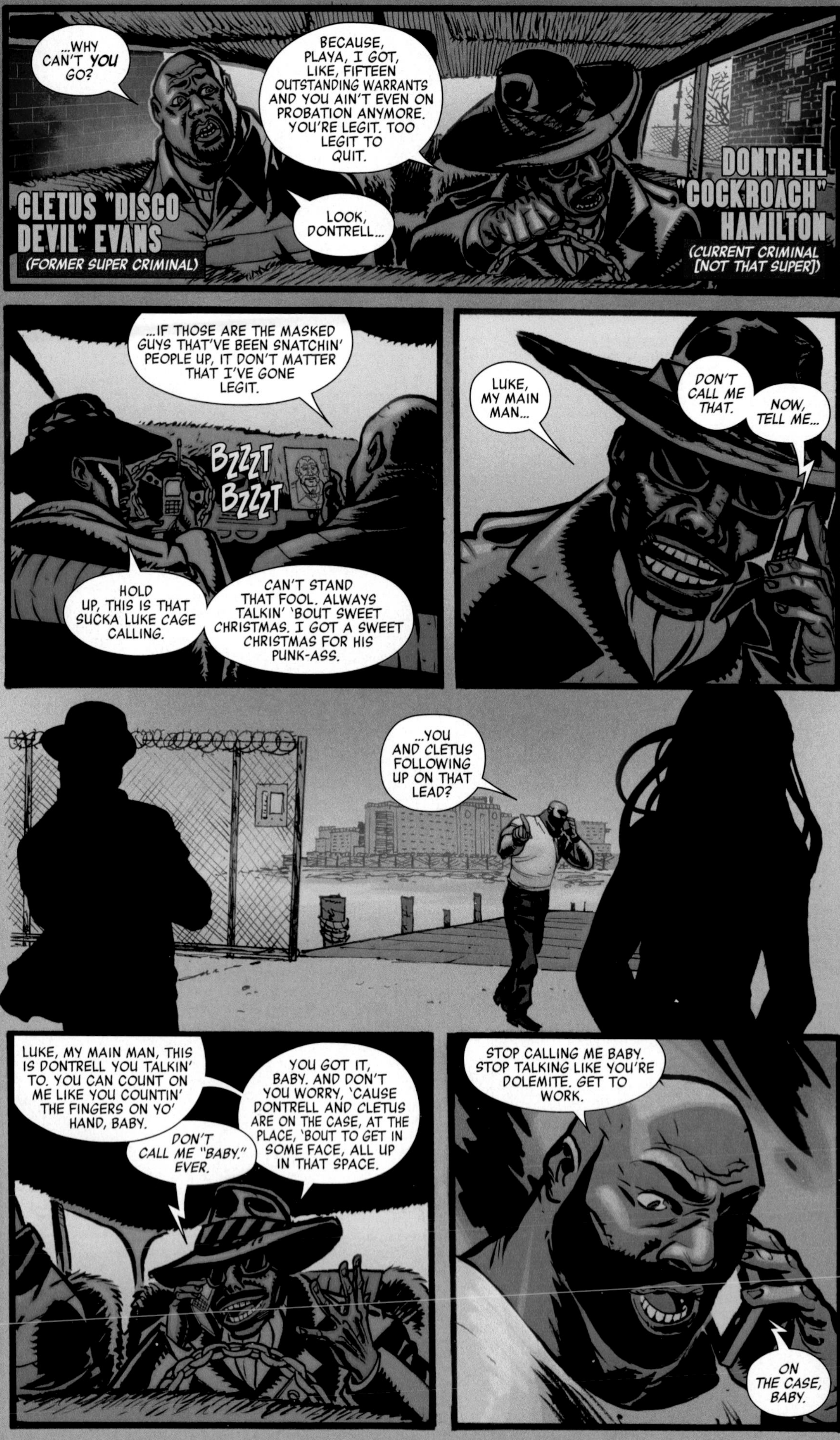
...WHY CAN'T YOU GO?
BECAUSE, PLAYA, I GOT, LIKE, FIFTEEN OUTSTANDING WARRANTS AND YOU AIN'T EVEN ON PROBATION ANYMORE. YOU'RE LEGIT. TOO LEGIT TO QUIT.
CLETUS "DISCO DEVIL" EVANS
(FORMER SUPER CRIMINAL)
LOOK, DONTRELL...
DONTRELL "COCKROACH" HAMILTON
(CURRENT CRIMINAL [NOT THAT SUPER])
...IF THOSE ARE THE MASKED GUYS THAT'VE BEEN SNATCHIN' PEOPLE UP, IT DON'T MATTER THAT I'VE GONE LEGIT.
BZZZT
BZZZT
HOLD UP, THIS IS THAT SUCKA LUKE CAGE CALLING.
CAN'T STAND THAT FOOL. ALWAYS TALKIN' 'BOUT SWEET CHRISTMAS. I GOT A SWEET CHRISTMAS FOR HIS PUNK-ASS.
LUKE, MY MAIN MAN...
DON'T CALL ME THAT.
NOW, TELL ME...
...YOU AND CLETUS FOLLOWING UP ON THAT LEAD?
LUKE, MY MAIN MAN, THIS IS DONTRELL YOU TALKIN' TO. YOU CAN COUNT ON ME LIKE YOU COUNTIN' THE FINGERS ON YO' HAND, BABY.
DON'T CALL ME "BABY." EVER.
YOU GOT IT, BABY. AND DON'T YOU WORRY, 'CAUSE DONTRELL AND CLETUS ARE ON THE CASE, AT THE PLACE, 'BOUT TO GET IN SOME FACE, ALL UP IN THAT SPACE.
STOP CALLING ME BABY. STOP TALKING LIKE YOU'RE DOLEMITE. GET TO WORK.
ON THE CASE, BABY.

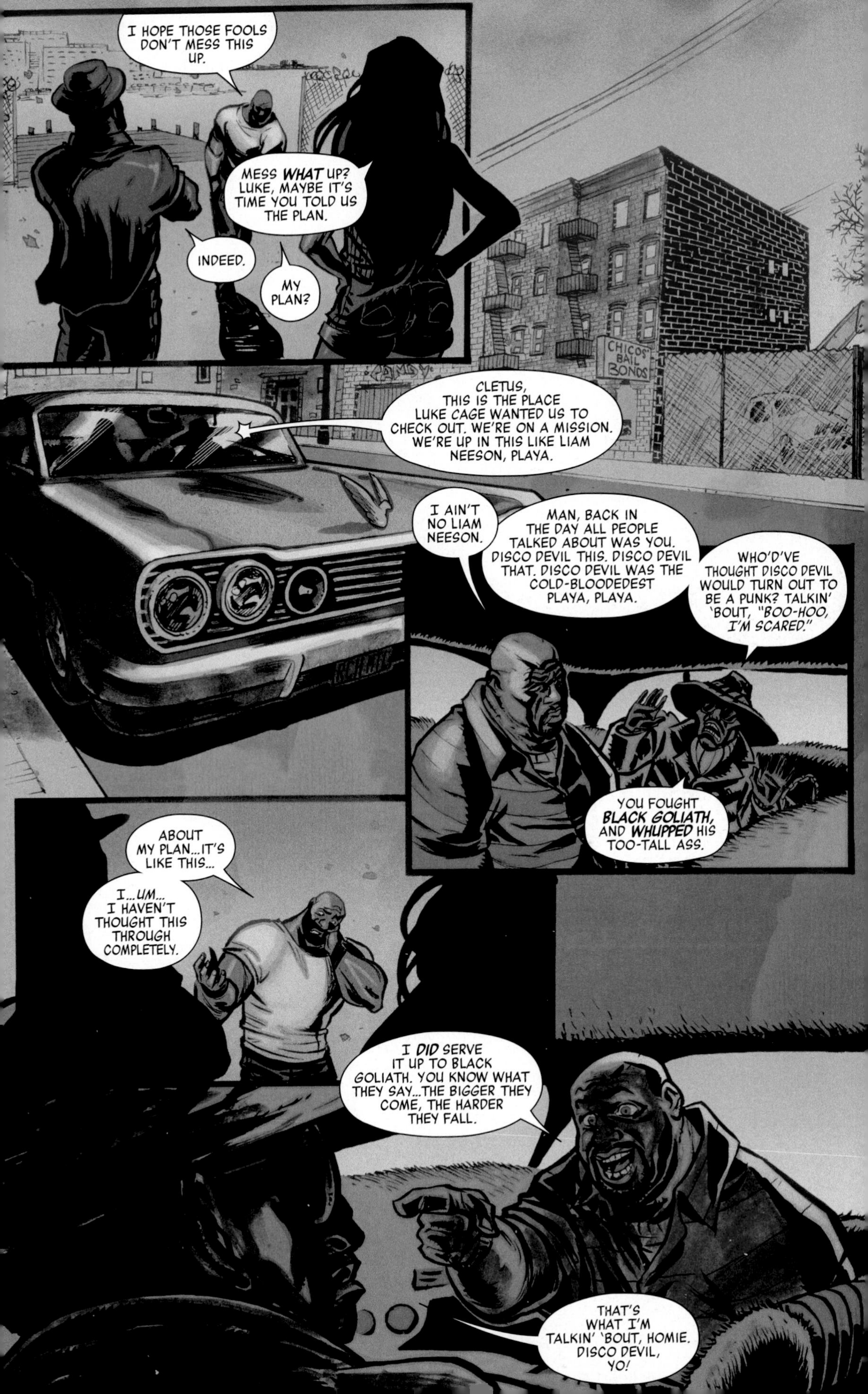
I HOPE THOSE FOOLS DON'T MESS THIS UP.
MESS WHAT UP? LUKE, MAYBE IT'S TIME YOU TOLD US THE PLAN.
INDEED.
MY PLAN?
CHICOS' BAIL BONDS
CLETUS, THIS IS THE PLACE LUKE CAGE WANTED US TO CHECK OUT. WE'RE ON A MISSION. WE'RE UP IN THIS LIKE LIAM NEESON, PLAYA.
I AIN'T NO LIAM NEESON.
MAN, BACK IN THE DAY ALL PEOPLE TALKED ABOUT WAS YOU. DISCO DEVIL THIS. DISCO DEVIL THAT. DISCO DEVIL WAS THE COLD-BLOODEDEST PLAYA, PLAYA.
WHO'D'VE THOUGHT DISCO DEVIL WOULD TURN OUT TO BE A PUNK? TALKIN' 'BOUT, "BOO-HOO, I'M SCARED."
YOU FOUGHT BLACK GOLIATH, AND WHUPPED HIS TOO-TALL ASS.
ABOUT MY PLAN...IT'S LIKE THIS...
I...UM... I HAVEN'T THOUGHT THIS THROUGH COMPLETELY.
I DID SERVE IT UP TO BLACK GOLIATH. YOU KNOW WHAT THEY SAY...THE BIGGER THEY COME, THE HARDER THEY FALL.
THAT'S WHAT I'M TALKIN' 'BOUT, HOMIE. DISCO DEVIL, YO!

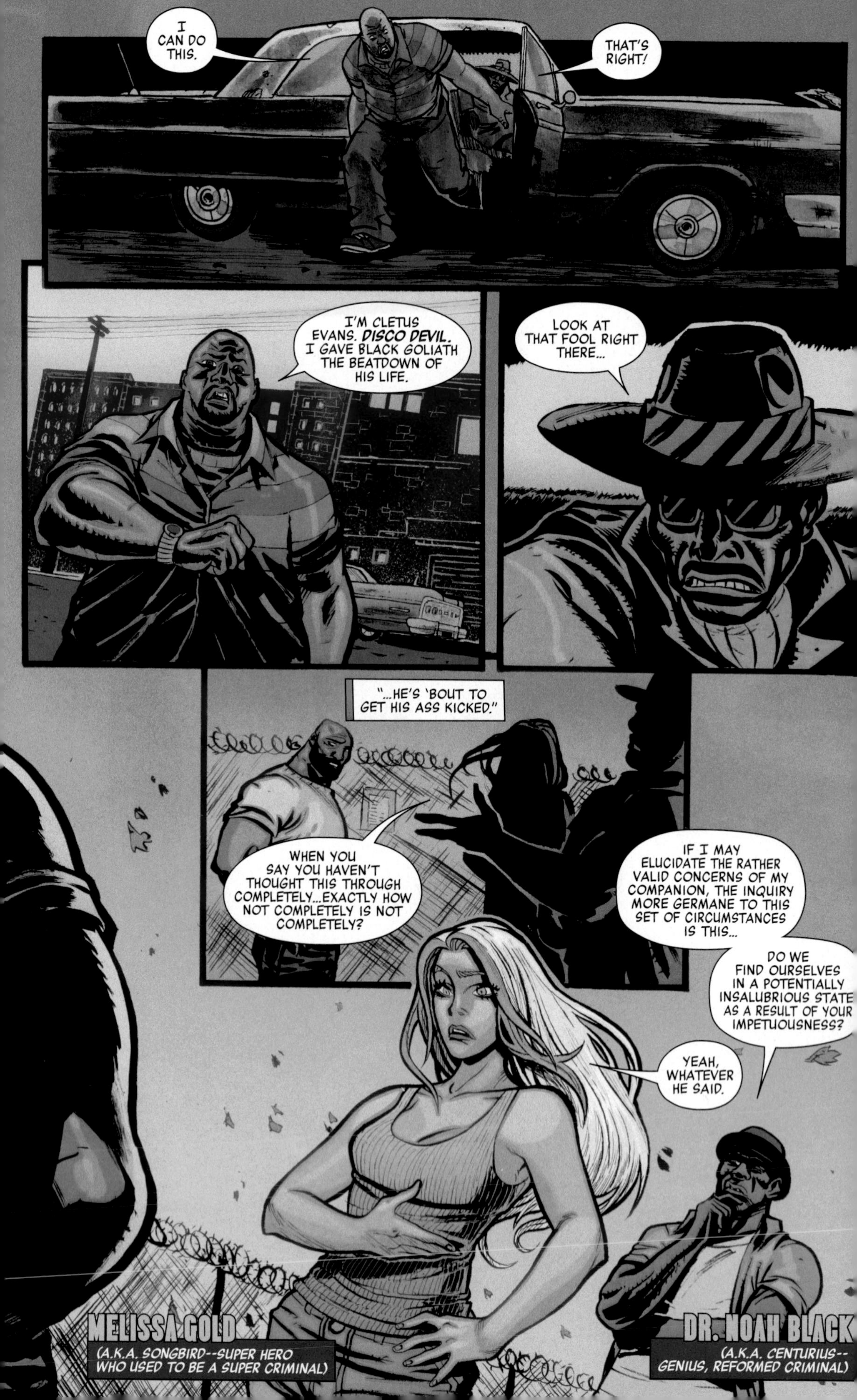
I CAN DO THIS.
THAT'S RIGHT!
I'M CLETUS EVANS. **DISCO DEVIL.** I GAVE BLACK GOLIATH THE BEATDOWN OF HIS LIFE.
LOOK AT THAT FOOL RIGHT THERE...
"...HE'S 'BOUT TO GET HIS ASS KICKED."
WHEN YOU SAY YOU HAVEN'T THOUGHT THIS THROUGH COMPLETELY...EXACTLY HOW NOT COMPLETELY IS NOT COMPLETELY?
IF I MAY ELUCIDATE THE RATHER VALID CONCERNS OF MY COMPANION, THE INQUIRY MORE GERMANE TO THIS SET OF CIRCUMSTANCES IS THIS...
DO WE FIND OURSELVES IN A POTENTIALLY INSALUBRIOUS STATE AS A RESULT OF YOUR IMPETUOUSNESS?
YEAH, WHATEVER HE SAID.
MELISSA GOLD
(A.K.A. SONGBIRD--SUPER HERO WHO USED TO BE A SUPER CRIMINAL)
DR. NOAH BLACK
(A.K.A. CENTURIUS--GENIUS, REFORMED CRIMINAL)

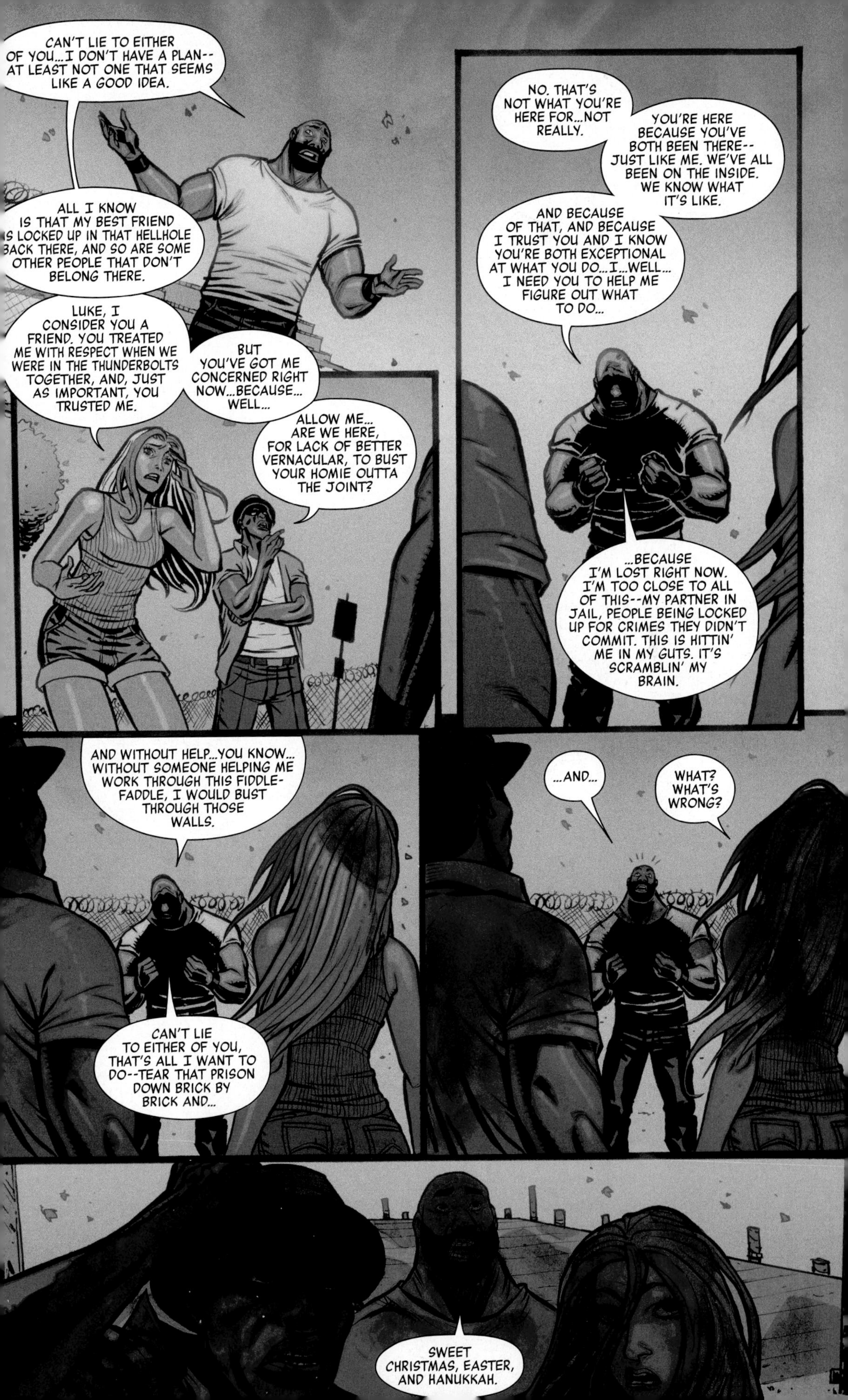
CAN'T LIE TO EITHER OF YOU...I DON'T HAVE A PLAN--AT LEAST NOT ONE THAT SEEMS LIKE A GOOD IDEA.
ALL I KNOW IS THAT MY BEST FRIEND IS LOCKED UP IN THAT HELLHOLE BACK THERE, AND SO ARE SOME OTHER PEOPLE THAT DON'T BELONG THERE.
LUKE, I CONSIDER YOU A FRIEND. YOU TREATED ME WITH RESPECT WHEN WE WERE IN THE THUNDERBOLTS TOGETHER, AND, JUST AS IMPORTANT, YOU TRUSTED ME.
BUT YOU'VE GOT ME CONCERNED RIGHT NOW...BECAUSE... WELL...
ALLOW ME... ARE WE HERE, FOR LACK OF BETTER VERNACULAR, TO BUST YOUR HOMIE OUTTA THE JOINT?
NO. THAT'S NOT WHAT YOU'RE HERE FOR...NOT REALLY.
YOU'RE HERE BECAUSE YOU'VE BOTH BEEN THERE--JUST LIKE ME. WE'VE ALL BEEN ON THE INSIDE. WE KNOW WHAT IT'S LIKE.
AND BECAUSE OF THAT, AND BECAUSE I TRUST YOU AND I KNOW YOU'RE BOTH EXCEPTIONAL AT WHAT YOU DO...I...WELL... I NEED YOU TO HELP ME FIGURE OUT WHAT TO DO...
...BECAUSE I'M LOST RIGHT NOW. I'M TOO CLOSE TO ALL OF THIS--MY PARTNER IN JAIL, PEOPLE BEING LOCKED UP FOR CRIMES THEY DIDN'T COMMIT. THIS IS HITTIN' ME IN MY GUTS. IT'S SCRAMBLIN' MY BRAIN.
AND WITHOUT HELP...YOU KNOW... WITHOUT SOMEONE HELPING ME WORK THROUGH THIS FIDDLE-FADDLE, I WOULD BUST THROUGH THOSE WALLS.
CAN'T LIE TO EITHER OF YOU, THAT'S ALL I WANT TO DO--TEAR THAT PRISON DOWN BRICK BY BRICK AND...
...AND...
WHAT? WHAT'S WRONG?
SWEET CHRISTMAS, EASTER, AND HANUKKAH.

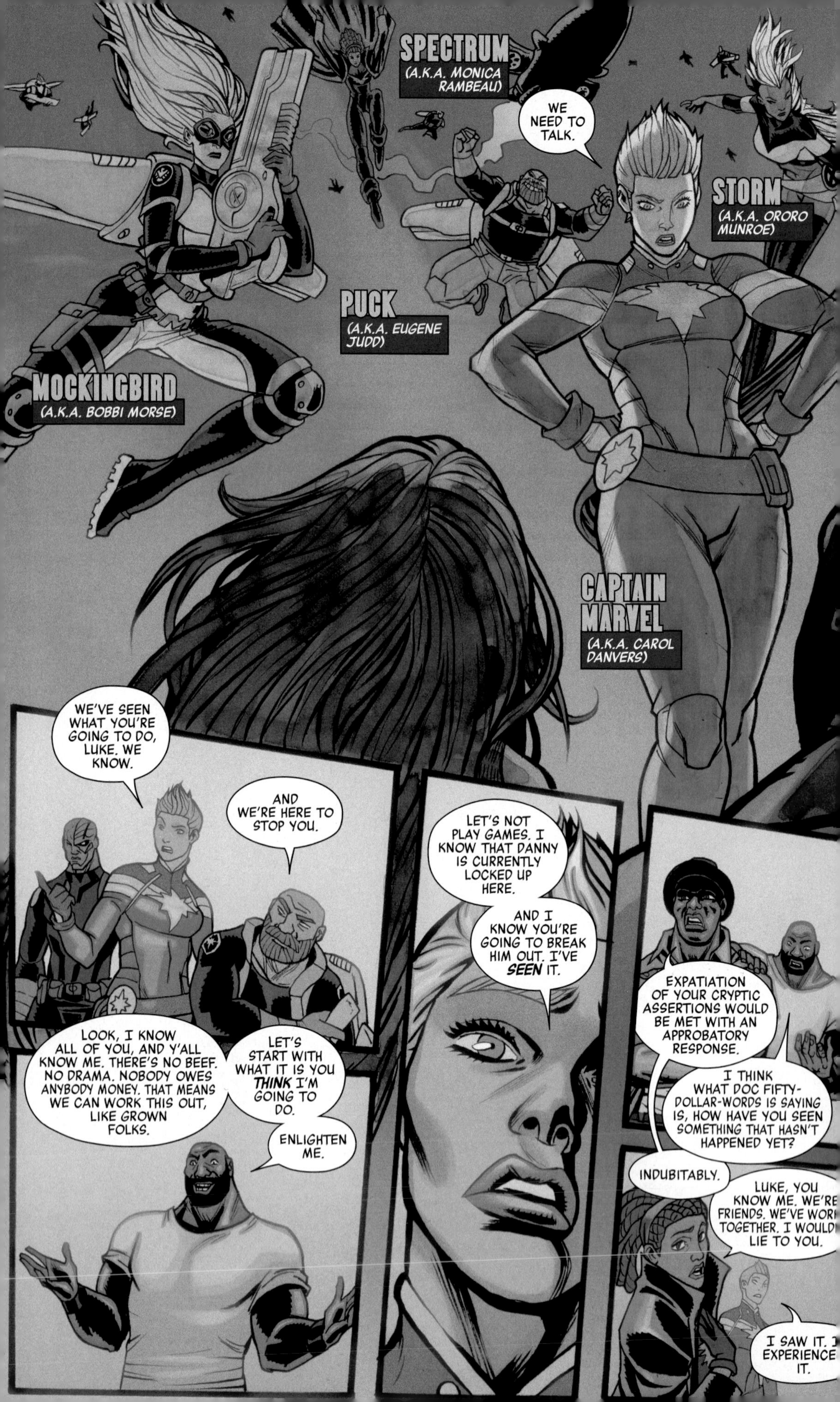

SPECTRUM
(A.K.A. MONICA RAMBEAU)
WE NEED TO TALK.
STORM
(A.K.A. ORORO MUNROE)
PUCK
(A.K.A. EUGENE JUDD)
MOCKINGBIRD
(A.K.A. BOBBI MORSE)
CAPTAIN MARVEL
(A.K.A. CAROL DANVERS)
WE'VE SEEN WHAT YOU'RE GOING TO DO, LUKE. WE KNOW.
AND WE'RE HERE TO STOP YOU.
LOOK, I KNOW ALL OF YOU, AND Y'ALL KNOW ME. THERE'S NO BEEF. NO DRAMA. NOBODY OWES ANYBODY MONEY. THAT MEANS WE CAN WORK THIS OUT, LIKE GROWN FOLKS.
LET'S START WITH WHAT IT IS YOU THINK I'M GOING TO DO.
ENLIGHTEN ME.
LET'S NOT PLAY GAMES. I KNOW THAT DANNY IS CURRENTLY LOCKED UP HERE.
AND I KNOW YOU'RE GOING TO BREAK HIM OUT. I'VE SEEN IT.
EXPATIATION OF YOUR CRYPTIC ASSERTIONS WOULD BE MET WITH AN APPROBATORY RESPONSE.
I THINK WHAT DOC FIFTY-DOLLAR-WORDS IS SAYING IS, HOW HAVE YOU SEEN SOMETHING THAT HASN'T HAPPENED YET?
INDUBITABLY.

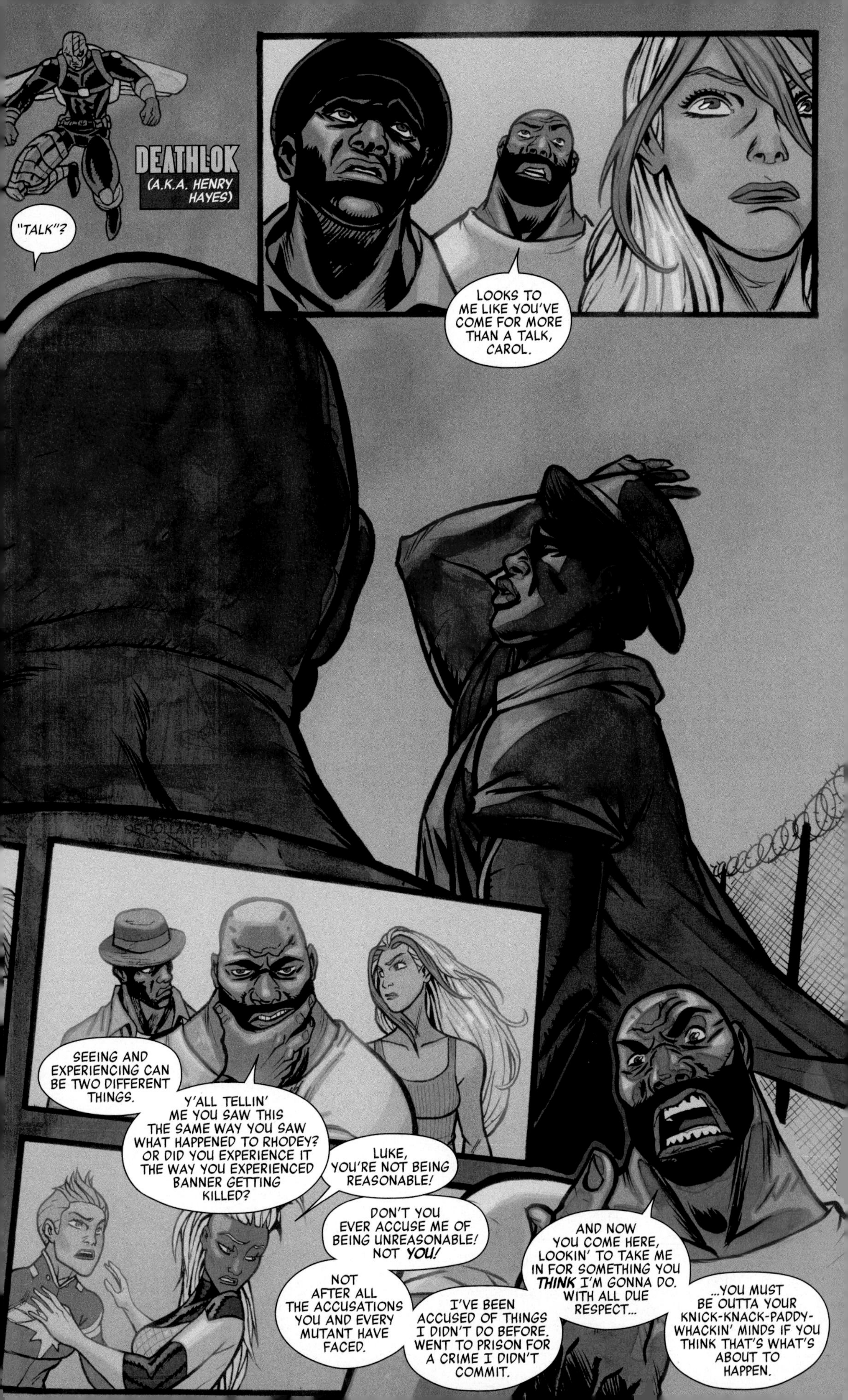
DEATHLOK
(A.K.A. HENRY HAYES)
"TALK"?
LOOKS TO ME LIKE YOU'VE COME FOR MORE THAN A TALK, CAROL.
SEEING AND EXPERIENCING CAN BE TWO DIFFERENT THINGS.
Y'ALL TELLIN' ME YOU SAW THIS THE SAME WAY YOU SAW WHAT HAPPENED TO RHODEY? OR DID YOU EXPERIENCE IT THE WAY YOU EXPERIENCED BANNER GETTING KILLED?
LUKE, YOU'RE NOT BEING REASONABLE!
DON'T YOU EVER ACCUSE ME OF BEING UNREASONABLE! NOT *YOU!*
NOT AFTER ALL THE ACCUSATIONS YOU AND EVERY MUTANT HAVE FACED.
I'VE BEEN ACCUSED OF THINGS I DIDN'T DO BEFORE. WENT TO PRISON FOR A CRIME I DIDN'T COMMIT.
AND NOW YOU COME HERE, LOOKIN' TO TAKE ME IN FOR SOMETHING YOU *THINK* I'M GONNA DO. WITH ALL DUE RESPECT...
...YOU MUST BE OUTTA YOUR KNICK-KNACK-PADDY-WHACKIN' MINDS IF YOU THINK THAT'S WHAT'S ABOUT TO HAPPEN.

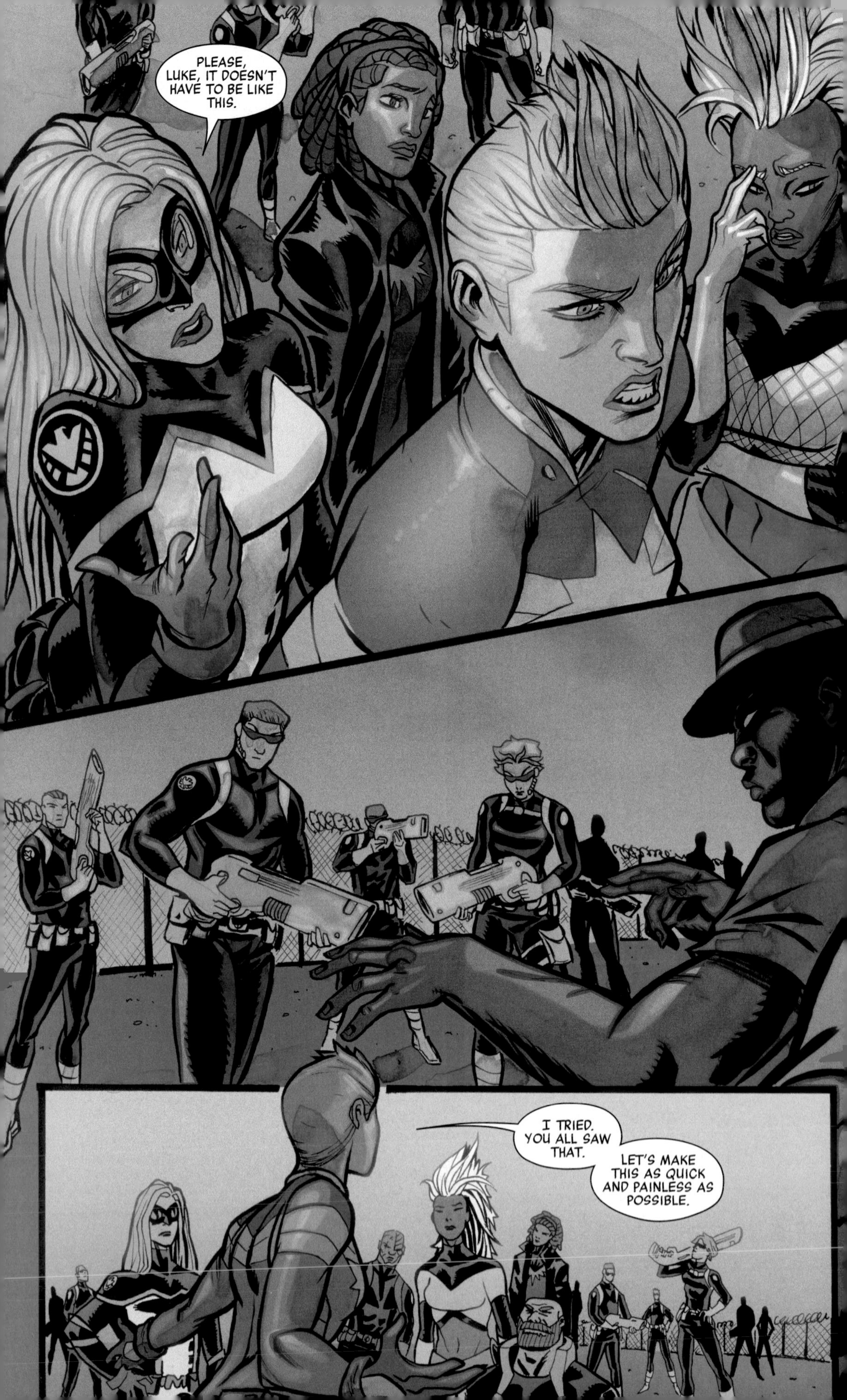
PLEASE, LUKE, IT DOESN'T HAVE TO BE LIKE THIS.
I TRIED. YOU ALL SAW THAT.
LET'S MAKE THIS AS QUICK AND PAINLESS AS POSSIBLE.

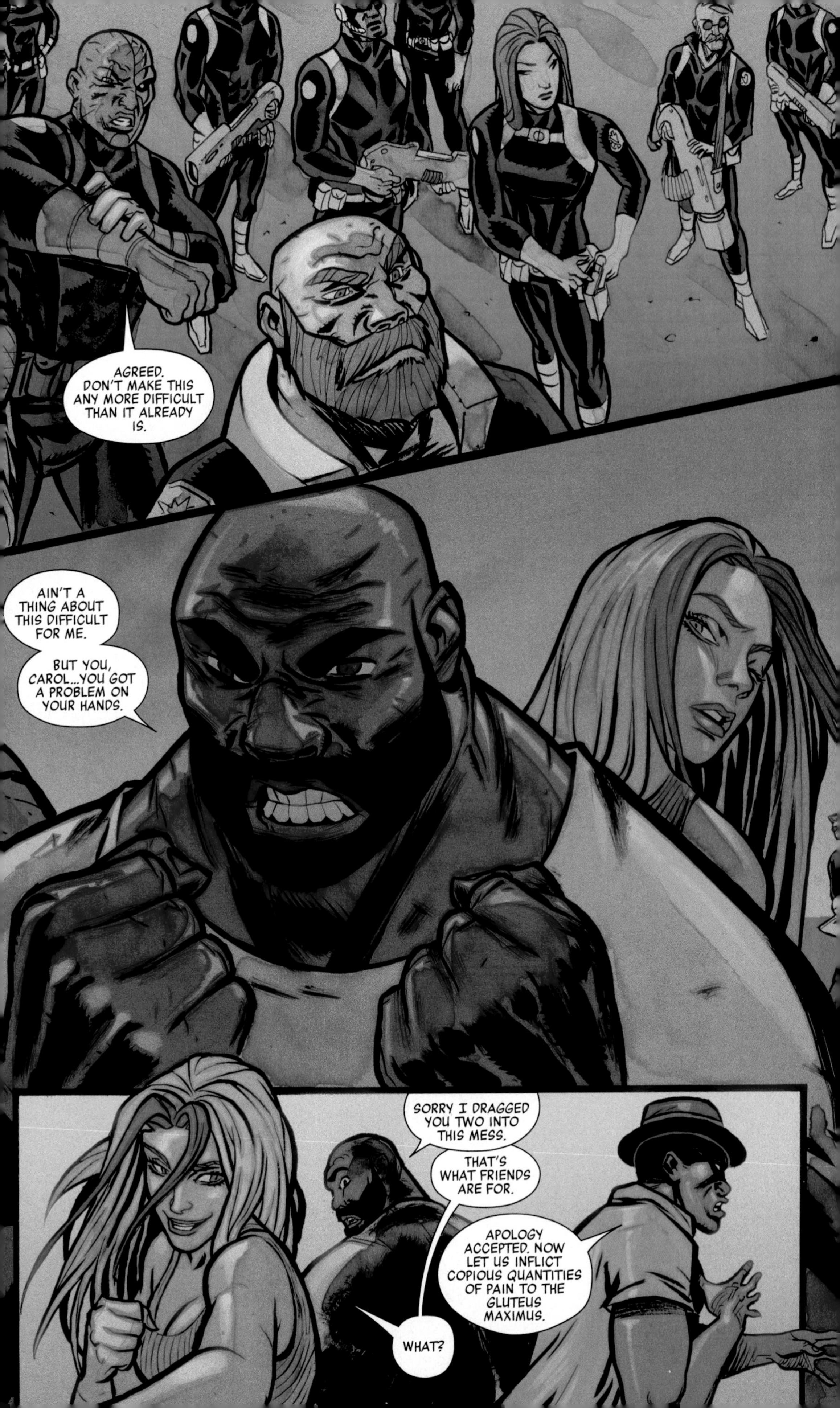

AGREED. DON'T MAKE THIS ANY MORE DIFFICULT THAN IT ALREADY IS.
AIN'T A THING ABOUT THIS DIFFICULT FOR ME.
BUT YOU, CAROL...YOU GOT A PROBLEM ON YOUR HANDS.
SORRY I DRAGGED YOU TWO INTO THIS MESS.
THAT'S WHAT FRIENDS ARE FOR.
APOLOGY ACCEPTED. NOW LET US INFLICT COPIOUS QUANTITIES OF PAIN TO THE GLUTEUS MAXIMUS.
WHAT?

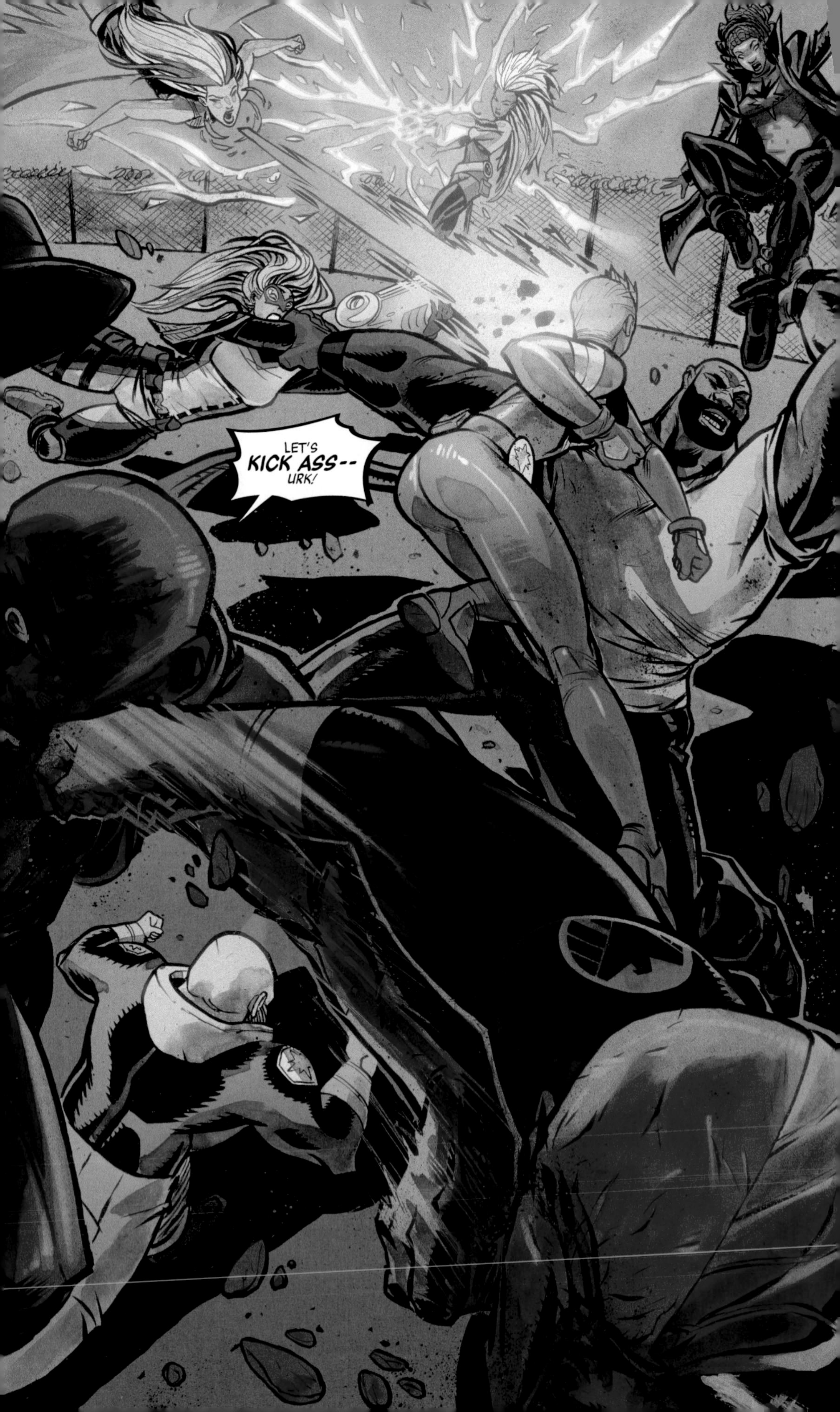
LET'S
KICK ASS--
URK!

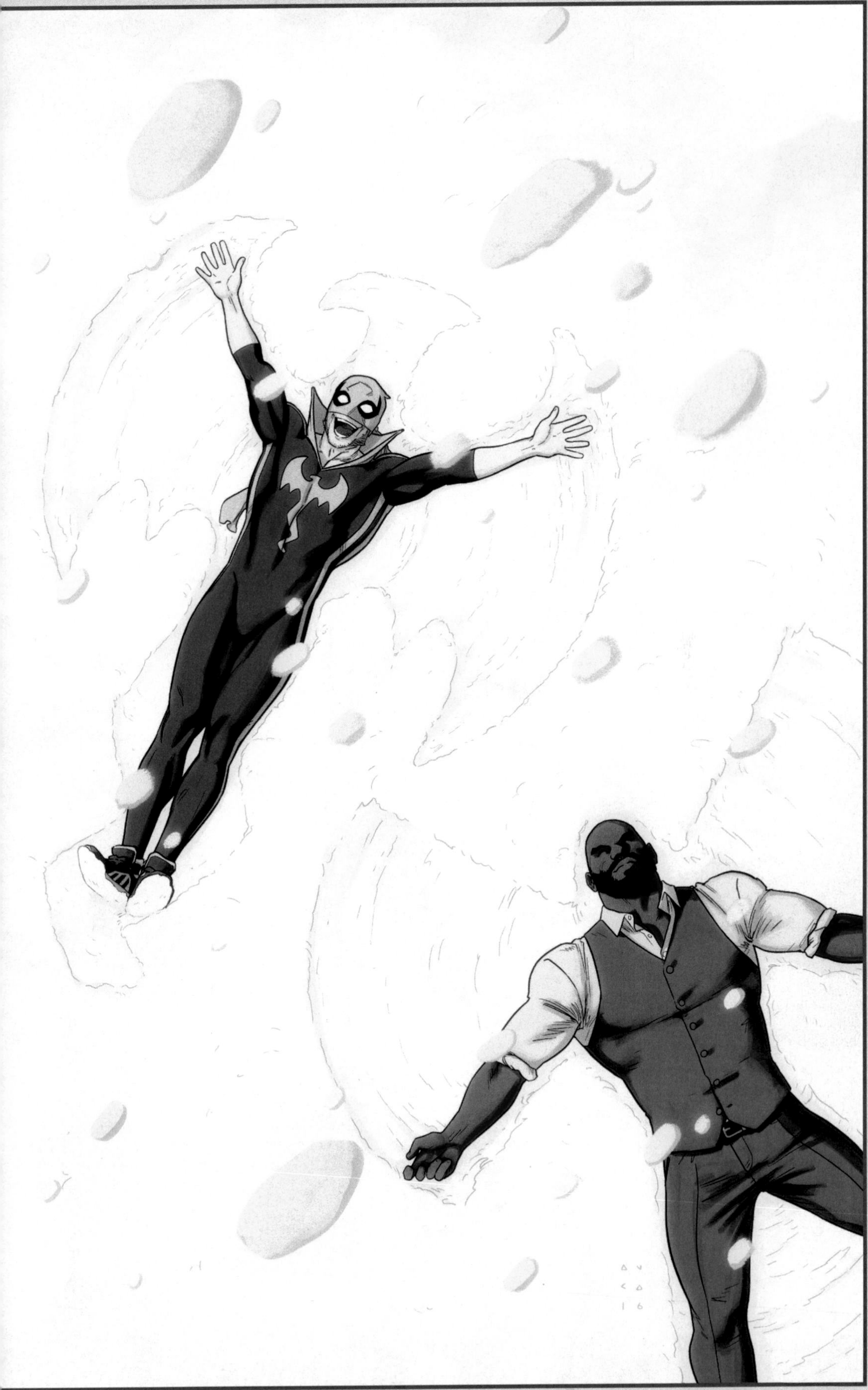

KRIS ANKA
SWEET CHRISTMAS ANNUAL 1 VARIANT

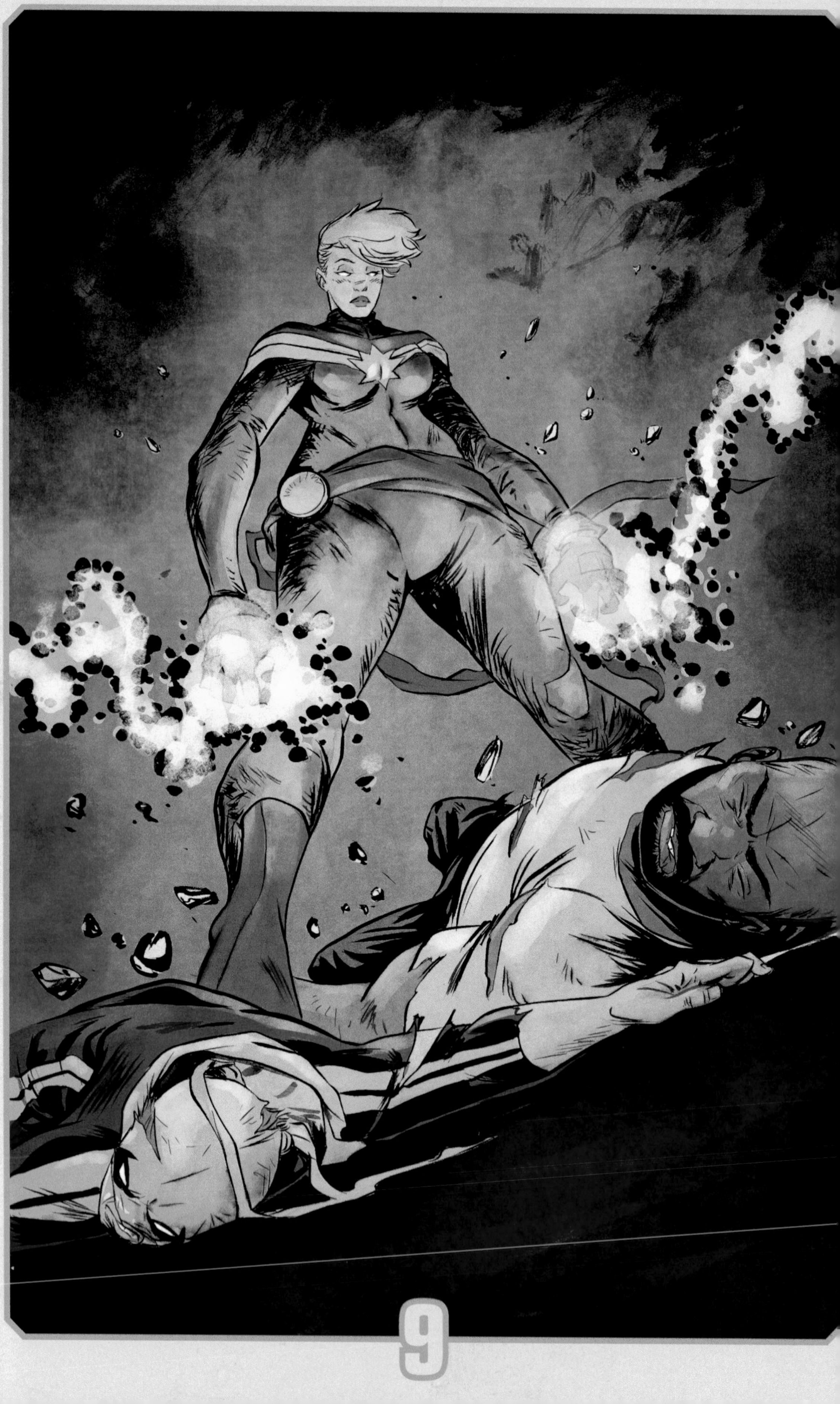
9

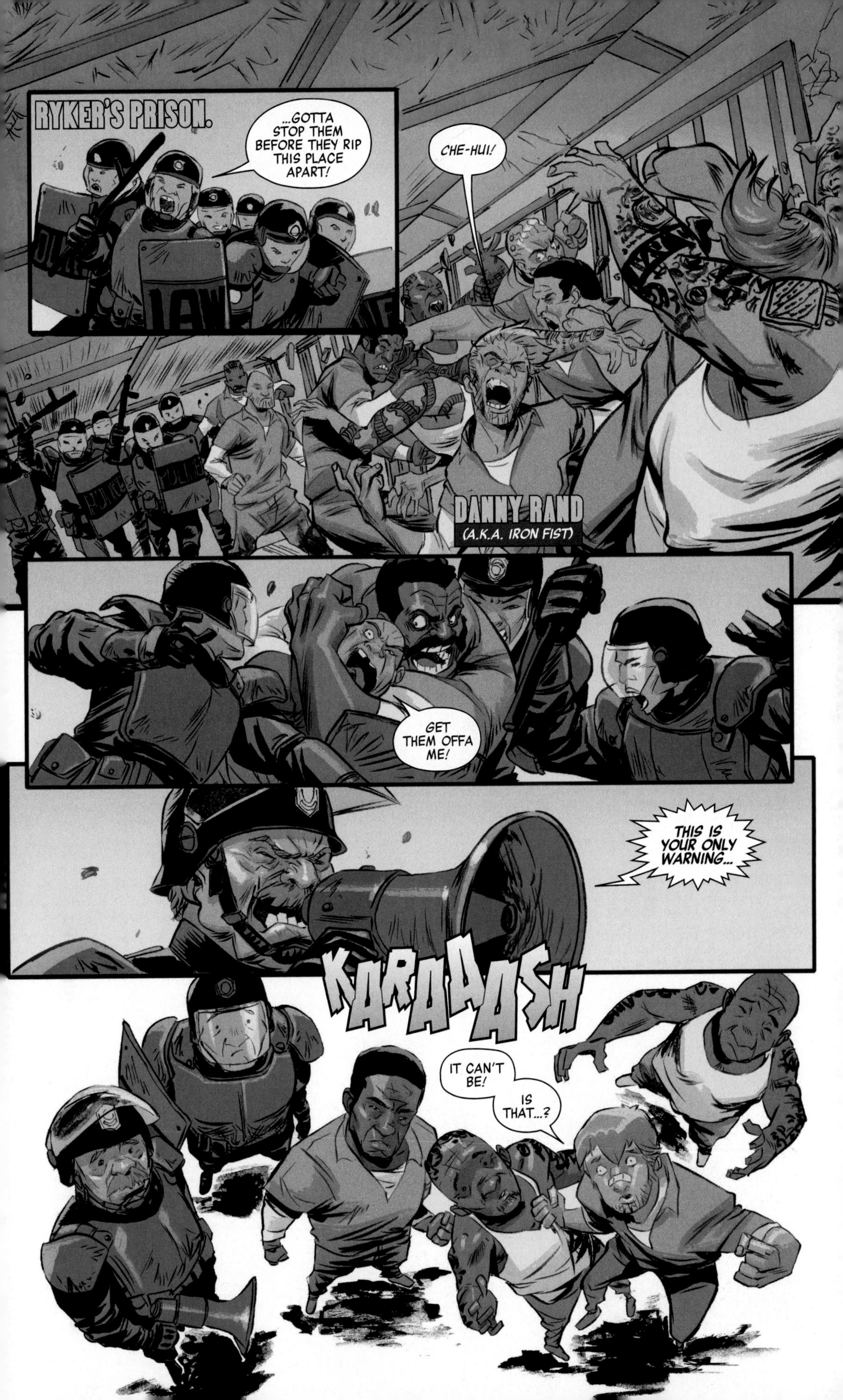
RYKER'S PRISON.
...GOTTA STOP THEM BEFORE THEY RIP THIS PLACE APART!
CHE-HUI!
DANNY RAND
(A.K.A. IRON FIST)
GET THEM OFFA ME!
THIS IS YOUR ONLY WARNING...
KARAAASH
IT CAN'T BE!
IS THAT...?

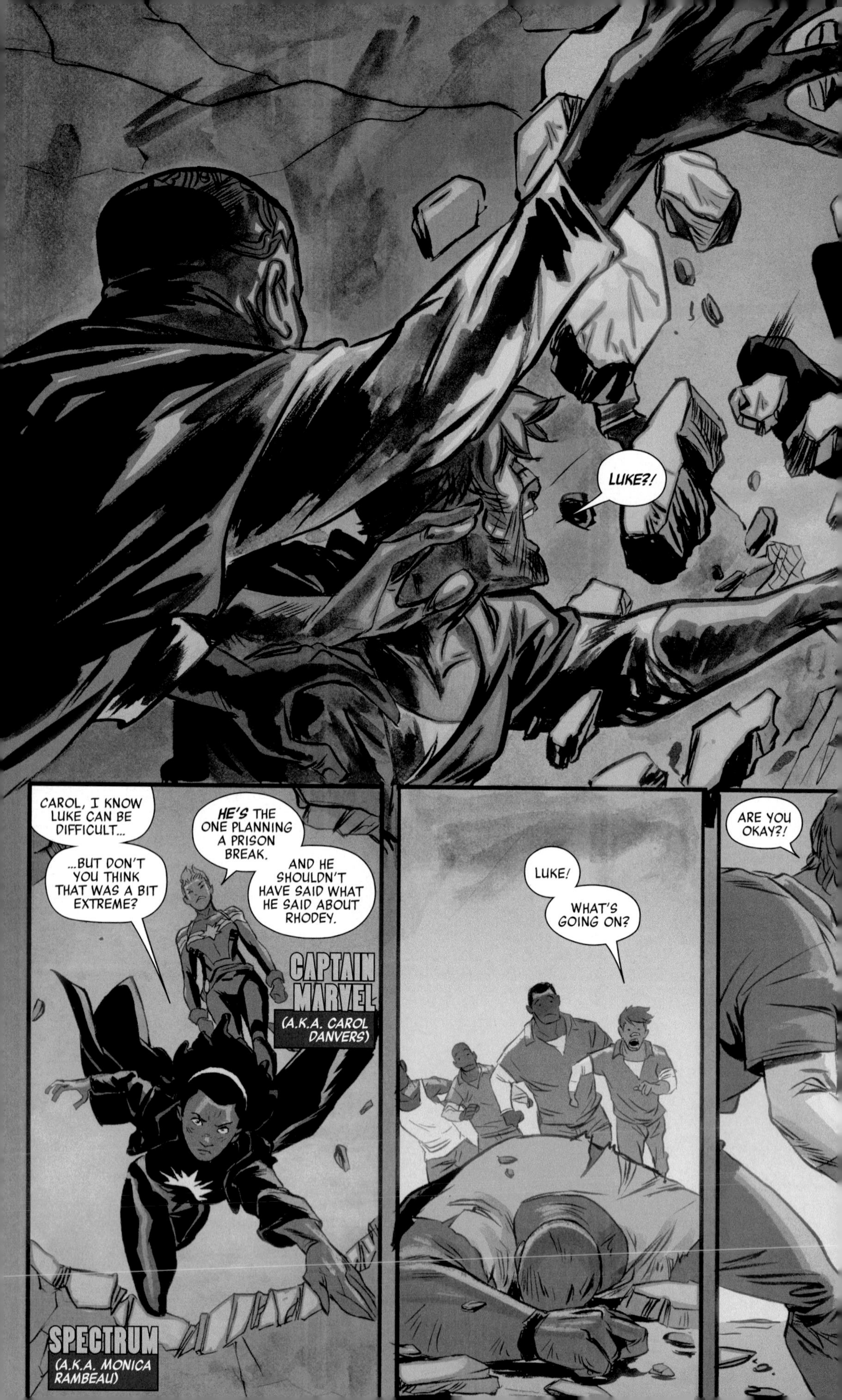

LUKE?!
CAROL, I KNOW LUKE CAN BE DIFFICULT...
...BUT DON'T YOU THINK THAT WAS A BIT EXTREME?
HE'S THE ONE PLANNING A PRISON BREAK.
AND HE SHOULDN'T HAVE SAID WHAT HE SAID ABOUT RHODEY.
CAPTAIN MARVEL
(A.K.A. CAROL DANVERS)
SPECTRUM
(A.K.A. MONICA RAMBEAU)
LUKE!
WHAT'S GOING ON?
ARE YOU OKAY?!

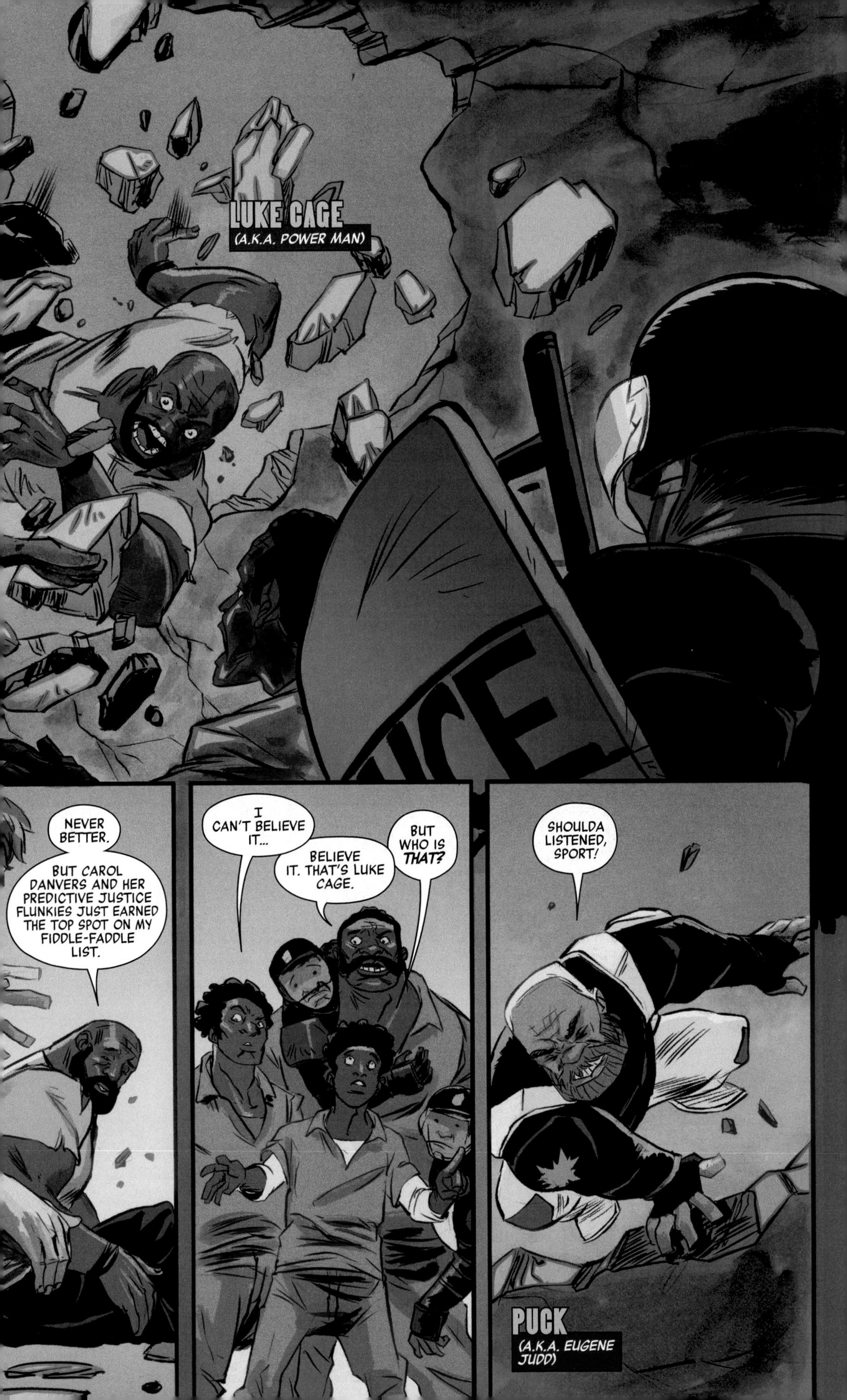

LUKE CAGE
(A.K.A. POWER MAN)
ICE
NEVER BETTER.
BUT CAROL DANVERS AND HER PREDICTIVE JUSTICE FLUNKIES JUST EARNED THE TOP SPOT ON MY FIDDLE-FADDLE LIST.
I CAN'T BELIEVE IT...
BELIEVE IT. THAT'S LUKE CAGE.
BUT WHO IS *THAT?*
SHOULDA LISTENED, SPORT!
PUCK
(A.K.A. EUGENE JUDD)

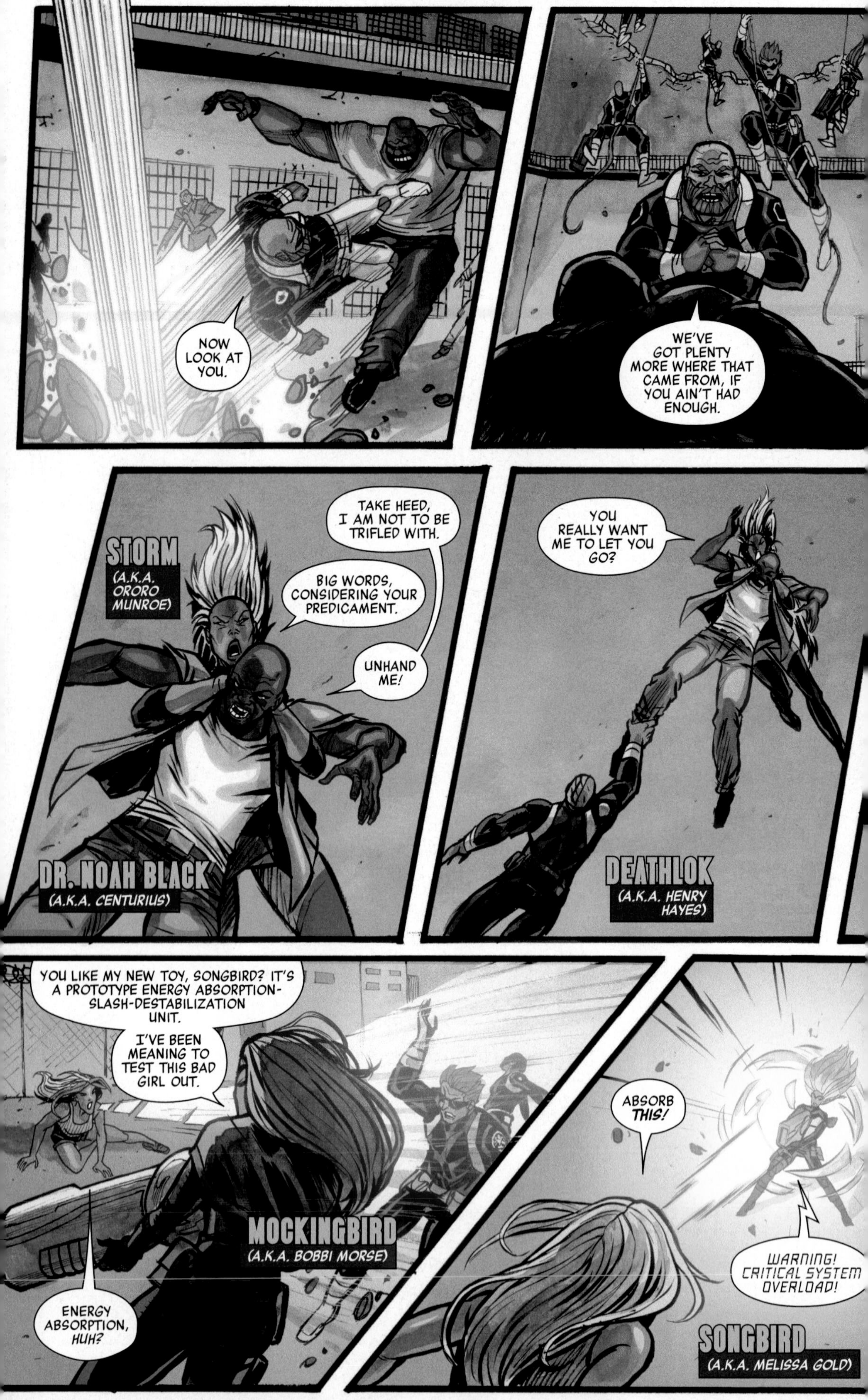
NOW LOOK AT YOU.
WE'VE GOT PLENTY MORE WHERE THAT CAME FROM, IF YOU AIN'T HAD ENOUGH.
STORM
(A.K.A. ORORO MUNROE)
TAKE HEED, I AM NOT TO BE TRIFLED WITH.
BIG WORDS, CONSIDERING YOUR PREDICAMENT.
UNHAND ME!
DR. NOAH BLACK
(A.K.A. CENTURIUS)
YOU REALLY WANT ME TO LET YOU GO?
DEATHLOK
(A.K.A. HENRY HAYES)
YOU LIKE MY NEW TOY, SONGBIRD? IT'S A PROTOTYPE ENERGY ABSORPTION-SLASH-DESTABILIZATION UNIT.
I'VE BEEN MEANING TO TEST THIS BAD GIRL OUT.
MOCKINGBIRD
(A.K.A. BOBBI MORSE)
ENERGY ABSORPTION, HUH?
ABSORB THIS!
WARNING! CRITICAL SYSTEM OVERLOAD!
SONGBIRD
(A.K.A. MELISSA GOLD)

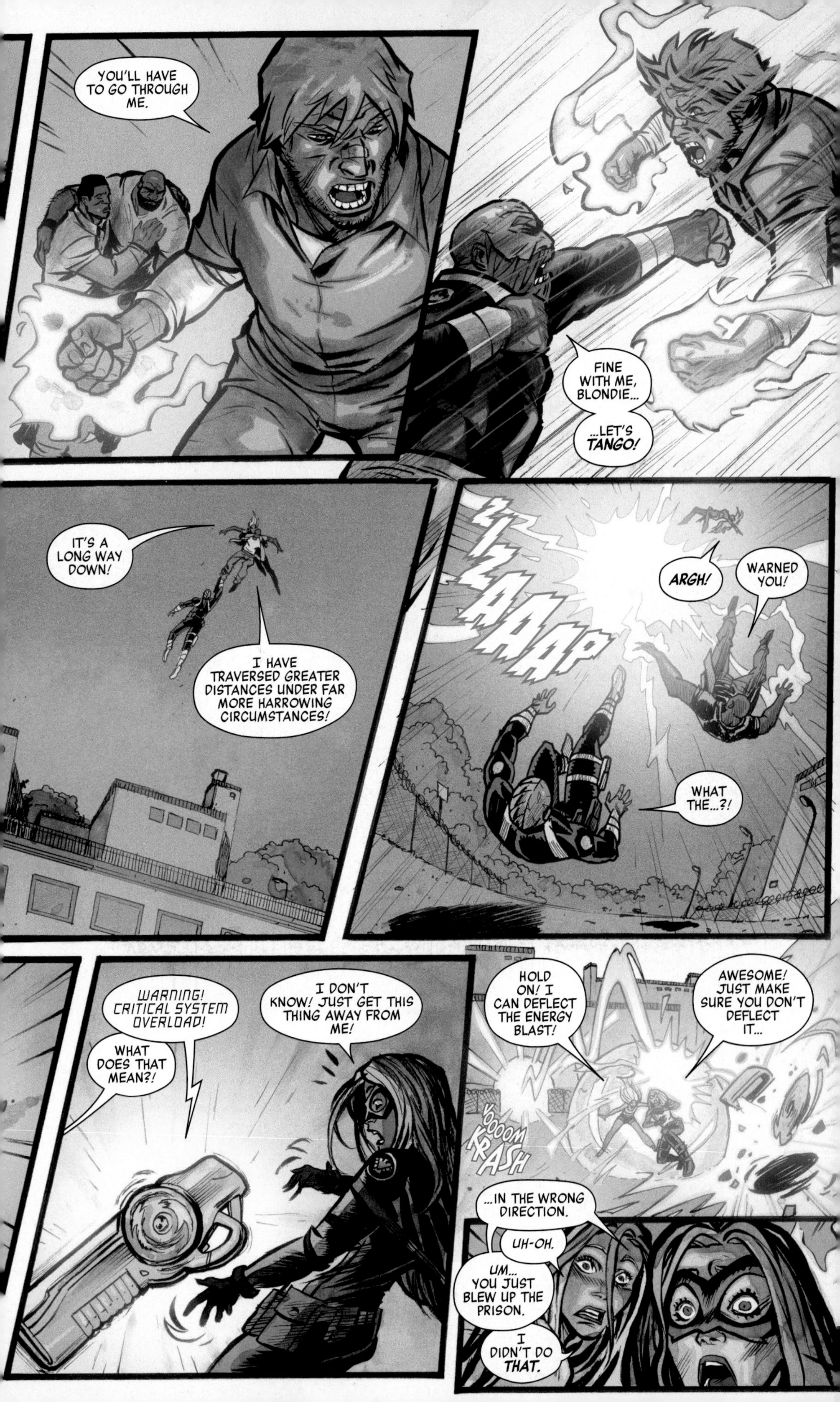
YOU'LL HAVE TO GO THROUGH ME.
FINE WITH ME, BLONDIE...
...LET'S *TANGO!*
IT'S A LONG WAY DOWN!
I HAVE TRAVERSED GREATER DISTANCES UNDER FAR MORE HARROWING CIRCUMSTANCES!
ZZAAAP
ARGH!
WARNED YOU!
WHAT THE...?!
WARNING! CRITICAL SYSTEM OVERLOAD!
WHAT DOES THAT MEAN?!
I DON'T KNOW! JUST GET THIS THING AWAY FROM ME!
HOLD ON! I CAN DEFLECT THE ENERGY BLAST!
AWESOME! JUST MAKE SURE YOU DON'T DEFLECT IT...
VOOOOM
KRASH
...IN THE WRONG DIRECTION.
UH-OH.
UM... YOU JUST BLEW UP THE PRISON.
I DIDN'T DO *THAT.*

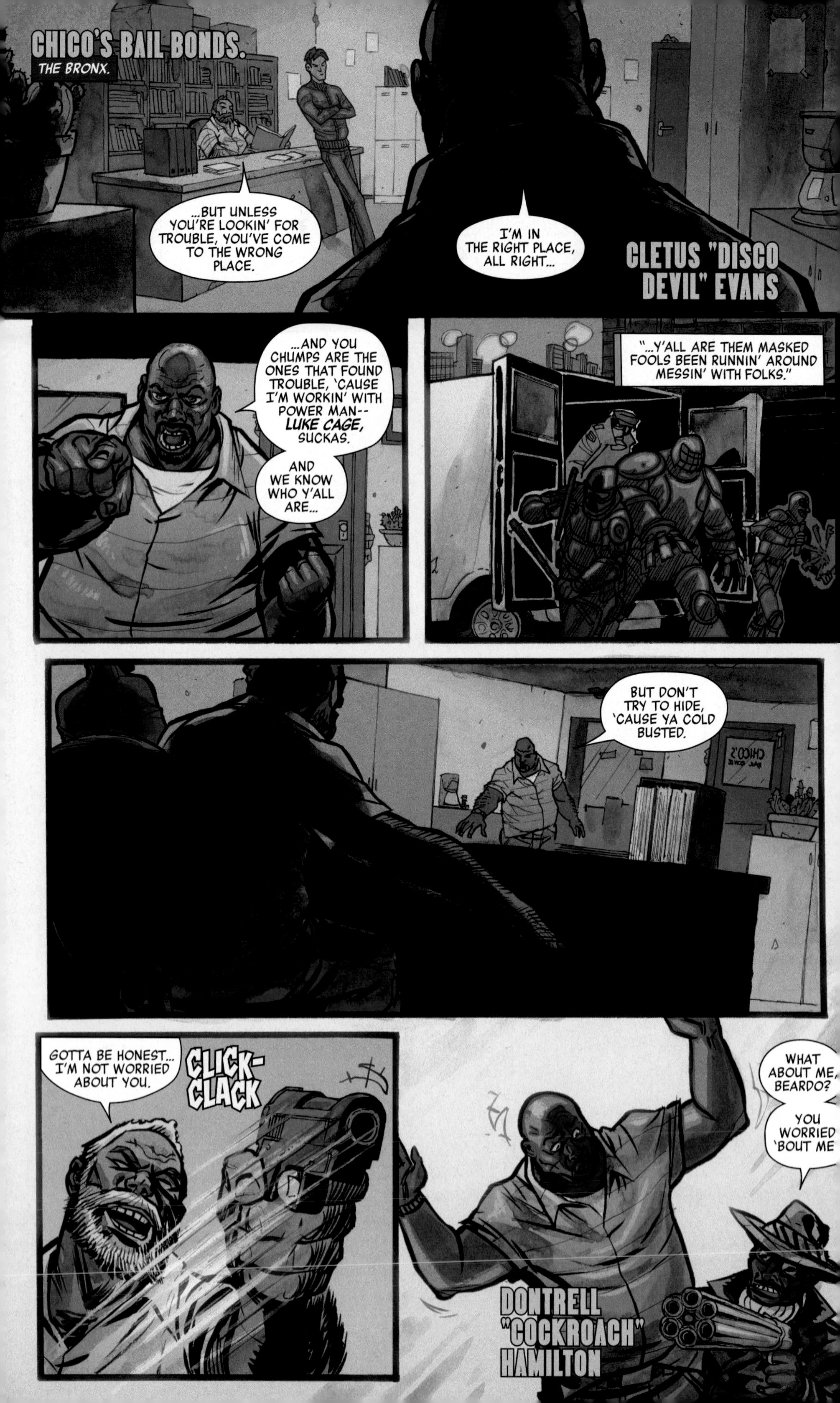

CHICO'S BAIL BONDS.
THE BRONX.
...BUT UNLESS YOU'RE LOOKIN' FOR TROUBLE, YOU'VE COME TO THE WRONG PLACE.
I'M IN THE RIGHT PLACE, ALL RIGHT...
CLETUS "DISCO DEVIL" EVANS
...AND YOU CHUMPS ARE THE ONES THAT FOUND TROUBLE, 'CAUSE I'M WORKIN' WITH POWER MAN-- LUKE CAGE, SUCKAS.
AND WE KNOW WHO Y'ALL ARE...
"...Y'ALL ARE THEM MASKED FOOLS BEEN RUNNIN' AROUND MESSIN' WITH FOLKS."
BUT DON'T TRY TO HIDE, 'CAUSE YA COLD BUSTED.
CHICO'S
GOTTA BE HONEST... I'M NOT WORRIED ABOUT YOU.
CLICK-CLACK
WHAT ABOUT ME, BEARDO?
YOU WORRIED 'BOUT ME
DONTRELL "COCKROACH" HAMILTON

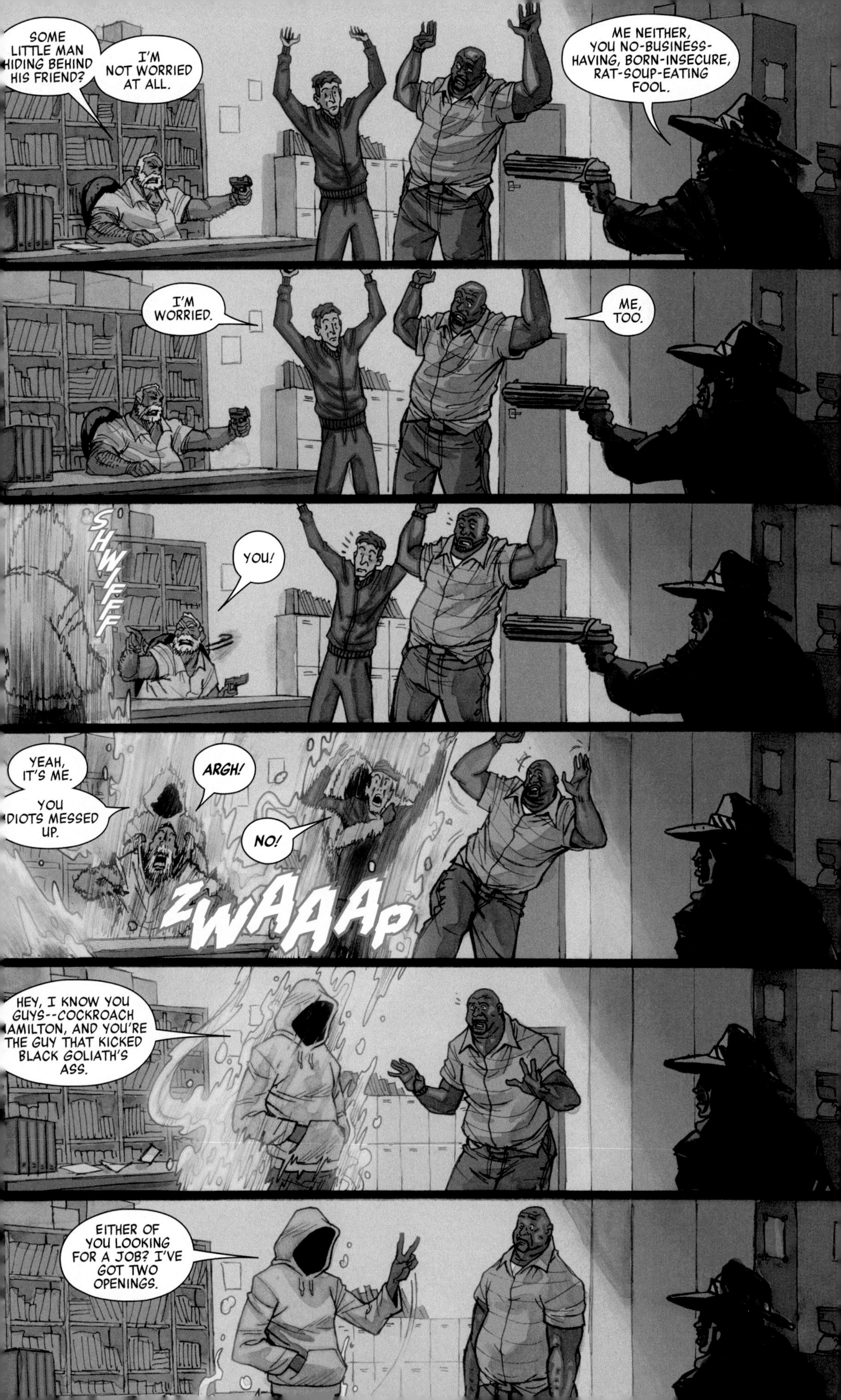

SOME LITTLE MAN HIDING BEHIND HIS FRIEND?
I'M NOT WORRIED AT ALL.
ME NEITHER, YOU NO-BUSINESS-HAVING, BORN-INSECURE, RAT-SOUP-EATING FOOL.
I'M WORRIED.
ME, TOO.
SHWIFFF
YOU!
YEAH, IT'S ME.
YOU IDIOTS MESSED UP.
ARGH!
NO!
ZWAAAP
HEY, I KNOW YOU GUYS--COCKROACH HAMILTON, AND YOU'RE THE GUY THAT KICKED BLACK GOLIATH'S ASS.
EITHER OF YOU LOOKING FOR A JOB? I'VE GOT TWO OPENINGS.

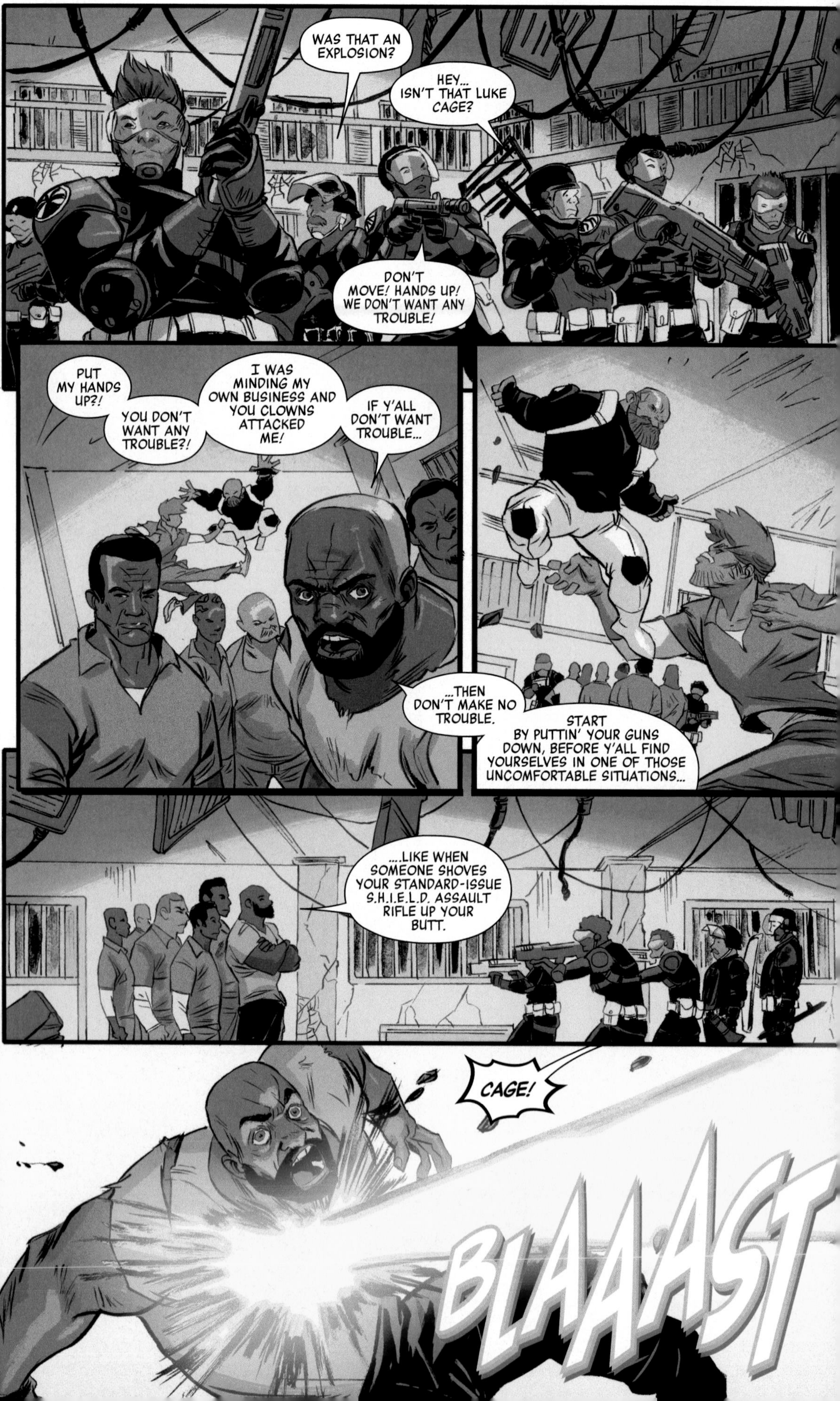

WAS THAT AN EXPLOSION?
HEY... ISN'T THAT LUKE CAGE?
DON'T MOVE! HANDS UP! WE DON'T WANT ANY TROUBLE!
PUT MY HANDS UP?!
YOU DON'T WANT ANY TROUBLE?!
I WAS MINDING MY OWN BUSINESS AND YOU CLOWNS ATTACKED ME!
IF Y'ALL DON'T WANT TROUBLE...
...THEN DON'T MAKE NO TROUBLE.
START BY PUTTIN' YOUR GUNS DOWN, BEFORE Y'ALL FIND YOURSELVES IN ONE OF THOSE UNCOMFORTABLE SITUATIONS...
....LIKE WHEN SOMEONE SHOVES YOUR STANDARD-ISSUE S.H.I.E.L.D. ASSAULT RIFLE UP YOUR BUTT.
CAGE!
BLAAAST

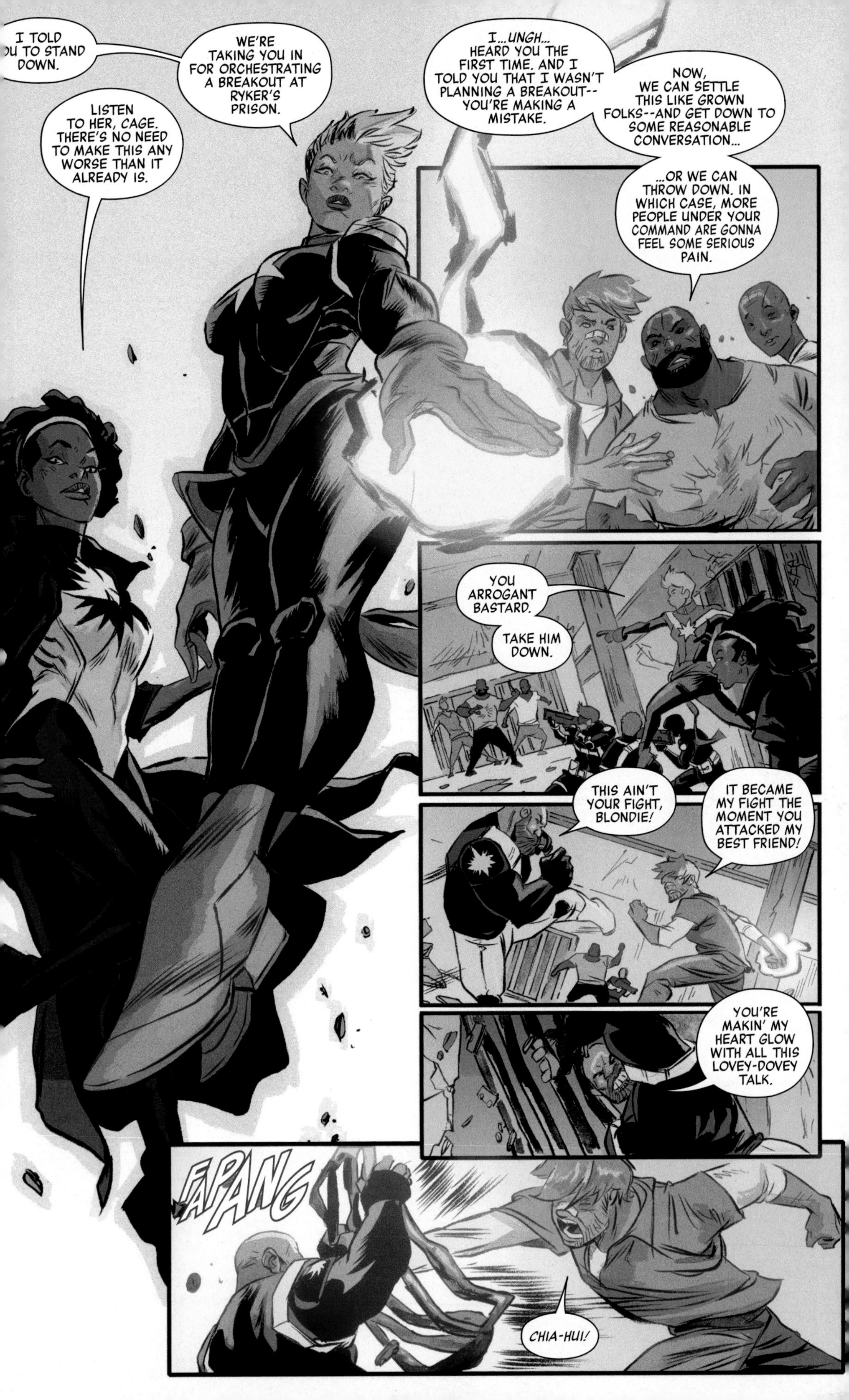
I TOLD
OU TO STAND
DOWN.
WE'RE
TAKING YOU IN
FOR ORCHESTRATING
A BREAKOUT AT
RYKER'S
PRISON.
LISTEN
TO HER, CAGE.
THERE'S NO NEED
TO MAKE THIS ANY
WORSE THAN IT
ALREADY IS.
I...UNGH...
HEARD YOU THE
FIRST TIME. AND I
TOLD YOU THAT I WASN'T
PLANNING A BREAKOUT--
YOU'RE MAKING A
MISTAKE.
NOW,
WE CAN SETTLE
THIS LIKE GROWN
FOLKS--AND GET DOWN TO
SOME REASONABLE
CONVERSATION...
...OR WE CAN
THROW DOWN. IN
WHICH CASE, MORE
PEOPLE UNDER YOUR
COMMAND ARE GONNA
FEEL SOME SERIOUS
PAIN.
YOU
ARROGANT
BASTARD.
TAKE HIM
DOWN.
THIS AIN'T
YOUR FIGHT,
BLONDIE!
IT BECAME
MY FIGHT THE
MOMENT YOU
ATTACKED MY
BEST FRIEND!
YOU'RE
MAKIN' MY
HEART GLOW
WITH ALL THIS
LOVEY-DOVEY
TALK.
FPANG
CHIA-HUI!

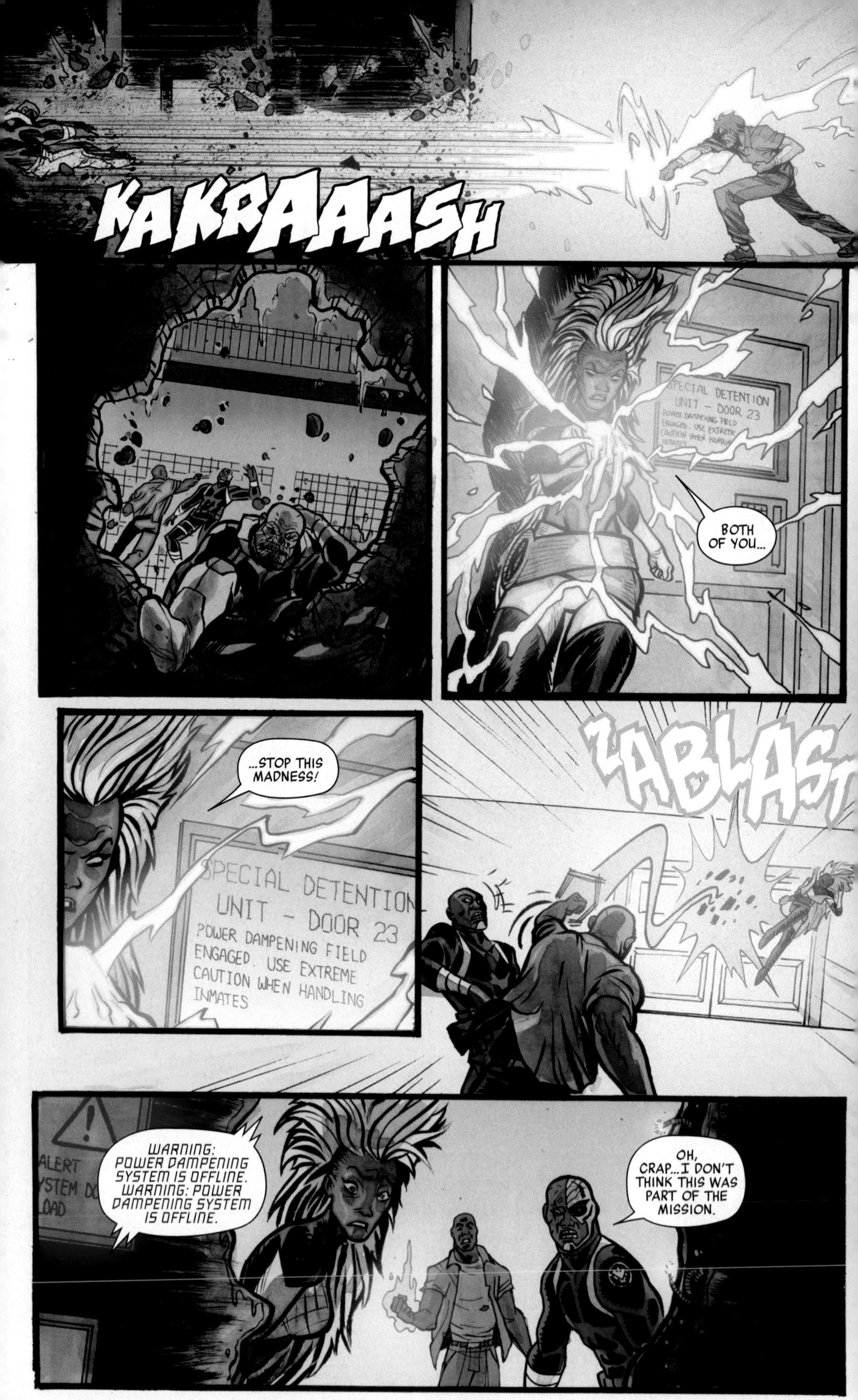
KAKRAAASH
BOTH OF YOU...
...STOP THIS MADNESS!
SPECIAL DETENTION UNIT - DOOR 23
POWER DAMPENING FIELD ENGAGED. USE EXTREME CAUTION WHEN HANDLING INMATES
ZABLAST
WARNING: POWER DAMPENING SYSTEM IS OFFLINE. WARNING: POWER DAMPENING SYSTEM IS OFFLINE.
OH, CRAP...I DON'T THINK THIS WAS PART OF THE MISSION.

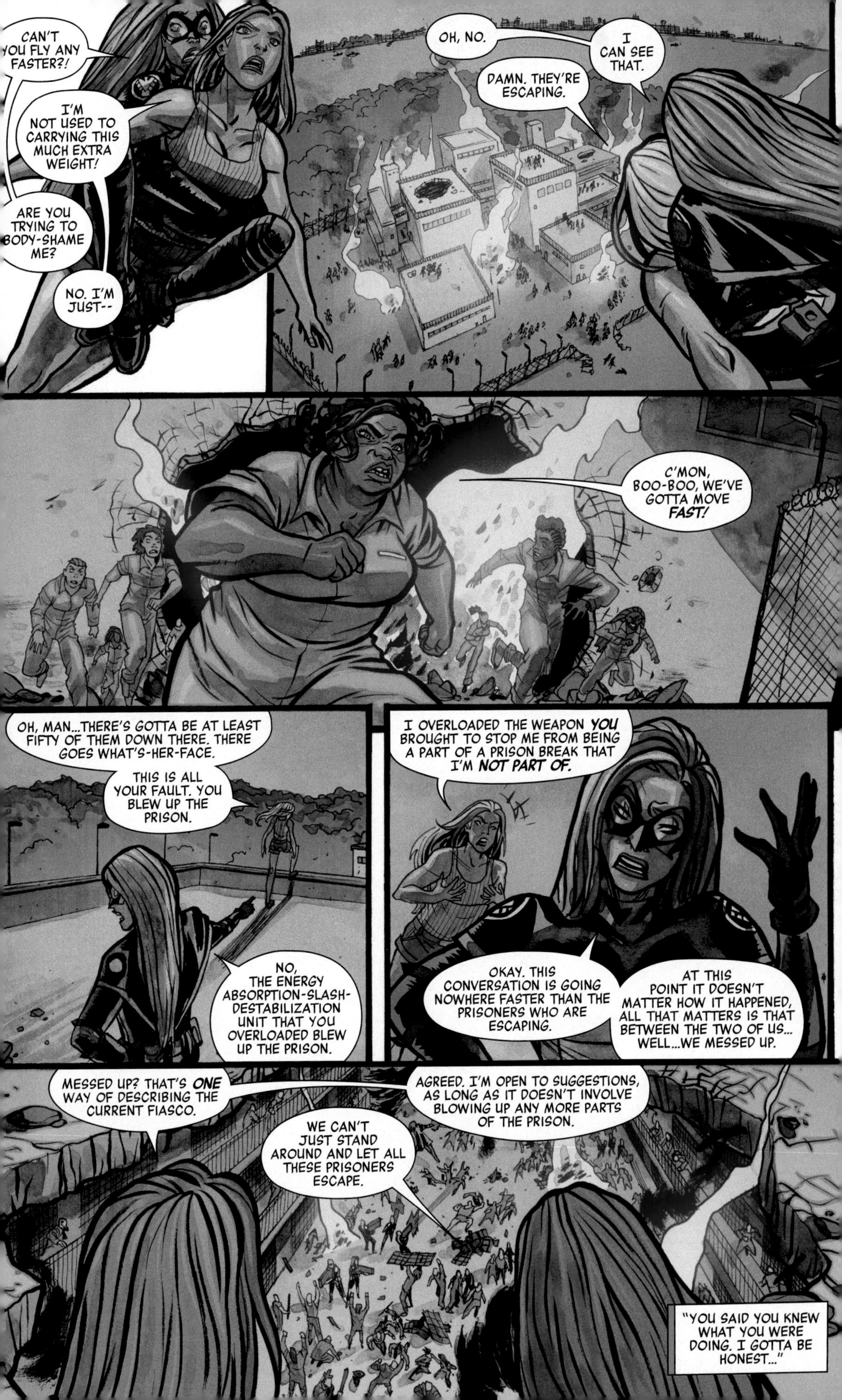

CAN'T YOU FLY ANY FASTER?!
I'M NOT USED TO CARRYING THIS MUCH EXTRA WEIGHT!
ARE YOU TRYING TO BODY-SHAME ME?
NO. I'M JUST--
OH, NO.
I CAN SEE THAT.
DAMN. THEY'RE ESCAPING.
C'MON, BOO-BOO, WE'VE GOTTA MOVE FAST!
OH, MAN...THERE'S GOTTA BE AT LEAST FIFTY OF THEM DOWN THERE. THERE GOES WHAT'S-HER-FACE.
THIS IS ALL YOUR FAULT. YOU BLEW UP THE PRISON.
NO, THE ENERGY ABSORPTION-SLASH-DESTABILIZATION UNIT THAT YOU OVERLOADED BLEW UP THE PRISON.
I OVERLOADED THE WEAPON YOU BROUGHT TO STOP ME FROM BEING A PART OF A PRISON BREAK THAT I'M NOT PART OF.
OKAY. THIS CONVERSATION IS GOING NOWHERE FASTER THAN THE PRISONERS WHO ARE ESCAPING.
AT THIS POINT IT DOESN'T MATTER HOW IT HAPPENED, ALL THAT MATTERS IS THAT BETWEEN THE TWO OF US... WELL...WE MESSED UP.
MESSED UP? THAT'S ONE WAY OF DESCRIBING THE CURRENT FIASCO.
AGREED. I'M OPEN TO SUGGESTIONS, AS LONG AS IT DOESN'T INVOLVE BLOWING UP ANY MORE PARTS OF THE PRISON.
WE CAN'T JUST STAND AROUND AND LET ALL THESE PRISONERS ESCAPE.
"YOU SAID YOU KNEW WHAT YOU WERE DOING. I GOTTA BE HONEST..."

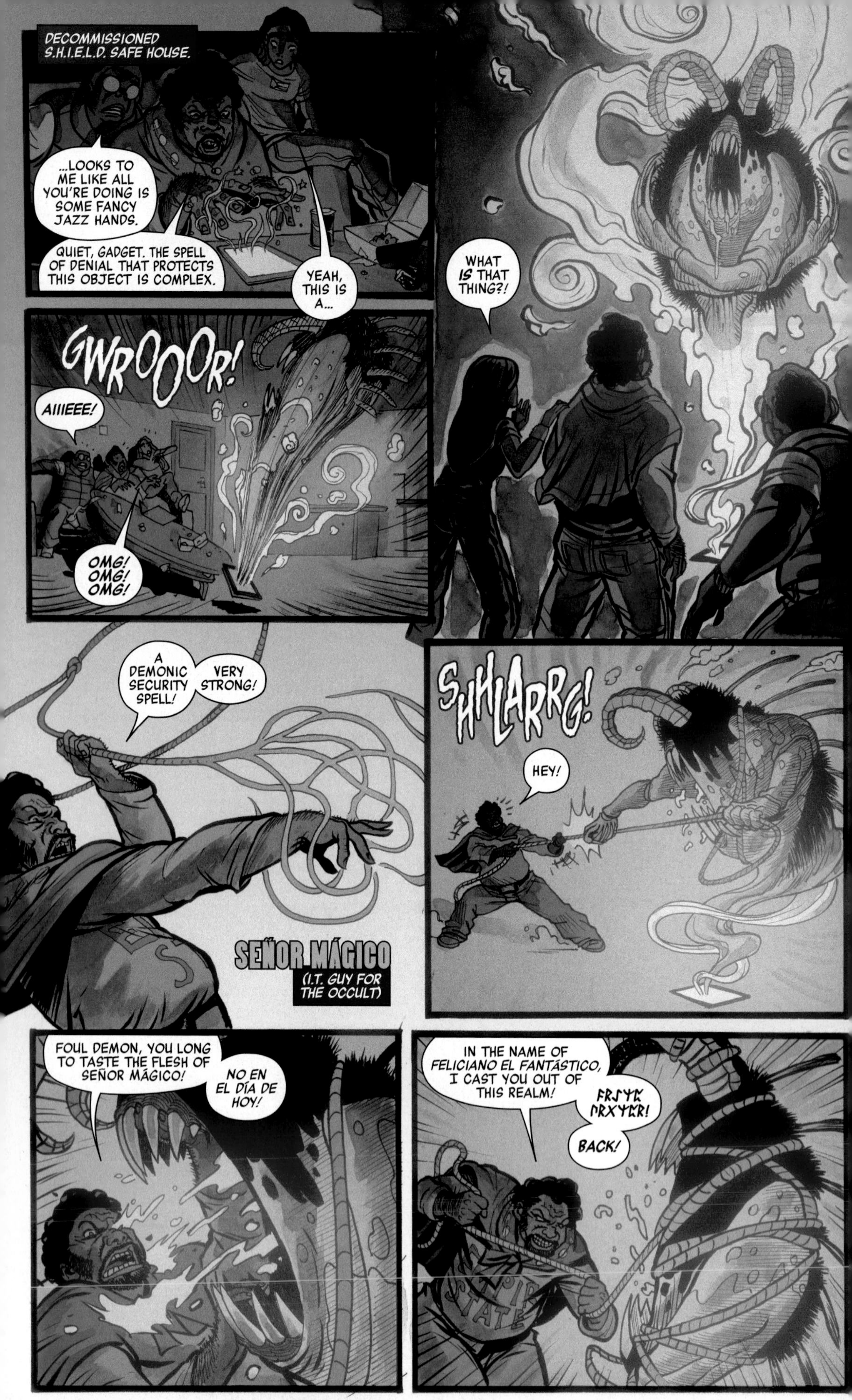
DECOMMISSIONED S.H.I.E.L.D. SAFE HOUSE.
...LOOKS TO ME LIKE ALL YOU'RE DOING IS SOME FANCY JAZZ HANDS.
QUIET, GADGET. THE SPELL OF DENIAL THAT PROTECTS THIS OBJECT IS COMPLEX.
YEAH, THIS IS A...
GWROOOR!
AIIIEEE!
OMG! OMG! OMG!
WHAT IS THAT THING?!
A DEMONIC SECURITY SPELL!
VERY STRONG!
SEÑOR MÁGICO
(I.T. GUY FOR THE OCCULT)
SHHLARRG!
HEY!
FOUL DEMON, YOU LONG TO TASTE THE FLESH OF SEÑOR MÁGICO!
NO EN EL DÍA DE HOY!
IN THE NAME OF FELICIANO EL FANTÁSTICO, I CAST YOU OUT OF THIS REALM!
BACK!
STATE

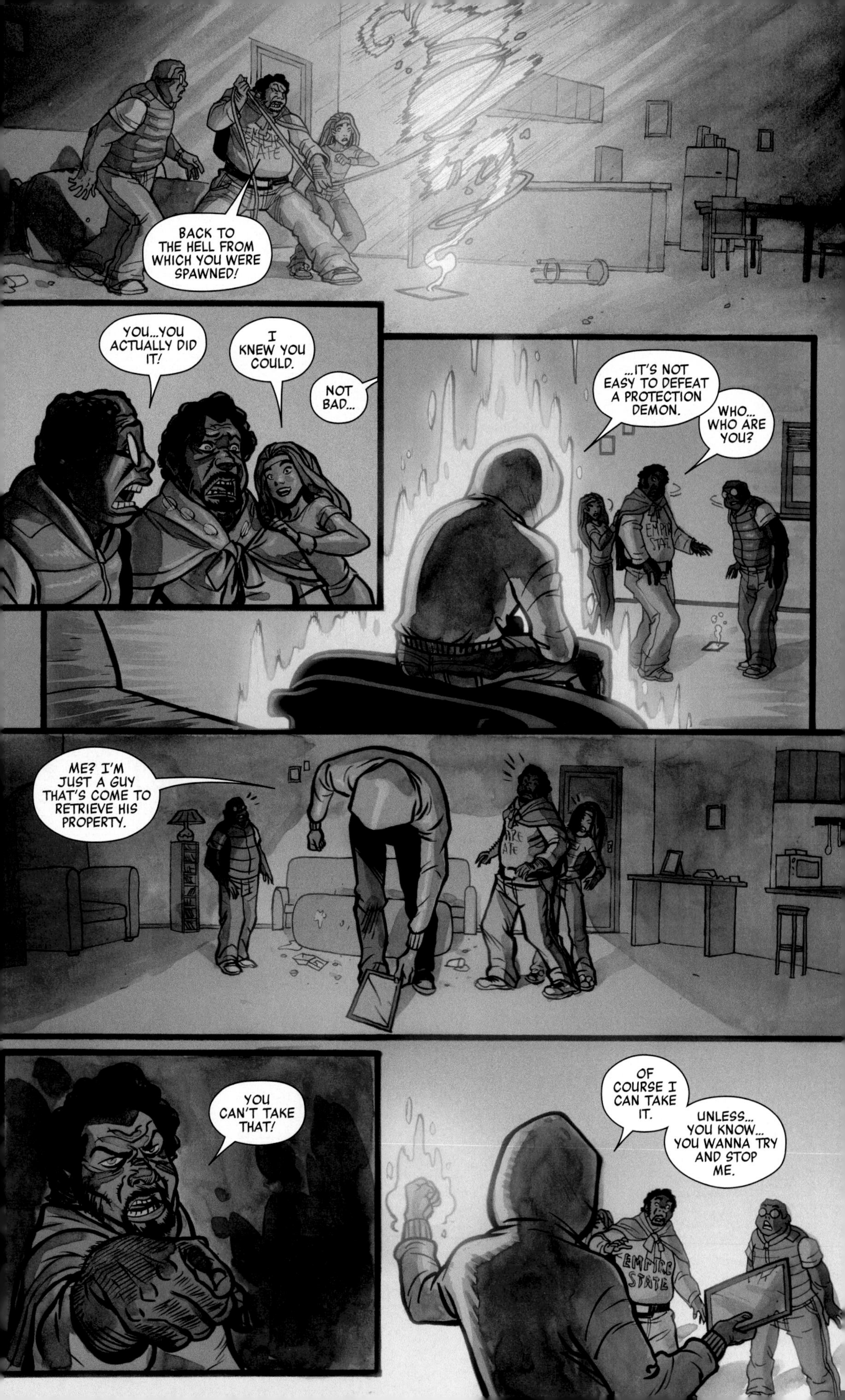
BACK TO THE HELL FROM WHICH YOU WERE SPAWNED!
YOU...YOU ACTUALLY DID IT!
I KNEW YOU COULD.
NOT BAD...
...IT'S NOT EASY TO DEFEAT A PROTECTION DEMON.
WHO... WHO ARE YOU?
EMPIRE STATE
ME? I'M JUST A GUY THAT'S COME TO RETRIEVE HIS PROPERTY.
YOU CAN'T TAKE THAT!
OF COURSE I CAN TAKE IT.
UNLESS... YOU KNOW... YOU WANNA TRY AND STOP ME.
EMPIRE STATE

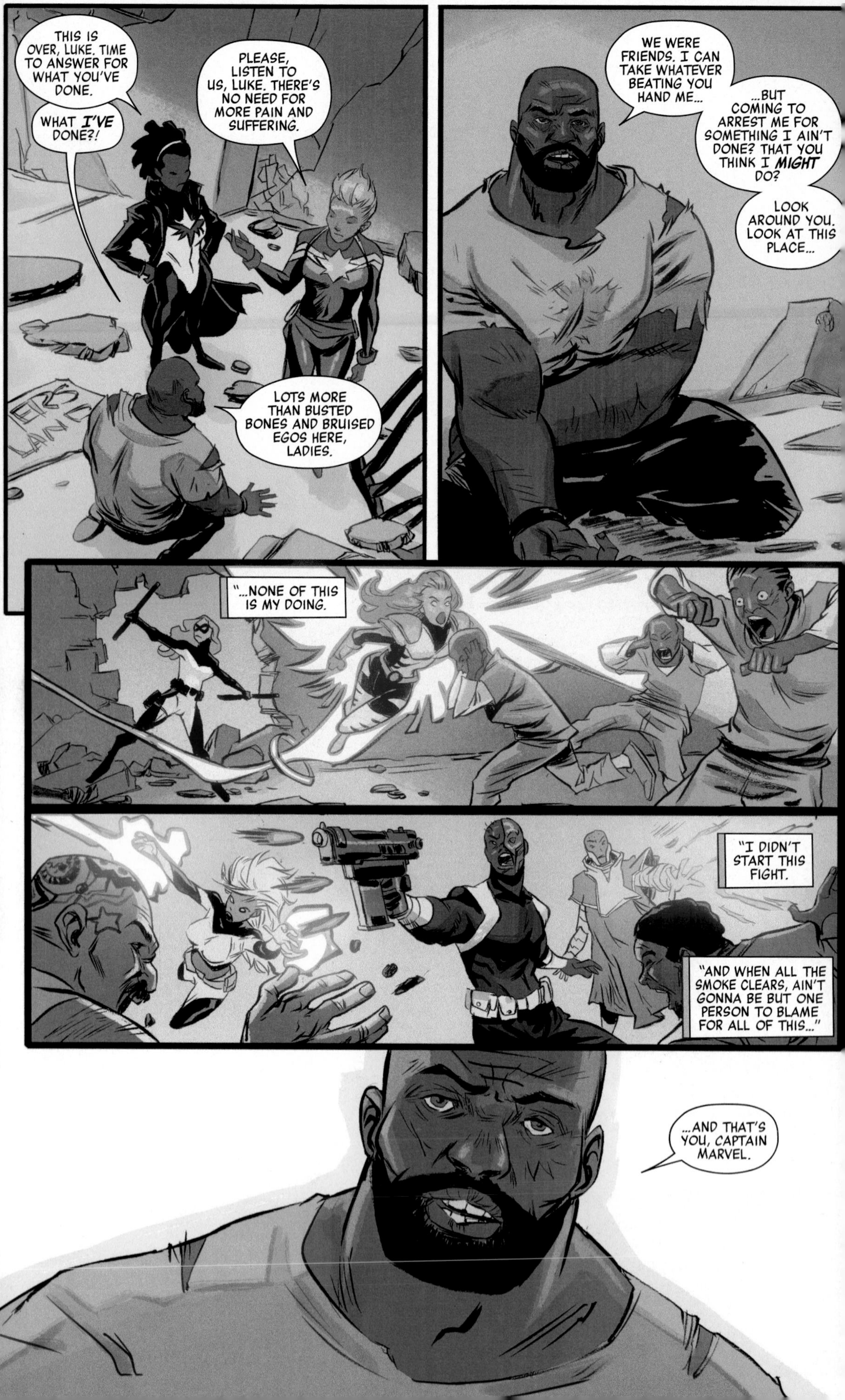

THIS IS OVER, LUKE. TIME TO ANSWER FOR WHAT YOU'VE DONE.
WHAT I'VE DONE?!
PLEASE, LISTEN TO US, LUKE. THERE'S NO NEED FOR MORE PAIN AND SUFFERING.
LOTS MORE THAN BUSTED BONES AND BRUISED EGOS HERE, LADIES.
WE WERE FRIENDS. I CAN TAKE WHATEVER BEATING YOU HAND ME...
...BUT COMING TO ARREST ME FOR SOMETHING I AIN'T DONE? THAT YOU THINK I MIGHT DO?
LOOK AROUND YOU. LOOK AT THIS PLACE...
"...NONE OF THIS IS MY DOING.
"I DIDN'T START THIS FIGHT.
"AND WHEN ALL THE SMOKE CLEARS, AIN'T GONNA BE BUT ONE PERSON TO BLAME FOR ALL OF THIS..."
...AND THAT'S YOU, CAPTAIN MARVEL.

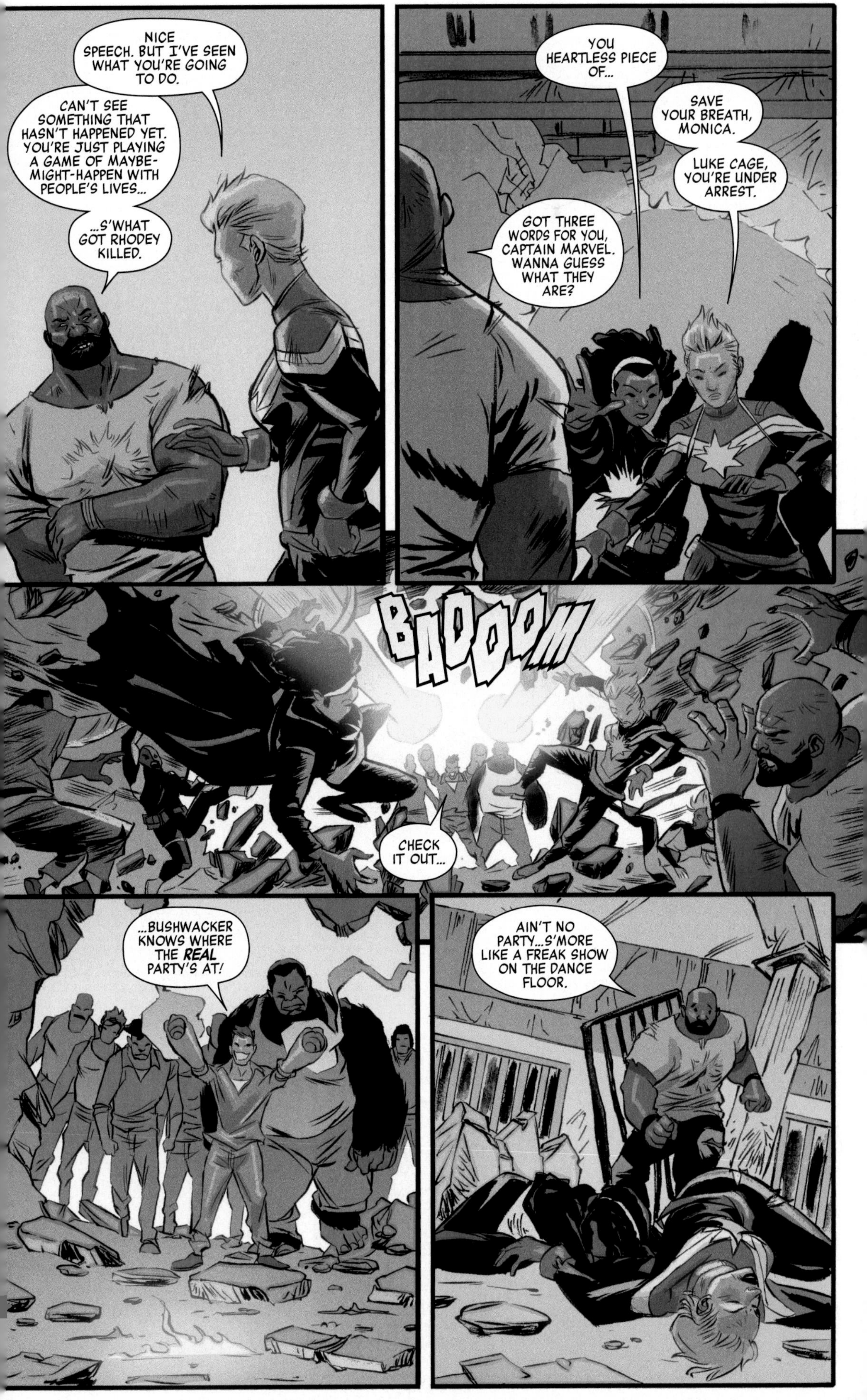
NICE SPEECH. BUT I'VE SEEN WHAT YOU'RE GOING TO DO.
CAN'T SEE SOMETHING THAT HASN'T HAPPENED YET. YOU'RE JUST PLAYING A GAME OF MAYBE-MIGHT-HAPPEN WITH PEOPLE'S LIVES...
...S'WHAT GOT RHODEY KILLED.
YOU HEARTLESS PIECE OF...
SAVE YOUR BREATH, MONICA.
LUKE CAGE, YOU'RE UNDER ARREST.
GOT THREE WORDS FOR YOU, CAPTAIN MARVEL. WANNA GUESS WHAT THEY ARE?
BADOOOM
CHECK IT OUT...
...BUSHWACKER KNOWS WHERE THE REAL PARTY'S AT!
AIN'T NO PARTY...S'MORE LIKE A FREAK SHOW ON THE DANCE FLOOR.

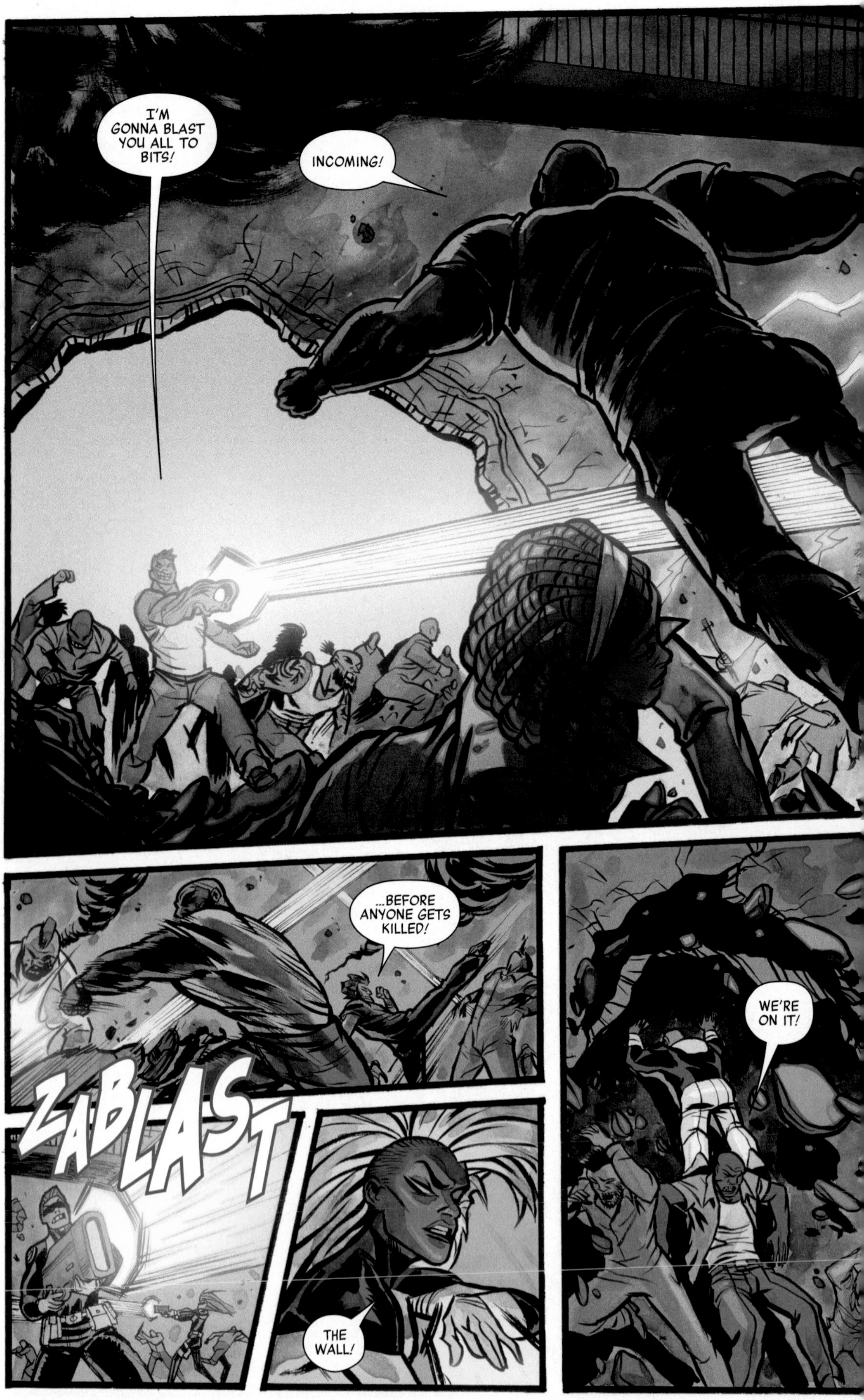
I'M GONNA BLAST YOU ALL TO BITS!
INCOMING!
...BEFORE ANYONE GETS KILLED!
ZABLAST
THE WALL!
WE'RE ON IT!

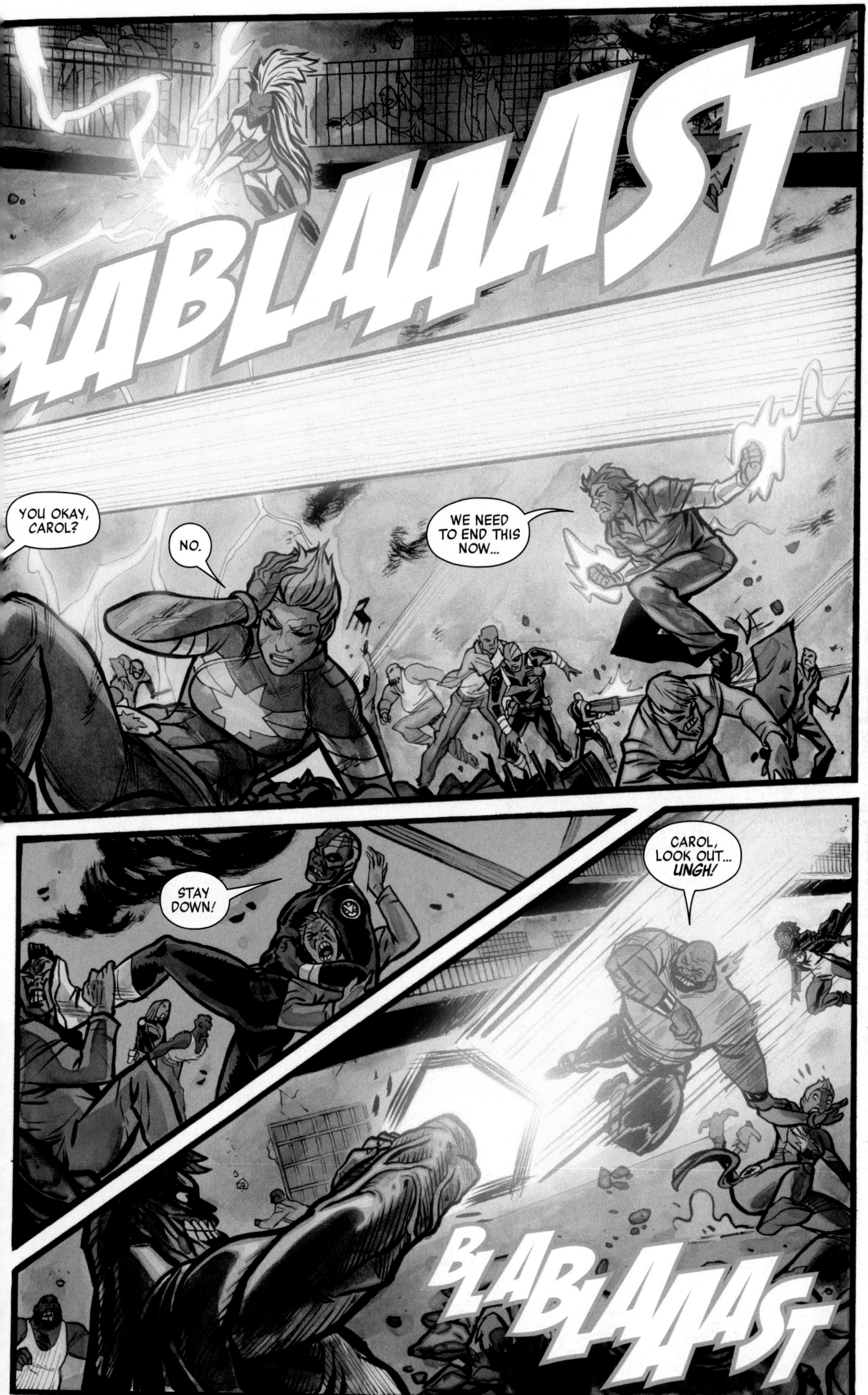
BLABLAAAST
YOU OKAY, CAROL?
NO.
WE NEED TO END THIS NOW...
STAY DOWN!
CAROL, LOOK OUT... **UNGH!**
BLABLAAAST

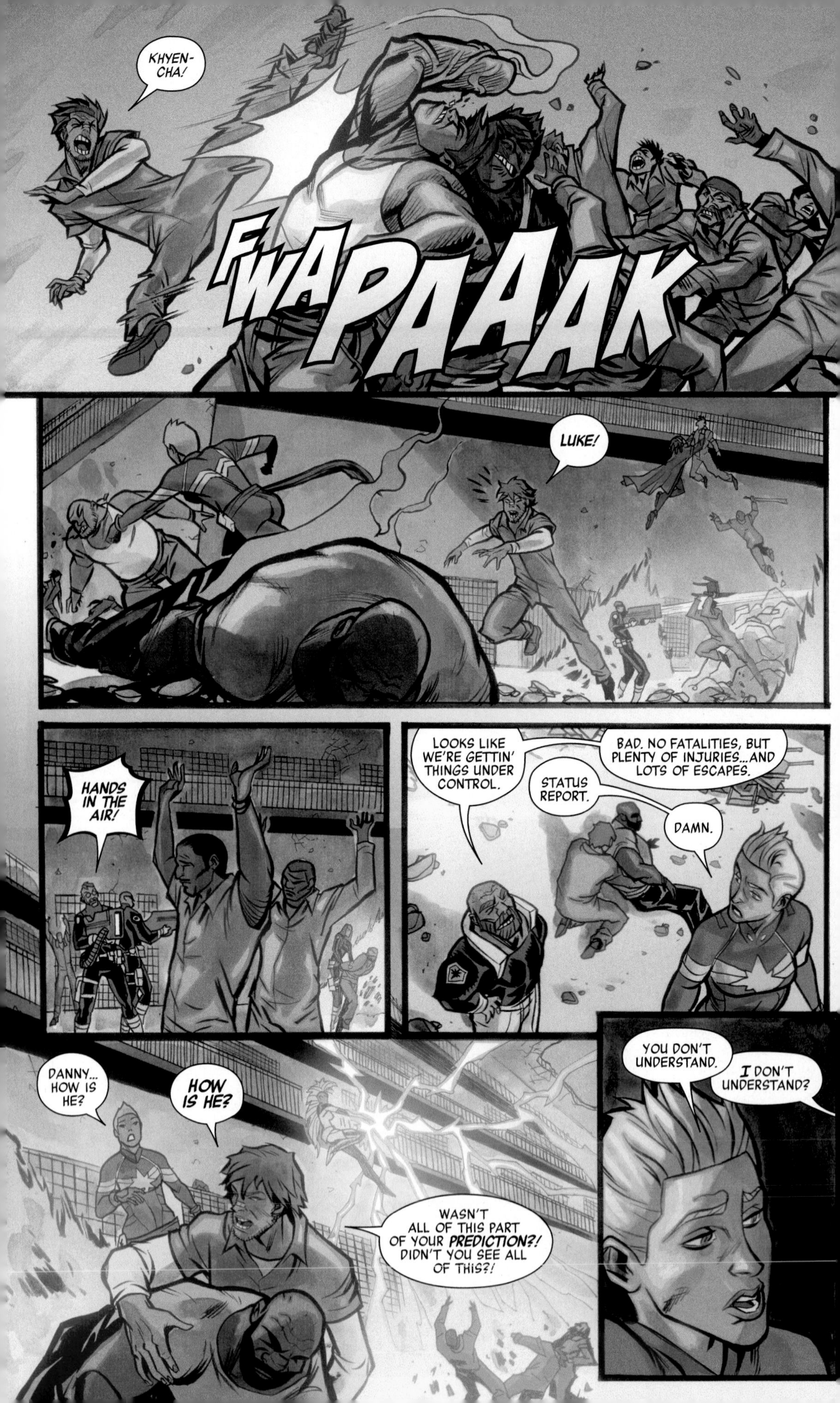
KHYEN-CHA!
FWAPAAAK
LUKE!
HANDS IN THE AIR!
LOOKS LIKE WE'RE GETTIN' THINGS UNDER CONTROL.
STATUS REPORT.
BAD. NO FATALITIES, BUT PLENTY OF INJURIES...AND LOTS OF ESCAPES.
DAMN.
DANNY... HOW IS HE?
HOW IS HE?
WASN'T ALL OF THIS PART OF YOUR PREDICTION?! DIDN'T YOU SEE ALL OF THIS?!
YOU DON'T UNDERSTAND.
I DON'T UNDERSTAND?

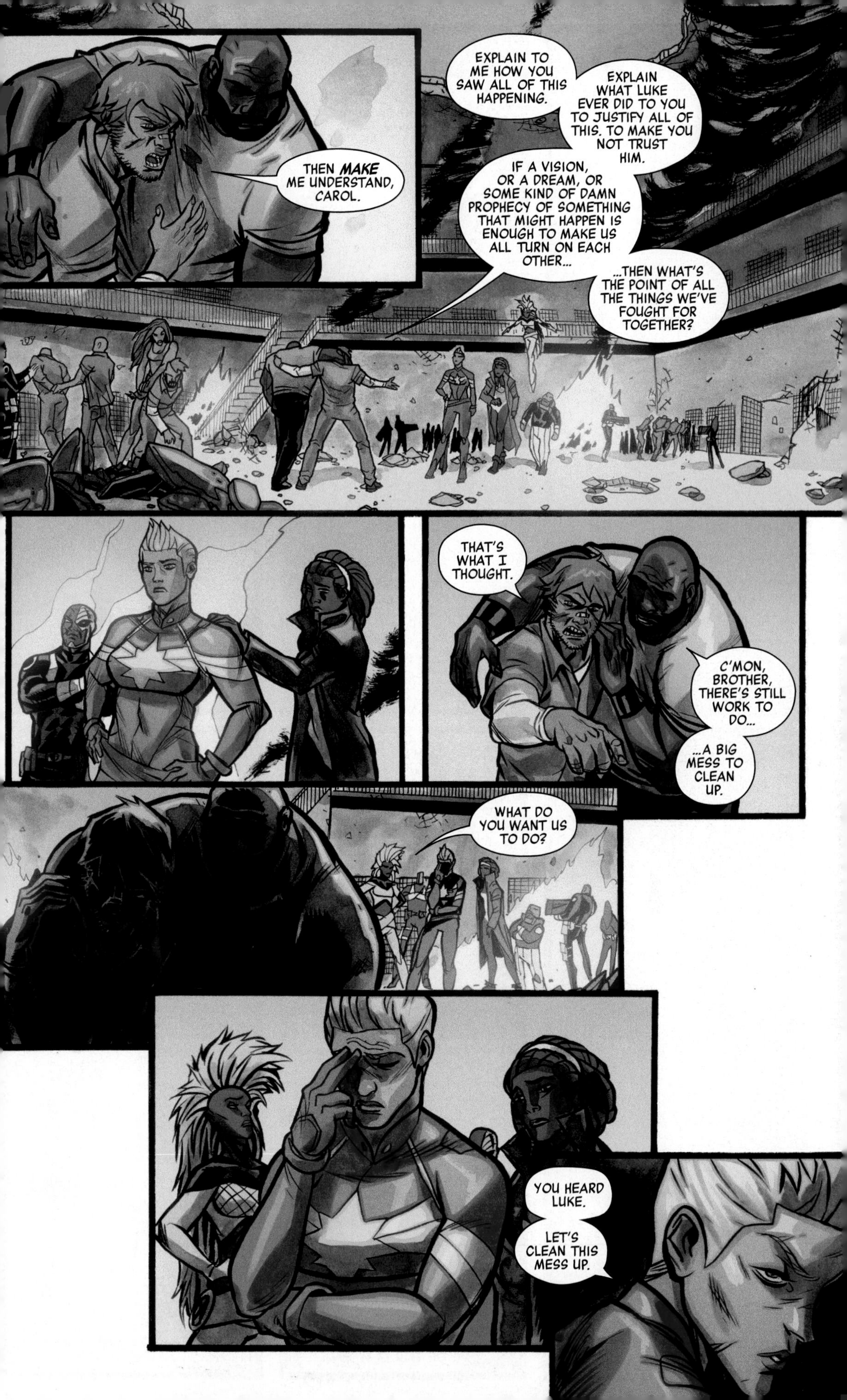
THEN MAKE ME UNDERSTAND, CAROL.
EXPLAIN TO ME HOW YOU SAW ALL OF THIS HAPPENING.
EXPLAIN WHAT LUKE EVER DID TO YOU TO JUSTIFY ALL OF THIS. TO MAKE YOU NOT TRUST HIM.
IF A VISION, OR A DREAM, OR SOME KIND OF DAMN PROPHECY OF SOMETHING THAT MIGHT HAPPEN IS ENOUGH TO MAKE US ALL TURN ON EACH OTHER...
...THEN WHAT'S THE POINT OF ALL THE THINGS WE'VE FOUGHT FOR TOGETHER?
THAT'S WHAT I THOUGHT.
C'MON, BROTHER, THERE'S STILL WORK TO DO...
...A BIG MESS TO CLEAN UP.
WHAT DO YOU WANT US TO DO?
YOU HEARD LUKE.
LET'S CLEAN THIS MESS UP.

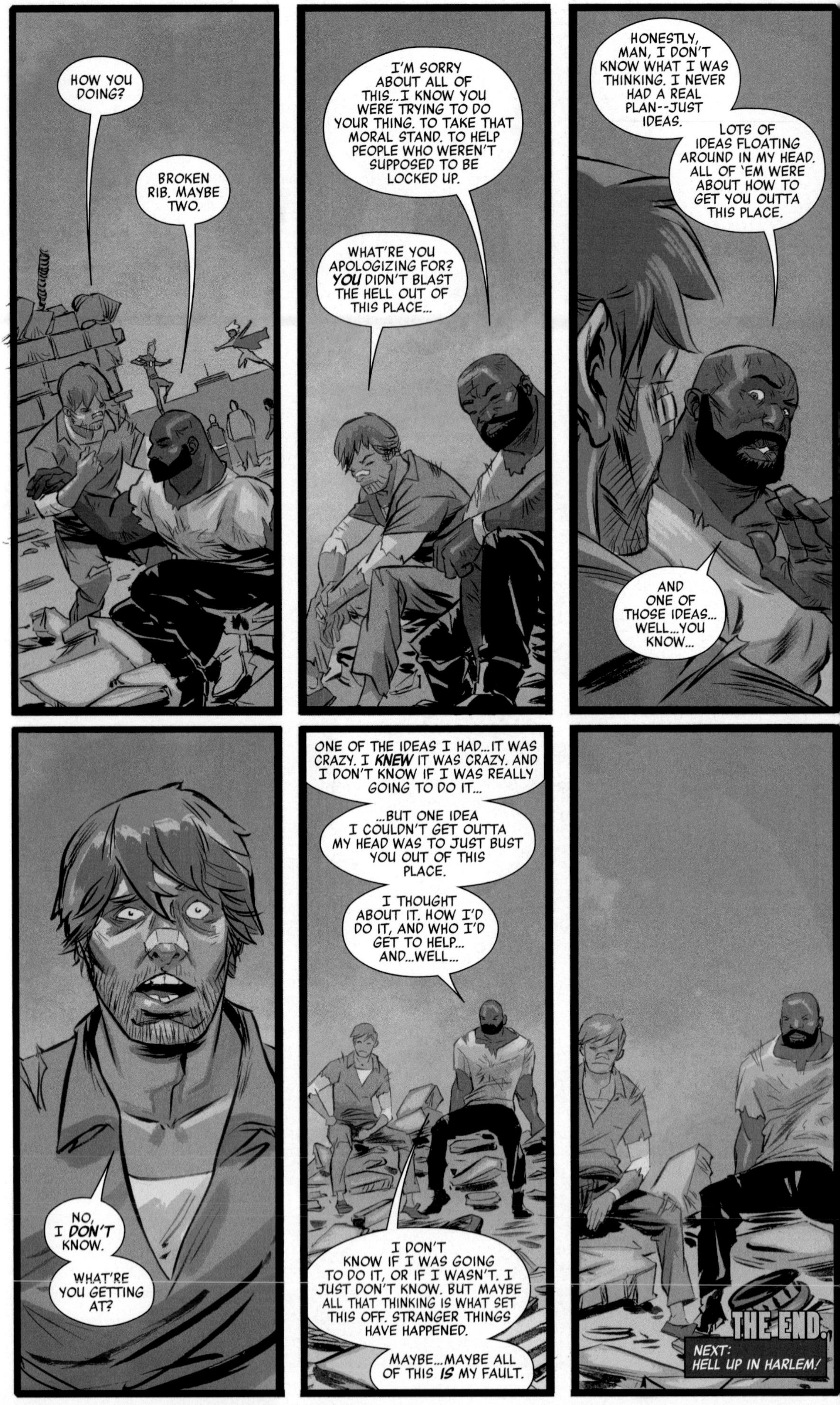
HOW YOU DOING?
BROKEN RIB. MAYBE TWO.
I'M SORRY ABOUT ALL OF THIS...I KNOW YOU WERE TRYING TO DO YOUR THING. TO TAKE THAT MORAL STAND. TO HELP PEOPLE WHO WEREN'T SUPPOSED TO BE LOCKED UP.
WHAT'RE YOU APOLOGIZING FOR? YOU DIDN'T BLAST THE HELL OUT OF THIS PLACE...
HONESTLY, MAN, I DON'T KNOW WHAT I WAS THINKING. I NEVER HAD A REAL PLAN--JUST IDEAS.
LOTS OF IDEAS FLOATING AROUND IN MY HEAD. ALL OF 'EM WERE ABOUT HOW TO GET YOU OUTTA THIS PLACE.
AND ONE OF THOSE IDEAS... WELL...YOU KNOW...
NO, I DON'T KNOW.
WHAT'RE YOU GETTING AT?
ONE OF THE IDEAS I HAD...IT WAS CRAZY. I KNEW IT WAS CRAZY. AND I DON'T KNOW IF I WAS REALLY GOING TO DO IT...
...BUT ONE IDEA I COULDN'T GET OUTTA MY HEAD WAS TO JUST BUST YOU OUT OF THIS PLACE.
I THOUGHT ABOUT IT. HOW I'D DO IT, AND WHO I'D GET TO HELP... AND...WELL...
I DON'T KNOW IF I WAS GOING TO DO IT, OR IF I WASN'T. I JUST DON'T KNOW. BUT MAYBE ALL THAT THINKING IS WHAT SET THIS OFF. STRANGER THINGS HAVE HAPPENED.
MAYBE...MAYBE ALL OF THIS IS MY FAULT.
THE END.
NEXT: HELL UP IN HARLEM!

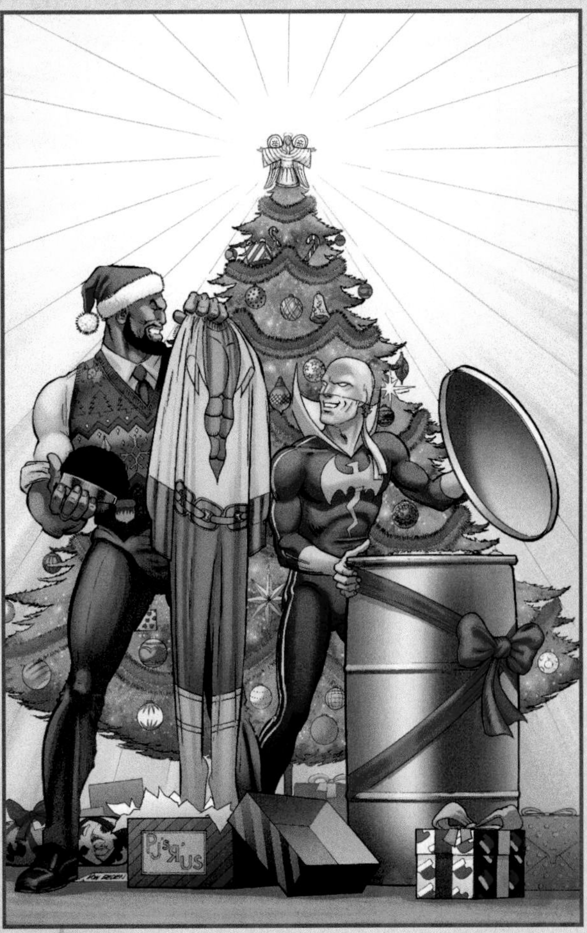

TREVOR VON EEDEN
& RACHELLE ROSENBERG
SWEET CHRISTMAS ANNUAL 1 VARIANT

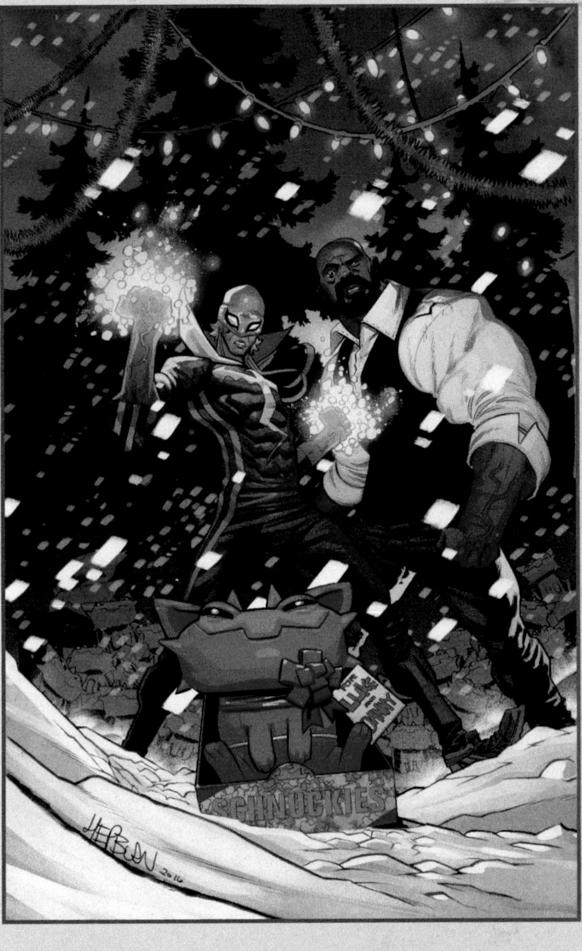
SCHNUCKIES
HEPBURN

SCOTT HEPBURN & MATT MILLA
SWEET CHRISTMAS ANNUAL 1 VARIANT

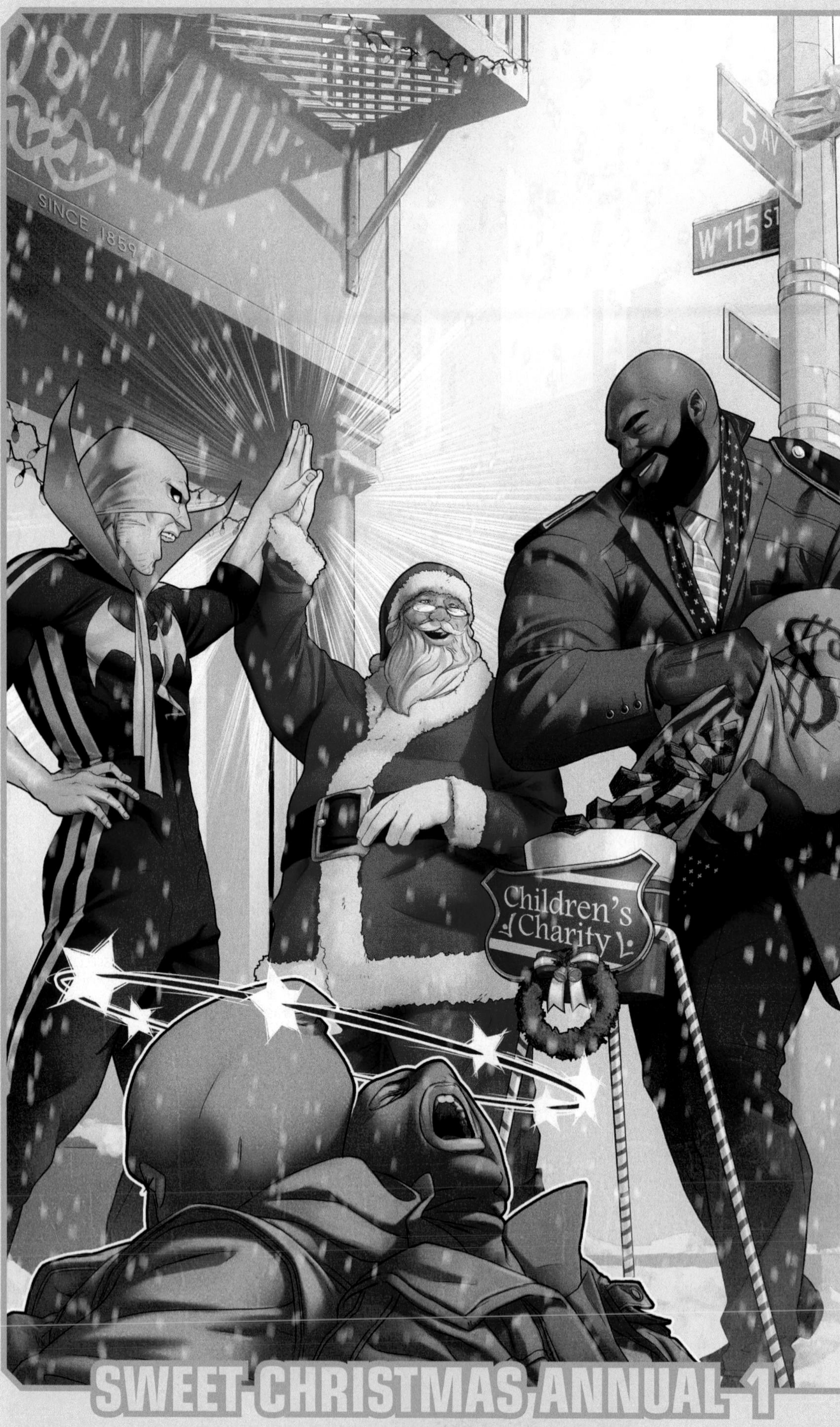
SINCE 1859
5 AV
W 115 ST
Children's Charity
SWEET CHRISTMAS ANNUAL 1

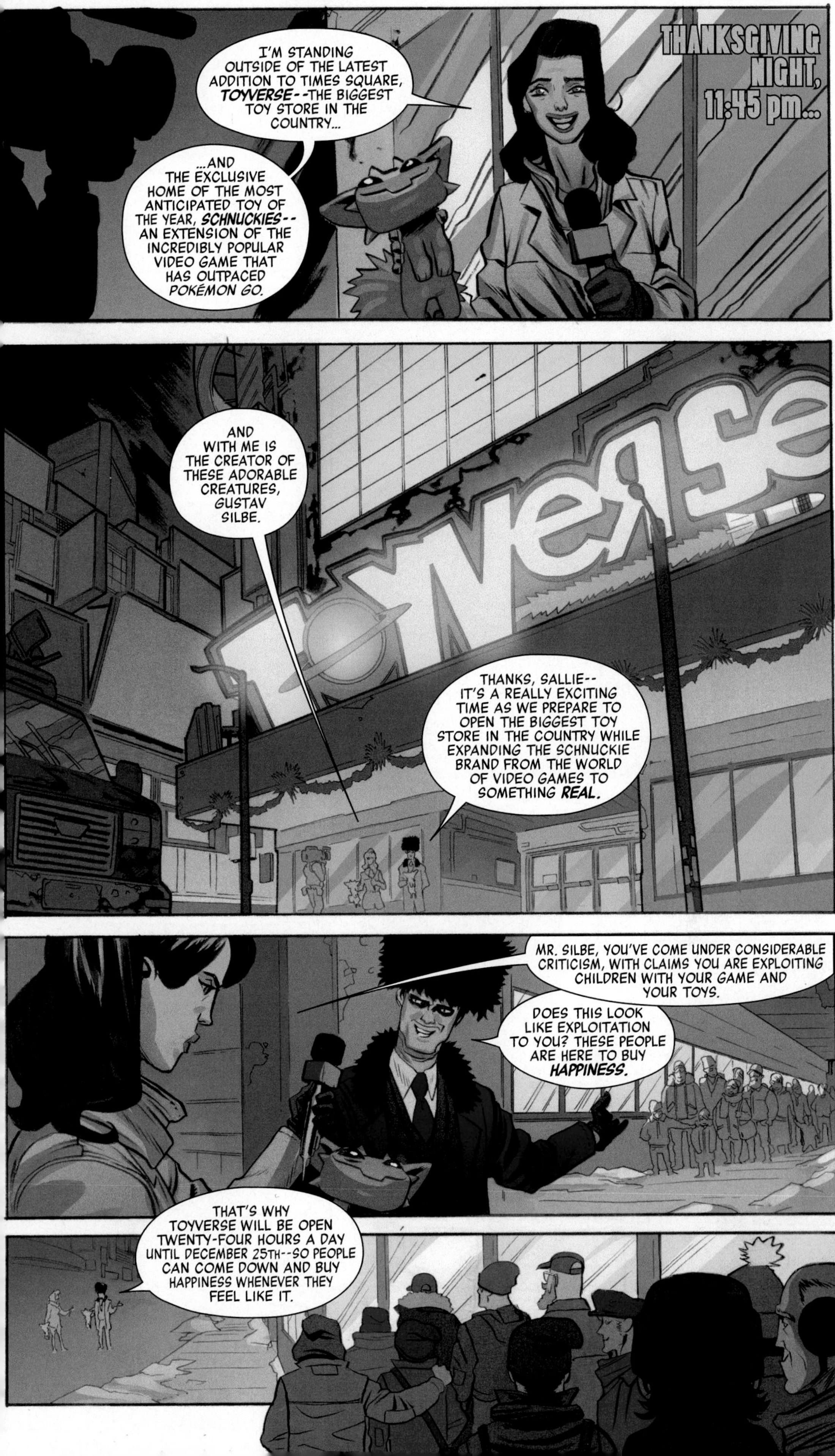
THANKSGIVING NIGHT, 11:45 pm...
I'M STANDING OUTSIDE OF THE LATEST ADDITION TO TIMES SQUARE, TOYVERSE--THE BIGGEST TOY STORE IN THE COUNTRY...
...AND HOME OF THE MOST ANTICIPATED TOY OF THE YEAR, SCHNUCKIES--AN EXTENSION OF THE INCREDIBLY POPULAR VIDEO GAME THAT HAS OUTPACED POKÉMON GO.
AND WITH ME IS THE CREATOR OF THESE ADORABLE CREATURES, GUSTAV SILBE.
THANKS, SALLIE--IT'S A REALLY EXCITING TIME AS WE PREPARE TO OPEN THE BIGGEST TOY STORE IN THE COUNTRY WHILE EXPANDING THE SCHNUCKIE BRAND FROM THE WORLD OF VIDEO GAMES TO SOMETHING REAL.
MR. SILBE, YOU'VE COME UNDER CONSIDERABLE CRITICISM, WITH CLAIMS YOU ARE EXPLOITING CHILDREN WITH YOUR GAME AND YOUR TOYS.
DOES THIS LOOK LIKE EXPLOITATION TO YOU? THESE PEOPLE ARE HERE TO BUY HAPPINESS.
THAT'S WHY TOYVERSE WILL BE OPEN TWENTY-FOUR HOURS A DAY UNTIL DECEMBER 25TH--SO PEOPLE CAN COME DOWN AND BUY HAPPINESS WHENEVER THEY FEEL LIKE IT.

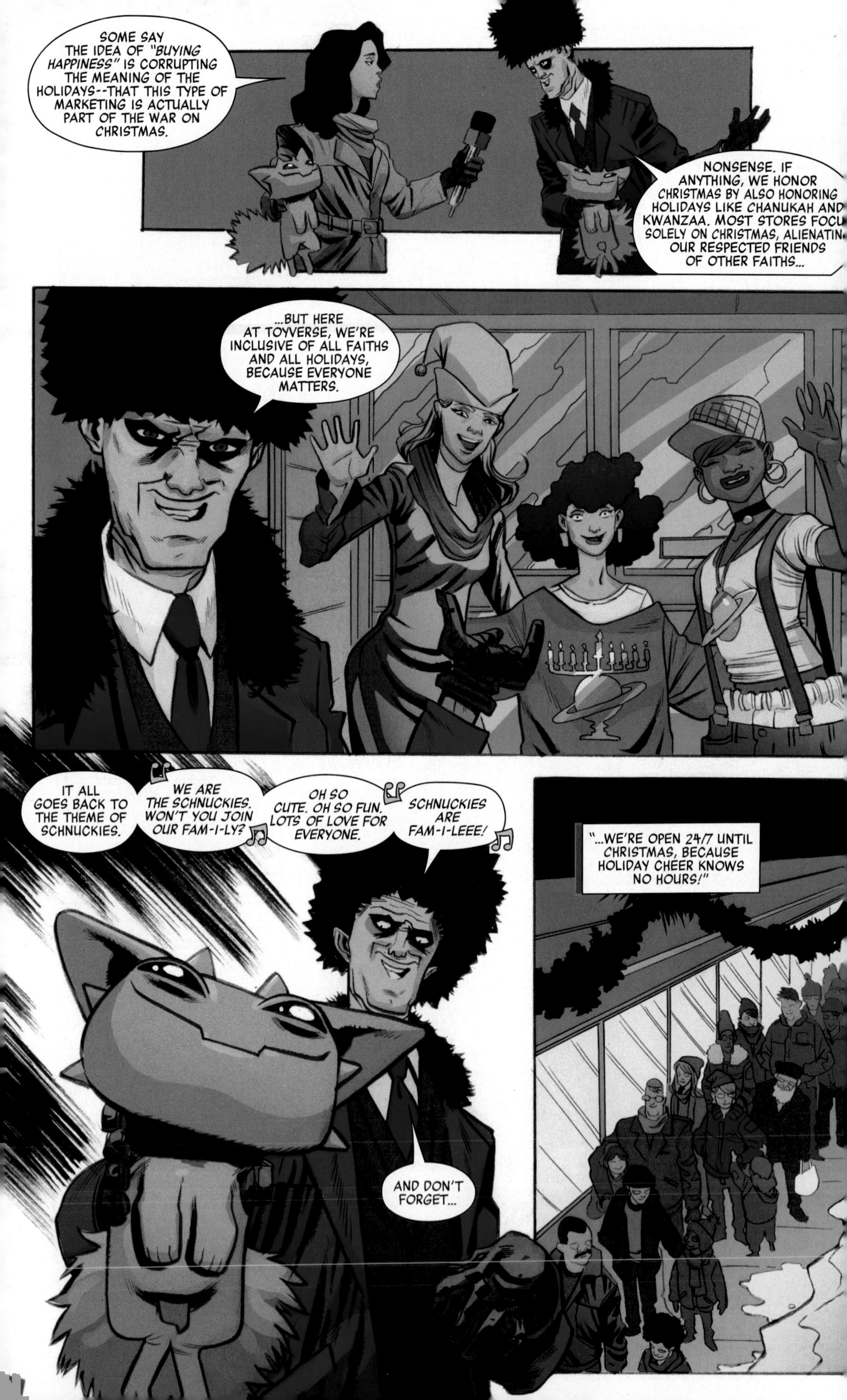
SOME SAY THE IDEA OF "BUYING HAPPINESS" IS CORRUPTING THE MEANING OF THE HOLIDAYS--THAT THIS TYPE OF MARKETING IS ACTUALLY PART OF THE WAR ON CHRISTMAS.
NONSENSE. IF ANYTHING, WE HONOR CHRISTMAS BY ALSO HONORING HOLIDAYS LIKE CHANUKAH AND KWANZAA. MOST STORES FOCU SOLELY ON CHRISTMAS, ALIENATIN OUR RESPECTED FRIENDS OF OTHER FAITHS...
...BUT HERE AT TOYVERSE, WE'RE INCLUSIVE OF ALL FAITHS AND ALL HOLIDAYS, BECAUSE EVERYONE MATTERS.
IT ALL GOES BACK TO THE THEME OF SCHNUCKIES.
WE ARE THE SCHNUCKIES. WON'T YOU JOIN OUR FAM-I-LY?
OH SO CUTE. OH SO FUN. LOTS OF LOVE FOR EVERYONE.
SCHNUCKIES ARE FAM-I-LEEE!
AND DON'T FORGET...
"...WE'RE OPEN 24/7 UNTIL CHRISTMAS, BECAUSE HOLIDAY CHEER KNOWS NO HOURS!"

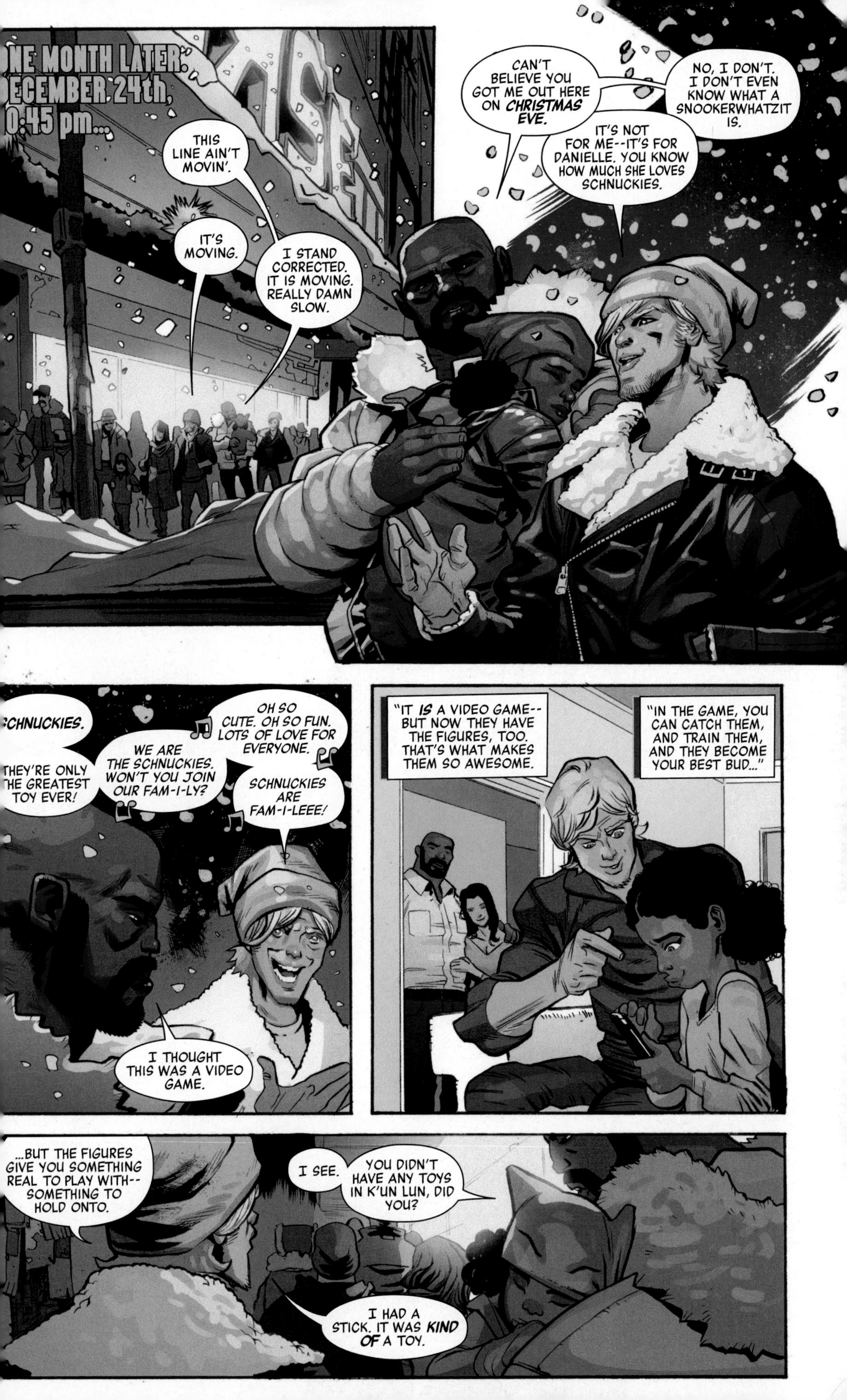
NE MONTH LATER: ECEMBER 24th, 0:45 pm...
THIS LINE AIN'T MOVIN'.
IT'S MOVING.
I STAND CORRECTED. IT IS MOVING. REALLY DAMN SLOW.
CAN'T BELIEVE YOU GOT ME OUT HERE ON CHRISTMAS EVE.
IT'S NOT FOR ME--IT'S FOR DANIELLE. YOU KNOW HOW MUCH SHE LOVES SCHNUCKIES.
NO, I DON'T. I DON'T EVEN KNOW WHAT A SNOOKERWHATZIT IS.
CHNUCKIES.
THEY'RE ONLY HE GREATEST TOY EVER!
WE ARE THE SCHNUCKIES. WON'T YOU JOIN OUR FAM-I-LY?
OH SO CUTE. OH SO FUN. LOTS OF LOVE FOR EVERYONE.
SCHNUCKIES ARE FAM-I-LEEE!
I THOUGHT THIS WAS A VIDEO GAME.
"IT IS A VIDEO GAME--BUT NOW THEY HAVE THE FIGURES, TOO. THAT'S WHAT MAKES THEM SO AWESOME.
"IN THE GAME, YOU CAN CATCH THEM, AND TRAIN THEM, AND THEY BECOME YOUR BEST BUD..."
...BUT THE FIGURES GIVE YOU SOMETHING REAL TO PLAY WITH--SOMETHING TO HOLD ONTO.
I SEE.
YOU DIDN'T HAVE ANY TOYS IN K'UN LUN, DID YOU?
I HAD A STICK. IT WAS KIND OF A TOY.

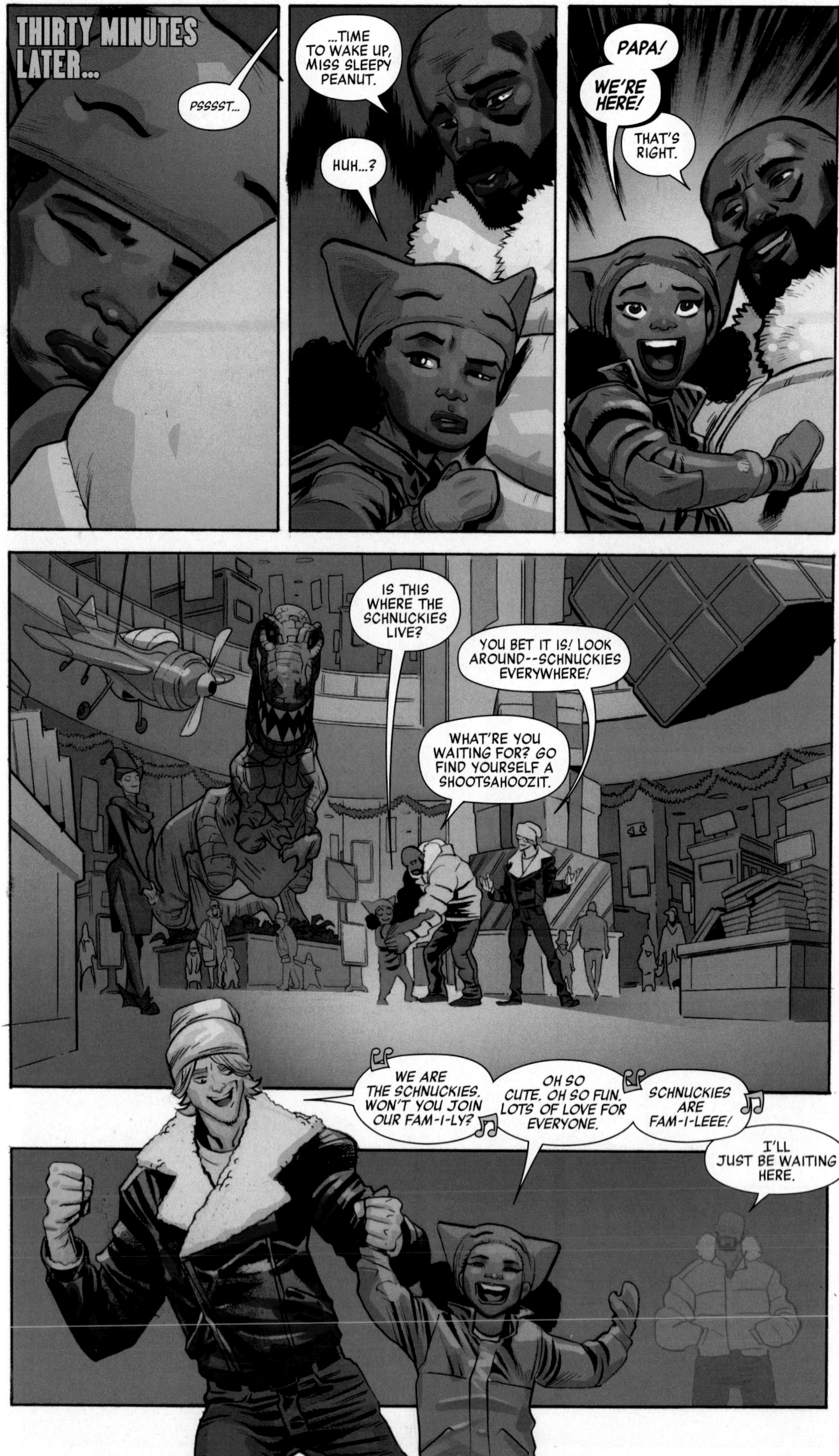
THIRTY MINUTES LATER...
PSSSST...
...TIME TO WAKE UP, MISS SLEEPY PEANUT.
HUH...?
PAPA!
WE'RE HERE!
THAT'S RIGHT.
IS THIS WHERE THE SCHNUCKIES LIVE?
YOU BET IT IS! LOOK AROUND--SCHNUCKIES EVERYWHERE!
WHAT'RE YOU WAITING FOR? GO FIND YOURSELF A SHOOTSAHOOZIT.
WE ARE THE SCHNUCKIES. WON'T YOU JOIN OUR FAM-I-LY?
OH SO CUTE. OH SO FUN. LOTS OF LOVE FOR EVERYONE.
SCHNUCKIES ARE FAM-I-LEEE!
I'LL JUST BE WAITING HERE.

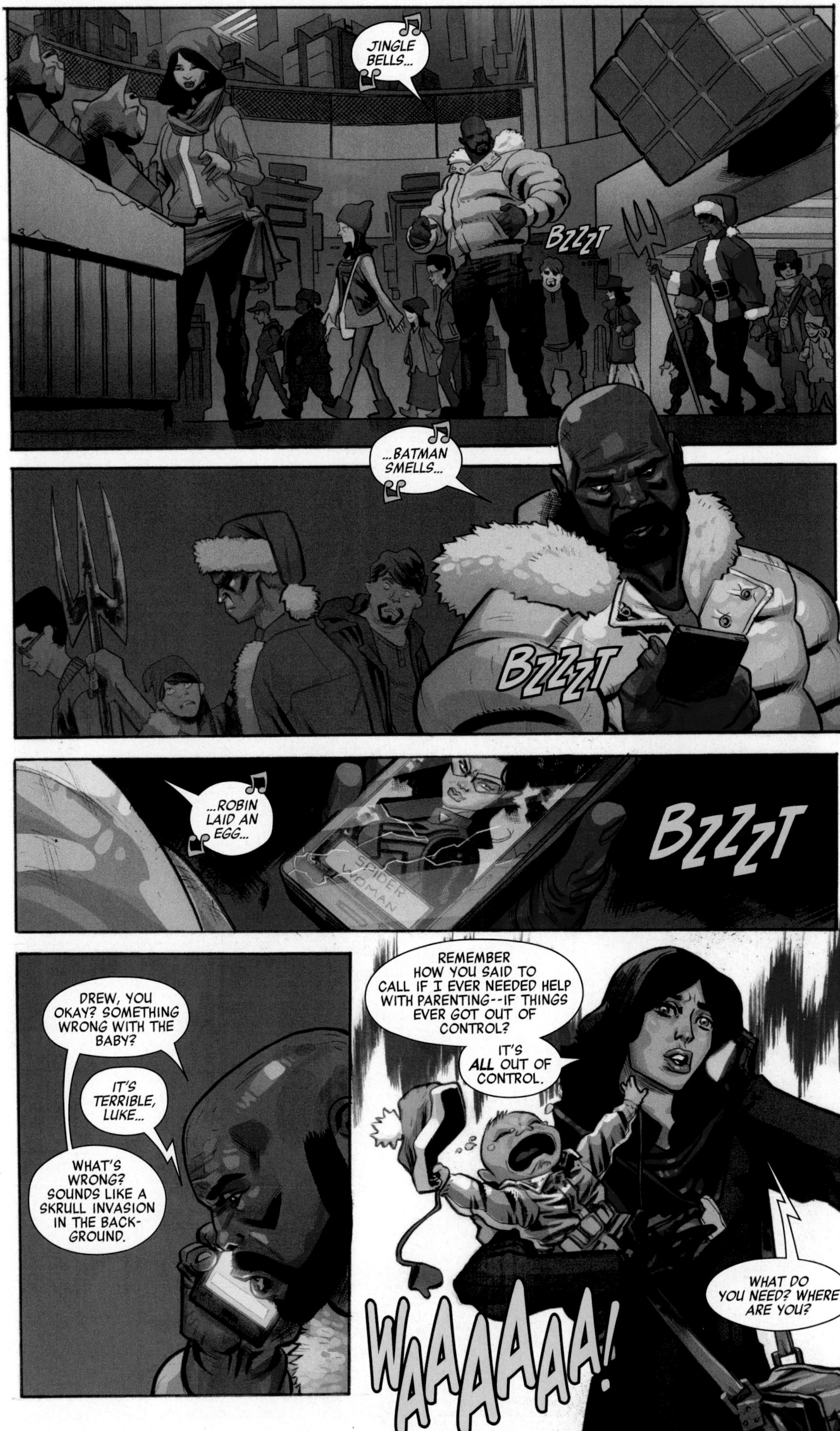
JINGLE BELLS...
BZZZT
...BATMAN SMELLS...
BZZZT
...ROBIN LAID AN EGG...
SPIDER WOMAN
BZZZT
DREW, YOU OKAY? SOMETHING WRONG WITH THE BABY?
IT'S TERRIBLE, LUKE...
WHAT'S WRONG? SOUNDS LIKE A SKRULL INVASION IN THE BACK-GROUND.
REMEMBER HOW YOU SAID TO CALL IF I EVER NEEDED HELP WITH PARENTING--IF THINGS EVER GOT OUT OF CONTROL?
IT'S ALL OUT OF CONTROL.
WHAT DO YOU NEED? WHERE ARE YOU?
WAAAAAAA!

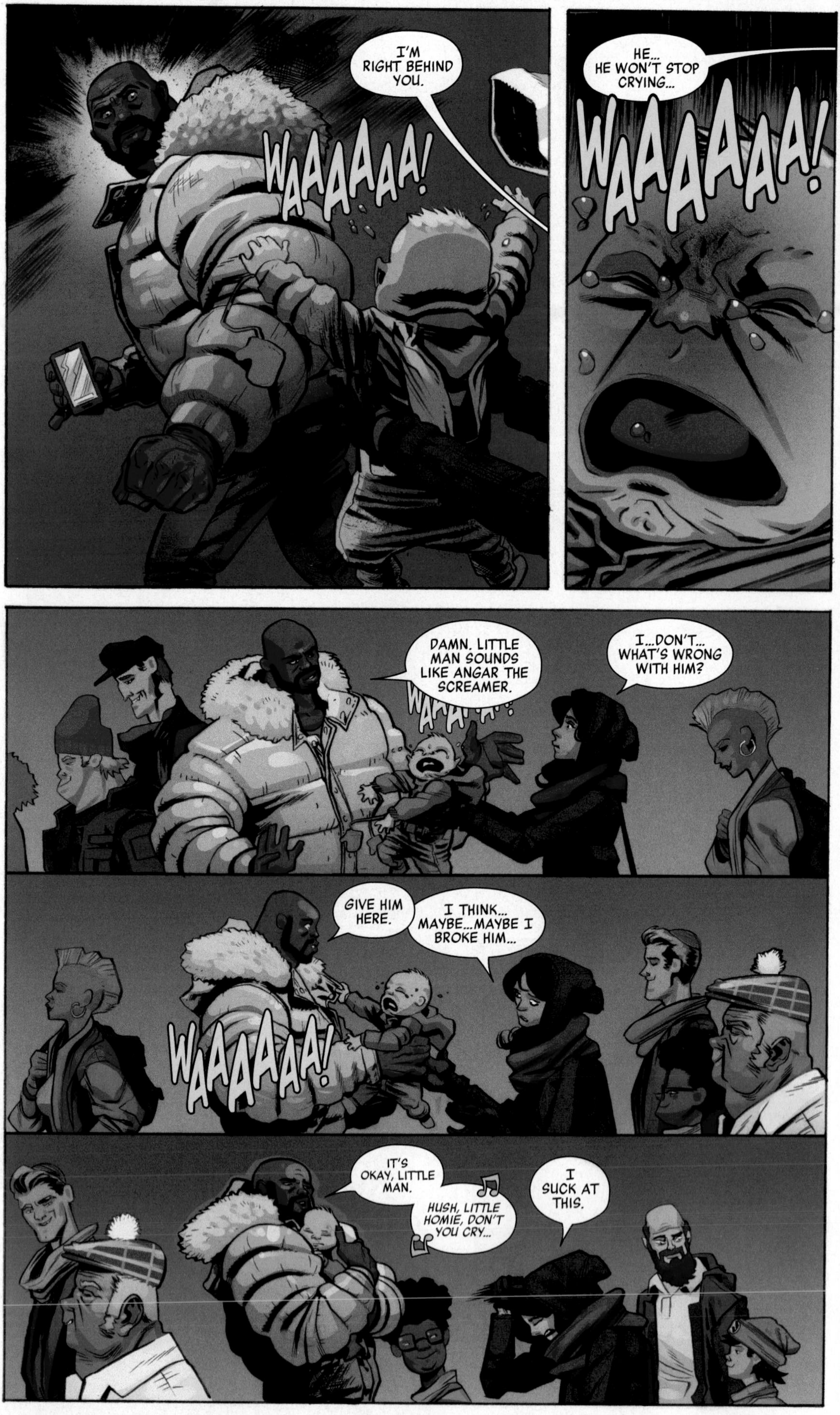
I'M RIGHT BEHIND YOU.
WAAAAAA!
HE... HE WON'T STOP CRYING...
WAAAAAAA!
DAMN. LITTLE MAN SOUNDS LIKE ANGAR THE SCREAMER.
I...DON'T... WHAT'S WRONG WITH HIM?
GIVE HIM HERE.
I THINK... MAYBE...MAYBE I BROKE HIM...
WAAAAAA!
IT'S OKAY, LITTLE MAN.
HUSH, LITTLE HOMIE, DON'T YOU CRY...
I SUCK AT THIS.

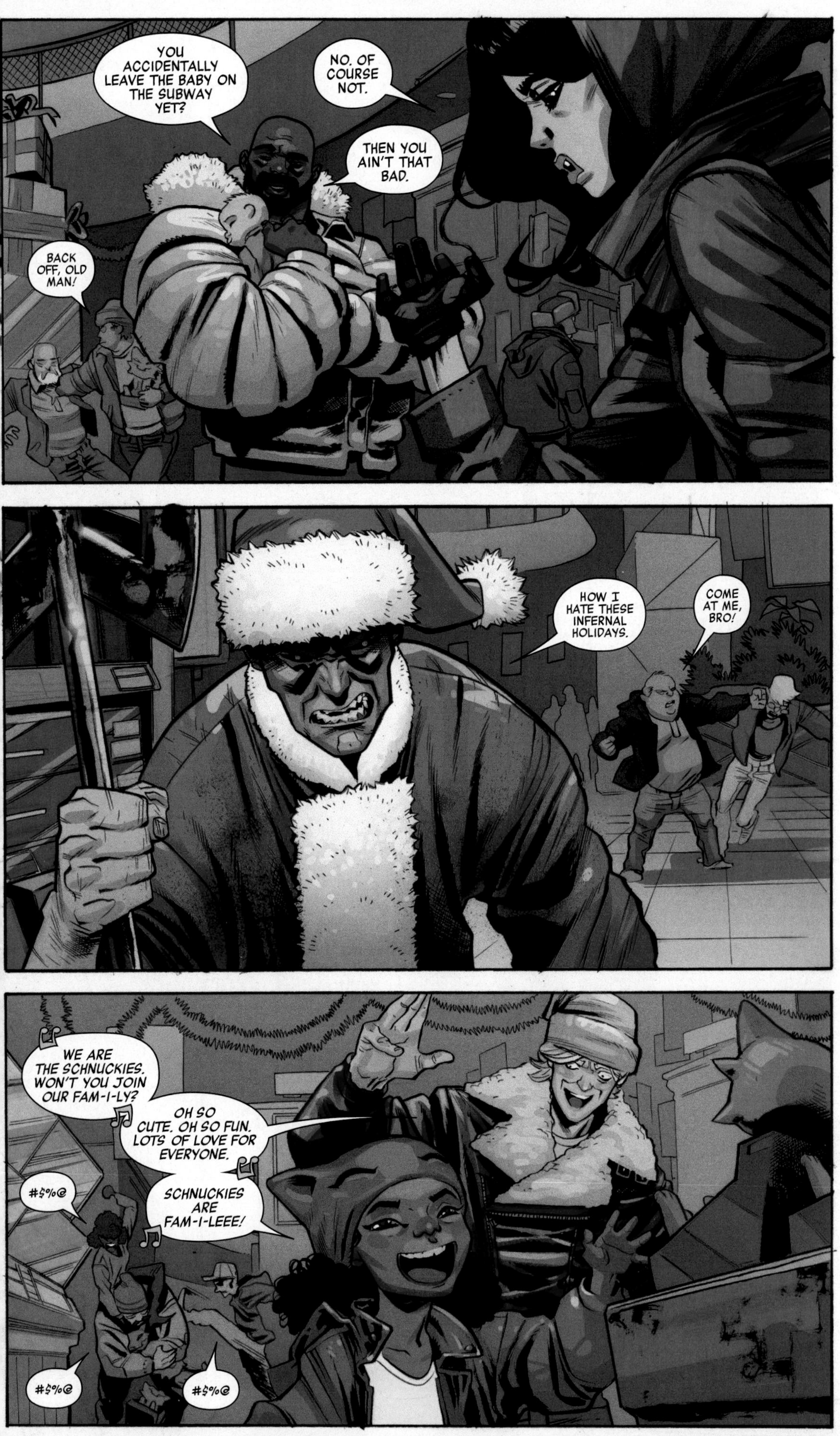

YOU ACCIDENTALLY LEAVE THE BABY ON THE SUBWAY YET?
NO. OF COURSE NOT.
THEN YOU AIN'T THAT BAD.
BACK OFF, OLD MAN!
HOW I HATE THESE INFERNAL HOLIDAYS.
COME AT ME, BRO!
WE ARE THE SCHNUCKIES. WON'T YOU JOIN OUR FAM-I-LY?
OH SO CUTE. OH SO FUN. LOTS OF LOVE FOR EVERYONE.
SCHNUCKIES ARE FAM-I-LEEE!
#$%@
#$%@
#$%@

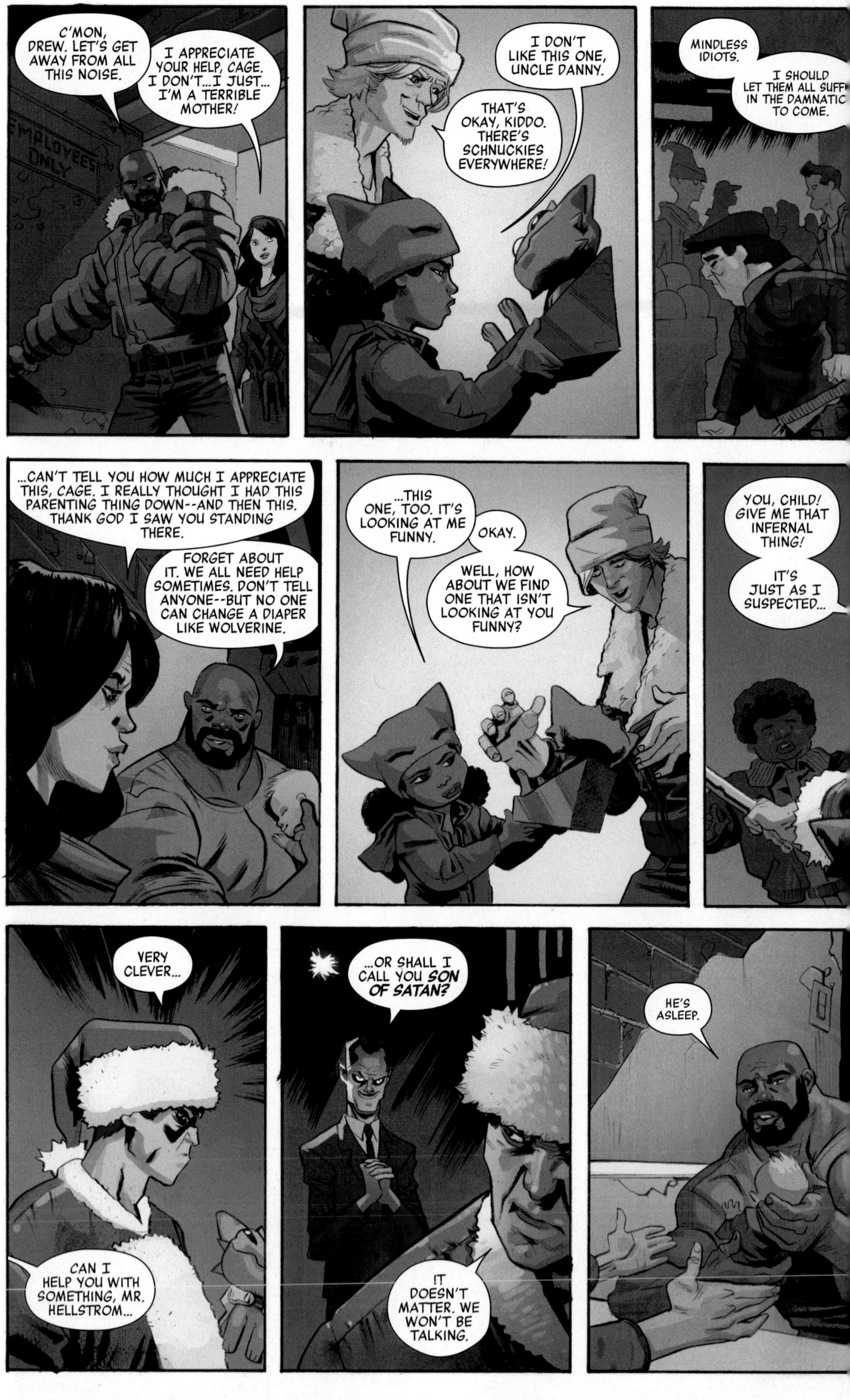
C'MON, DREW. LET'S GET AWAY FROM ALL THIS NOISE.
I APPRECIATE YOUR HELP, CAGE. I DON'T...I JUST... I'M A TERRIBLE MOTHER!
EMPLOYEES ONLY
I DON'T LIKE THIS ONE, UNCLE DANNY.
THAT'S OKAY, KIDDO. THERE'S SCHNUCKIES EVERYWHERE!
MINDLESS IDIOTS.
I SHOULD LET THEM ALL SUFF IN THE DAMNATIC TO COME.
...CAN'T TELL YOU HOW MUCH I APPRECIATE THIS, CAGE. I REALLY THOUGHT I HAD THIS PARENTING THING DOWN--AND THEN THIS. THANK GOD I SAW YOU STANDING THERE.
FORGET ABOUT IT. WE ALL NEED HELP SOMETIMES. DON'T TELL ANYONE--BUT NO ONE CAN CHANGE A DIAPER LIKE WOLVERINE.
...THIS ONE, TOO. IT'S LOOKING AT ME FUNNY.
OKAY.
WELL, HOW ABOUT WE FIND ONE THAT ISN'T LOOKING AT YOU FUNNY?
YOU, CHILD! GIVE ME THAT INFERNAL THING!
IT'S JUST AS I SUSPECTED...
VERY CLEVER...
CAN I HELP YOU WITH SOMETHING, MR. HELLSTROM...
...OR SHALL I CALL YOU SON OF SATAN?
!T DOESN'T MATTER. WE WON'T BE TALKING.
HE'S ASLEEP.

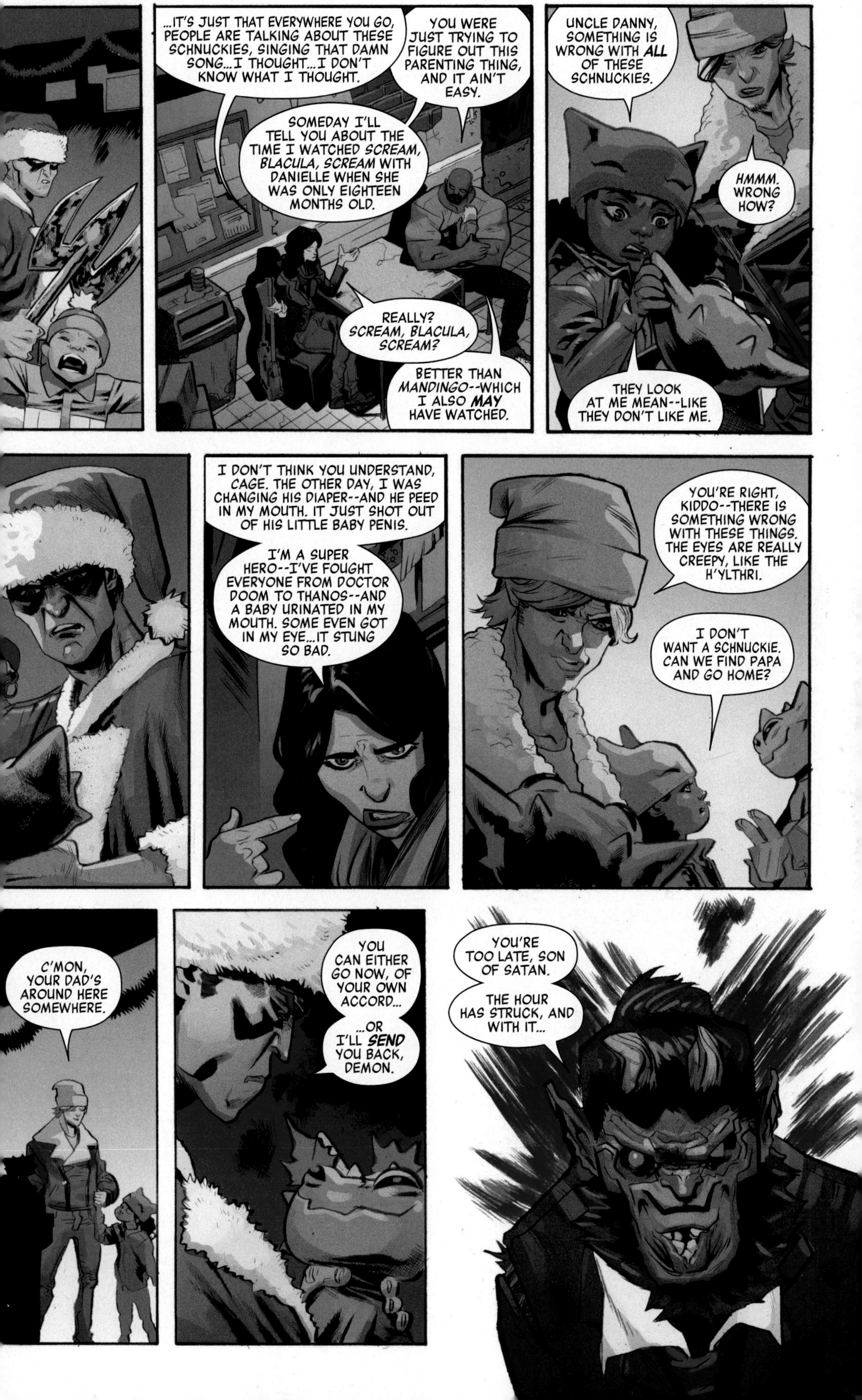
...IT'S JUST THAT EVERYWHERE YOU GO, PEOPLE ARE TALKING ABOUT THESE SCHNUCKIES, SINGING THAT DAMN SONG...I THOUGHT...I DON'T KNOW WHAT I THOUGHT.
YOU WERE JUST TRYING TO FIGURE OUT THIS PARENTING THING, AND IT AIN'T EASY.
SOMEDAY I'LL TELL YOU ABOUT THE TIME I WATCHED SCREAM, BLACULA, SCREAM WITH DANIELLE WHEN SHE WAS ONLY EIGHTEEN MONTHS OLD.
REALLY? SCREAM, BLACULA, SCREAM?
BETTER THAN MANDINGO--WHICH I ALSO MAY HAVE WATCHED.
UNCLE DANNY, SOMETHING IS WRONG WITH ALL OF THESE SCHNUCKIES.
HMMM. WRONG HOW?
THEY LOOK AT ME MEAN--LIKE THEY DON'T LIKE ME.
I DON'T THINK YOU UNDERSTAND, CAGE. THE OTHER DAY, I WAS CHANGING HIS DIAPER--AND HE PEED IN MY MOUTH. IT JUST SHOT OUT OF HIS LITTLE BABY PENIS.
I'M A SUPER HERO--I'VE FOUGHT EVERYONE FROM DOCTOR DOOM TO THANOS--AND A BABY URINATED IN MY MOUTH. SOME EVEN GOT IN MY EYE...IT STUNG SO BAD.
YOU'RE RIGHT, KIDDO--THERE IS SOMETHING WRONG WITH THESE THINGS. THE EYES ARE REALLY CREEPY, LIKE THE H'YLTHRI.
I DON'T WANT A SCHNUCKIE. CAN WE FIND PAPA AND GO HOME?
C'MON, YOUR DAD'S AROUND HERE SOMEWHERE.
YOU CAN EITHER GO NOW, OF YOUR OWN ACCORD...
...OR I'LL SEND YOU BACK, DEMON.
YOU'RE TOO LATE, SON OF SATAN.
THE HOUR HAS STRUCK, AND WITH IT...

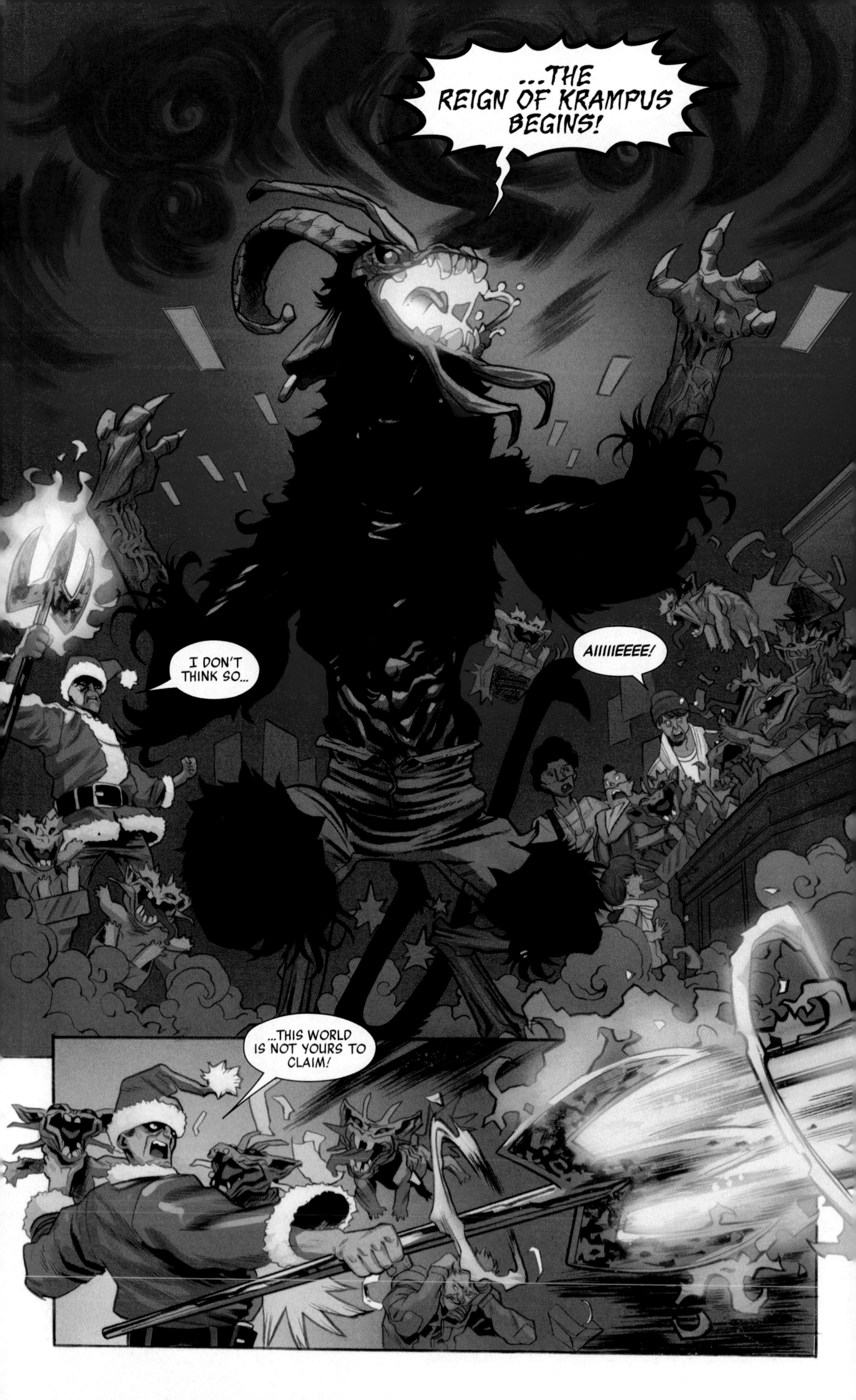
...THE REIGN OF KRAMPUS BEGINS!
I DON'T THINK SO...
AIIIIIEEEE!
...THIS WORLD IS NOT YOURS TO CLAIM!

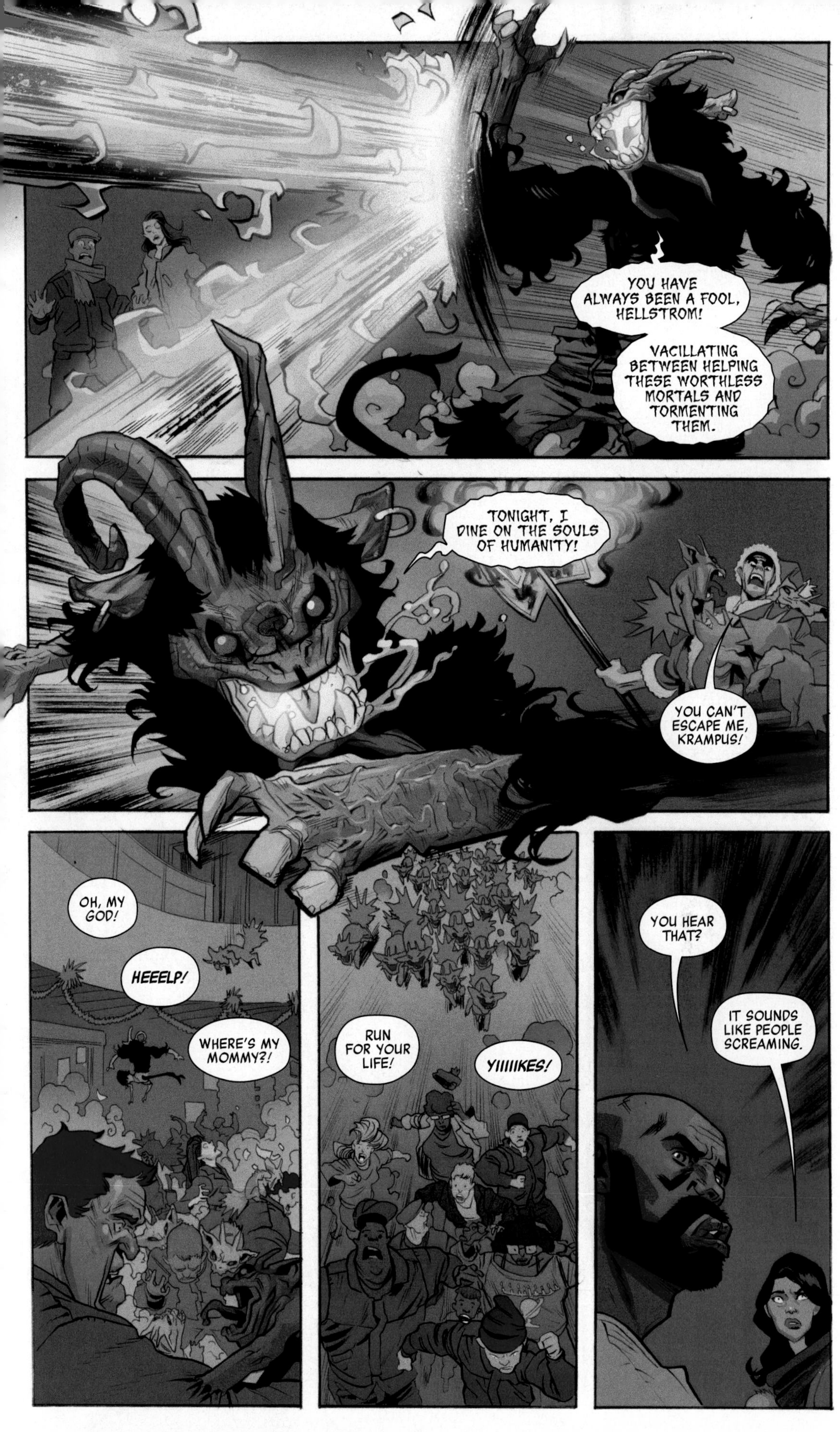
YOU HAVE ALWAYS BEEN A FOOL, HELLSTROM!
VACILLATING BETWEEN HELPING THESE WORTHLESS MORTALS AND TORMENTING THEM.
TONIGHT, I DINE ON THE SOULS OF HUMANITY!
YOU CAN'T ESCAPE ME, KRAMPUS!
OH, MY GOD!
HEEELP!
WHERE'S MY MOMMY?!
RUN FOR YOUR LIFE!
YIIIIIKES!
YOU HEAR THAT?
IT SOUNDS LIKE PEOPLE SCREAMING.

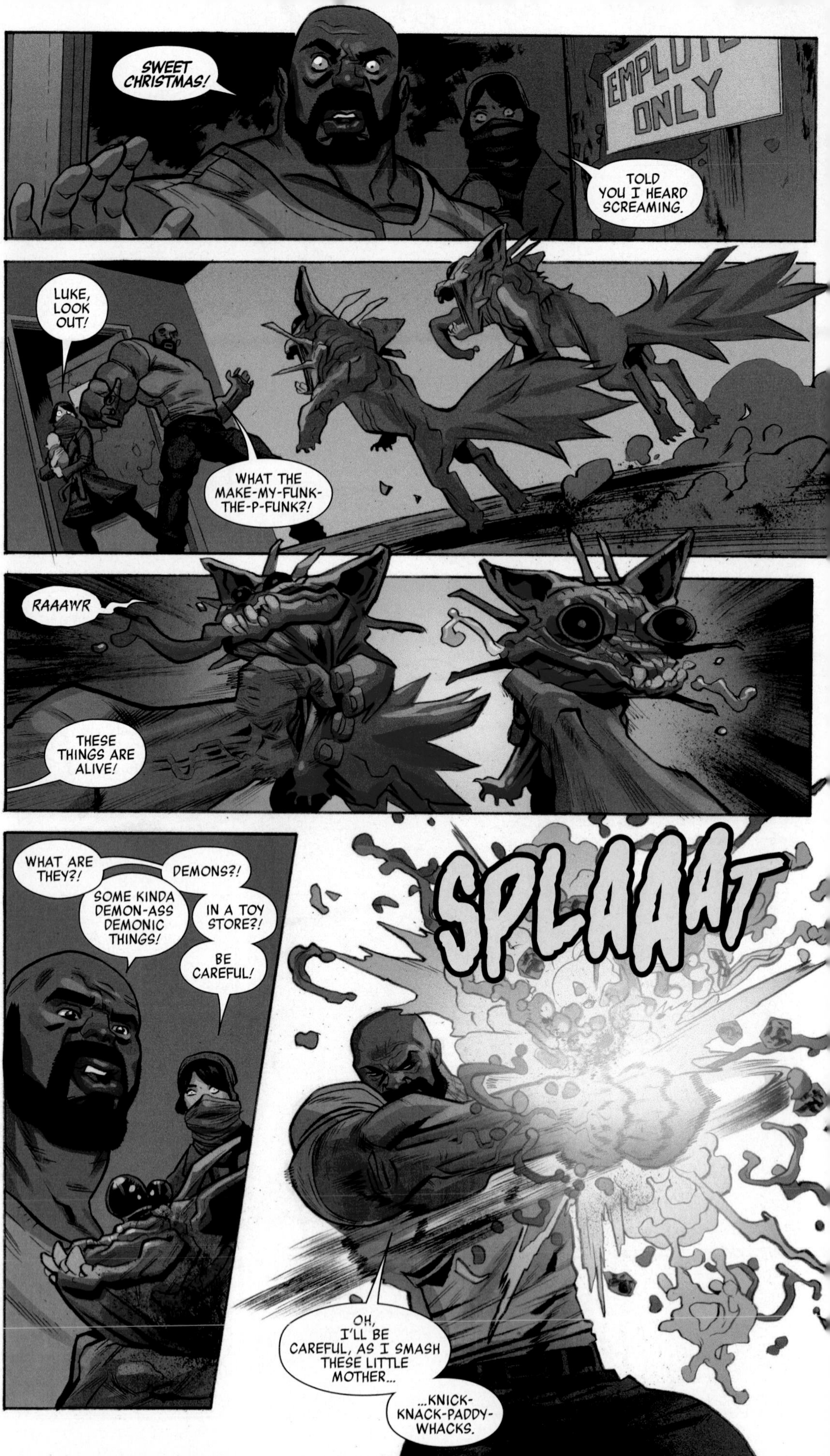
SWEET CHRISTMAS!
EMPLOYE ONLY
TOLD YOU I HEARD SCREAMING.
LUKE, LOOK OUT!
WHAT THE MAKE-MY-FUNK-THE-P-FUNK?!
RAAAWR
THESE THINGS ARE ALIVE!
WHAT ARE THEY?!
DEMONS?!
SOME KINDA DEMON-ASS DEMONIC THINGS!
IN A TOY STORE?!
BE CAREFUL!
SPLAAAT
OH, I'LL BE CAREFUL, AS I SMASH THESE LITTLE MOTHER...
...KNICK-KNACK-PADDY-WHACKS.

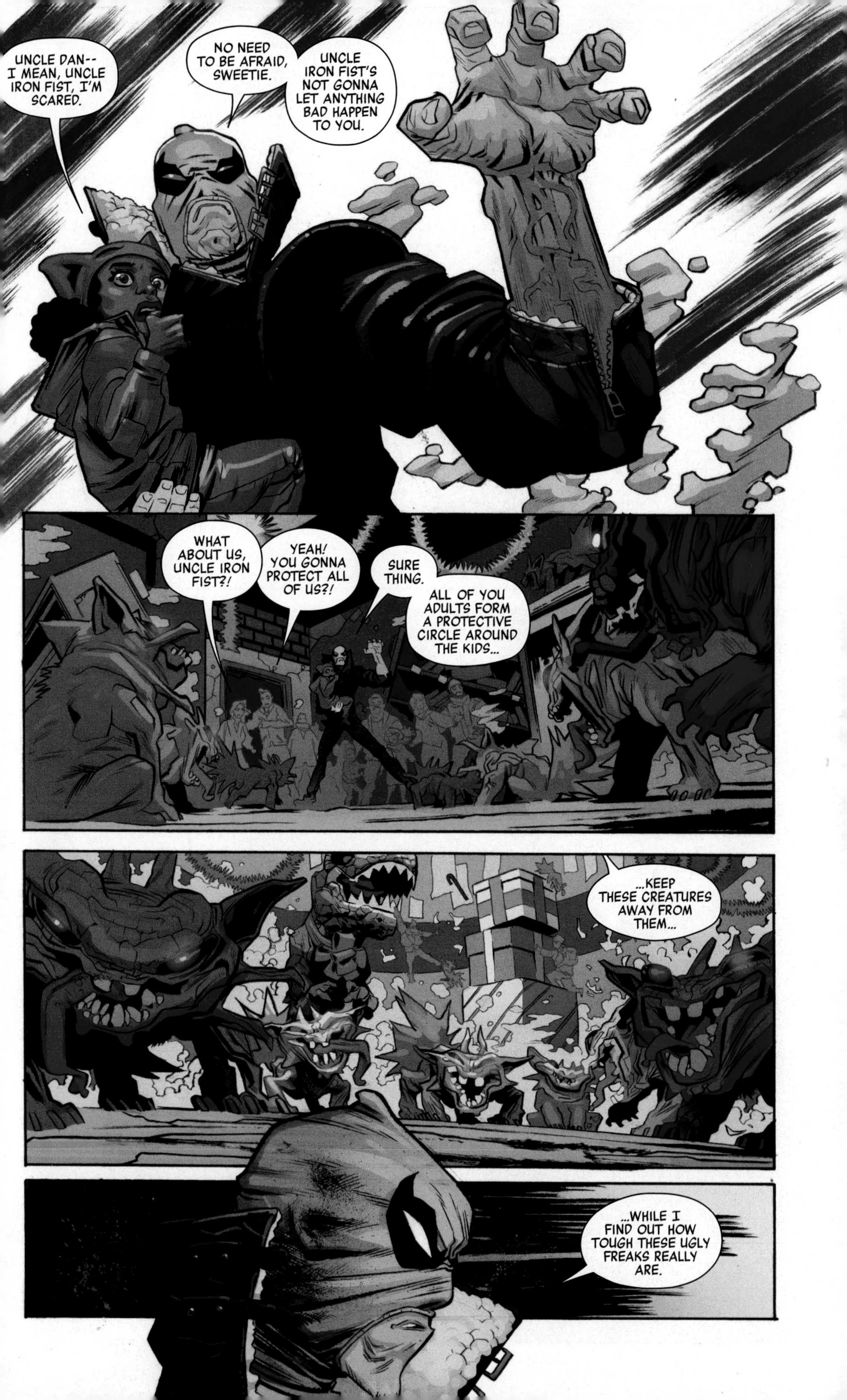
UNCLE DAN-- I MEAN, UNCLE IRON FIST, I'M SCARED.
NO NEED TO BE AFRAID, SWEETIE.
UNCLE IRON FIST'S NOT GONNA LET ANYTHING BAD HAPPEN TO YOU.
WHAT ABOUT US, UNCLE IRON FIST?!
YEAH! YOU GONNA PROTECT ALL OF US?!
SURE THING.
ALL OF YOU ADULTS FORM A PROTECTIVE CIRCLE AROUND THE KIDS...
...KEEP THESE CREATURES AWAY FROM THEM...
...WHILE I FIND OUT HOW TOUGH THESE UGLY FREAKS REALLY ARE.

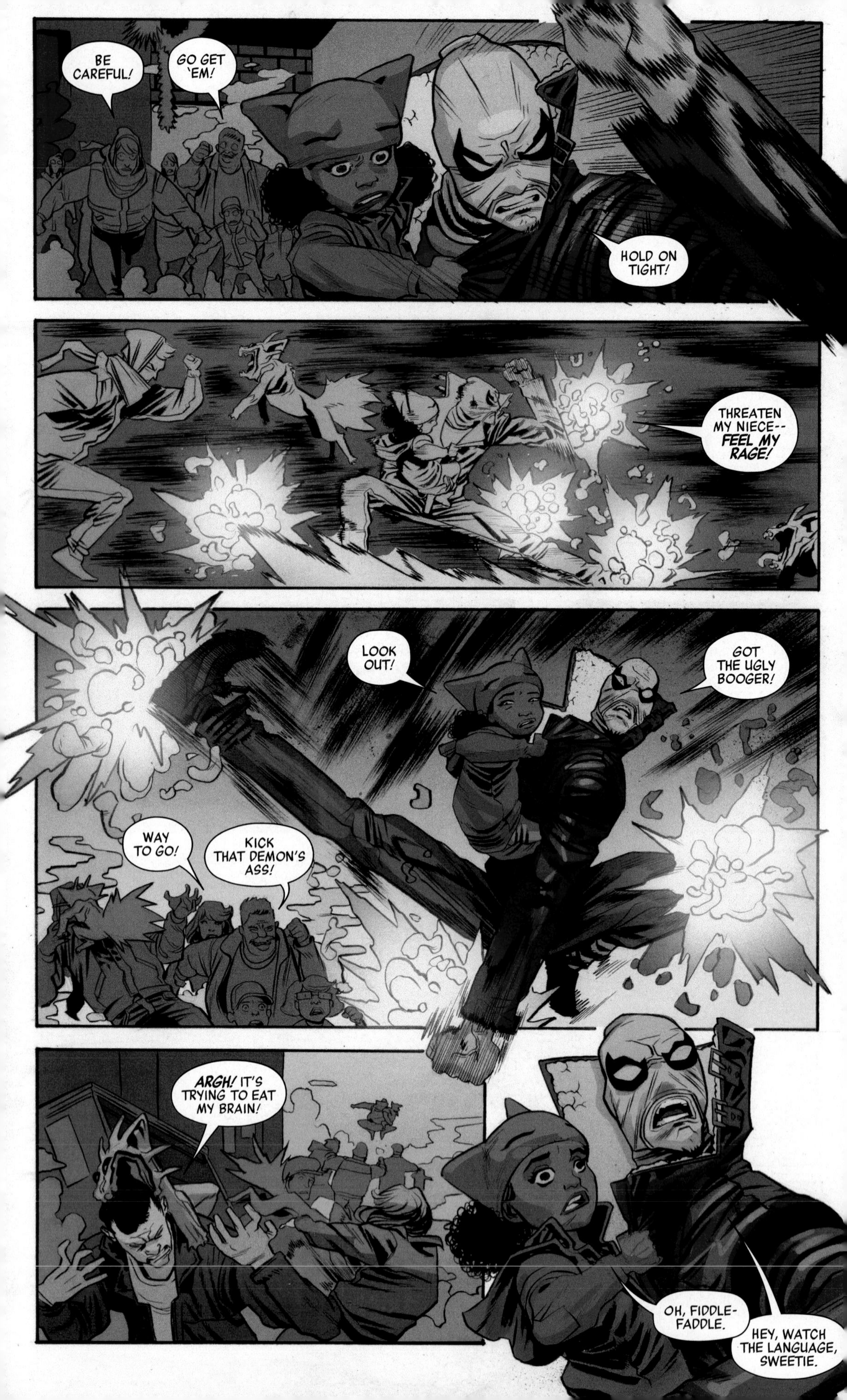
BE CAREFUL!
GO GET 'EM!
HOLD ON TIGHT!
THREATEN MY NIECE-- FEEL MY RAGE!
LOOK OUT!
GOT THE UGLY BOOGER!
WAY TO GO!
KICK THAT DEMON'S ASS!
ARGH! IT'S TRYING TO EAT MY BRAIN!
OH, FIDDLE-FADDLE.
HEY, WATCH THE LANGUAGE, SWEETIE.

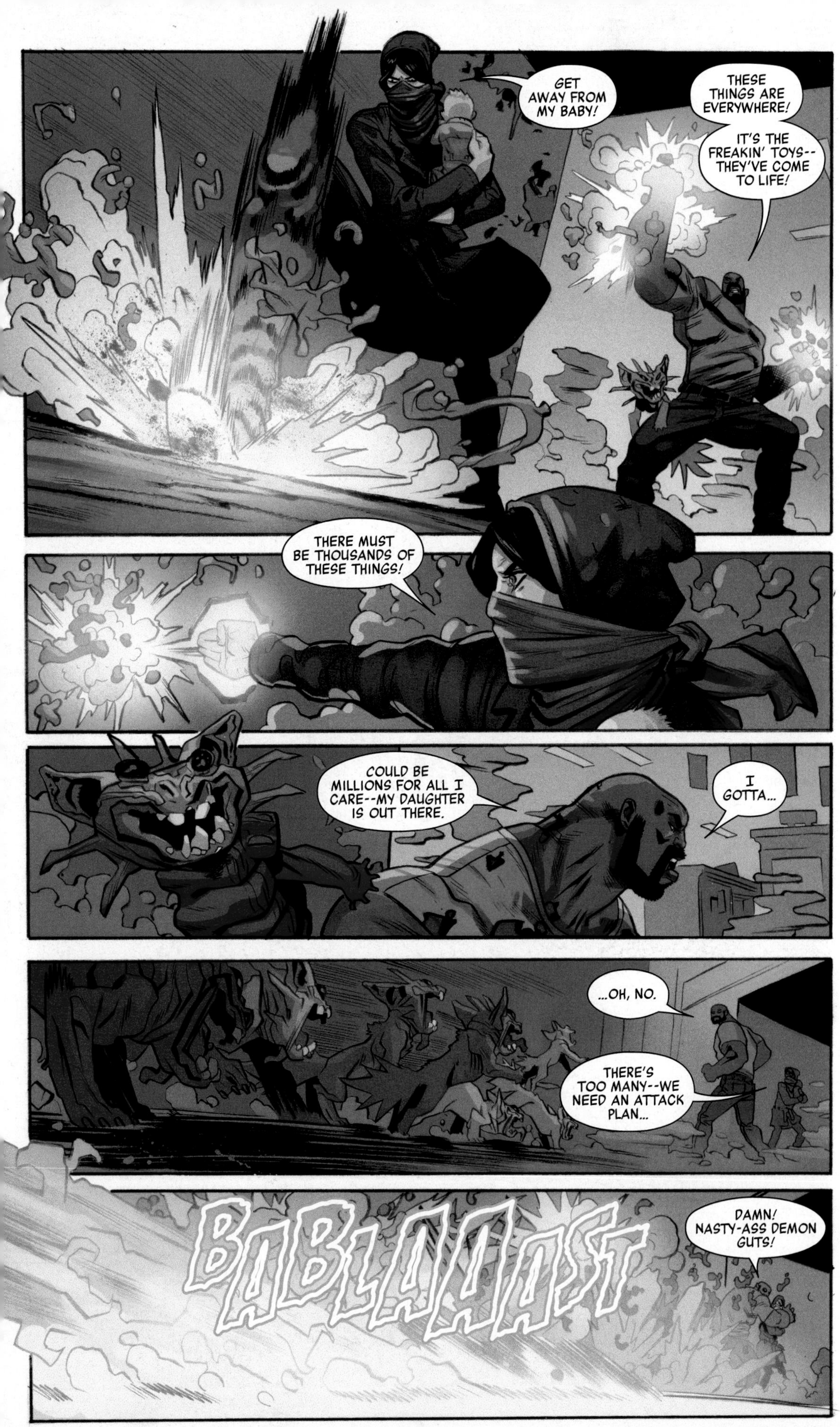
GET AWAY FROM MY BABY!
THESE THINGS ARE EVERYWHERE!
IT'S THE FREAKIN' TOYS-- THEY'VE COME TO LIFE!
THERE MUST BE THOUSANDS OF THESE THINGS!
COULD BE MILLIONS FOR ALL I CARE--MY DAUGHTER IS OUT THERE.
I GOTTA...
...OH, NO.
THERE'S TOO MANY--WE NEED AN ATTACK PLAN...
BOBLAAAST
DAMN! NASTY-ASS DEMON GUTS!

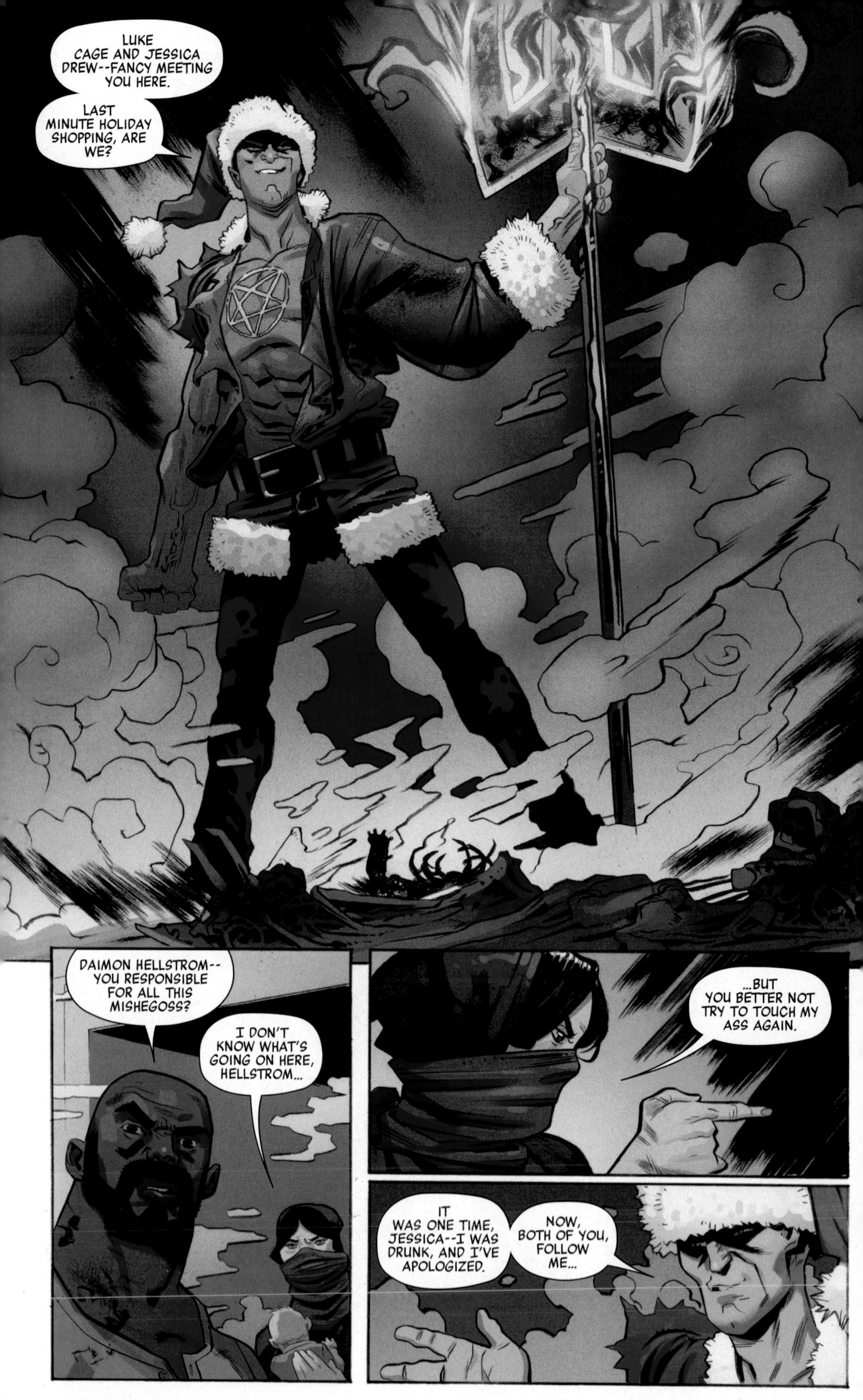

LUKE CAGE AND JESSICA DREW--FANCY MEETING YOU HERE.
LAST MINUTE HOLIDAY SHOPPING, ARE WE?
DAIMON HELLSTROM-- YOU RESPONSIBLE FOR ALL THIS MISHEGOSS?
I DON'T KNOW WHAT'S GOING ON HERE, HELLSTROM...
...BUT YOU BETTER NOT TRY TO TOUCH MY ASS AGAIN.
IT WAS ONE TIME, JESSICA--I WAS DRUNK, AND I'VE APOLOGIZED.
NOW, BOTH OF YOU, FOLLOW ME...

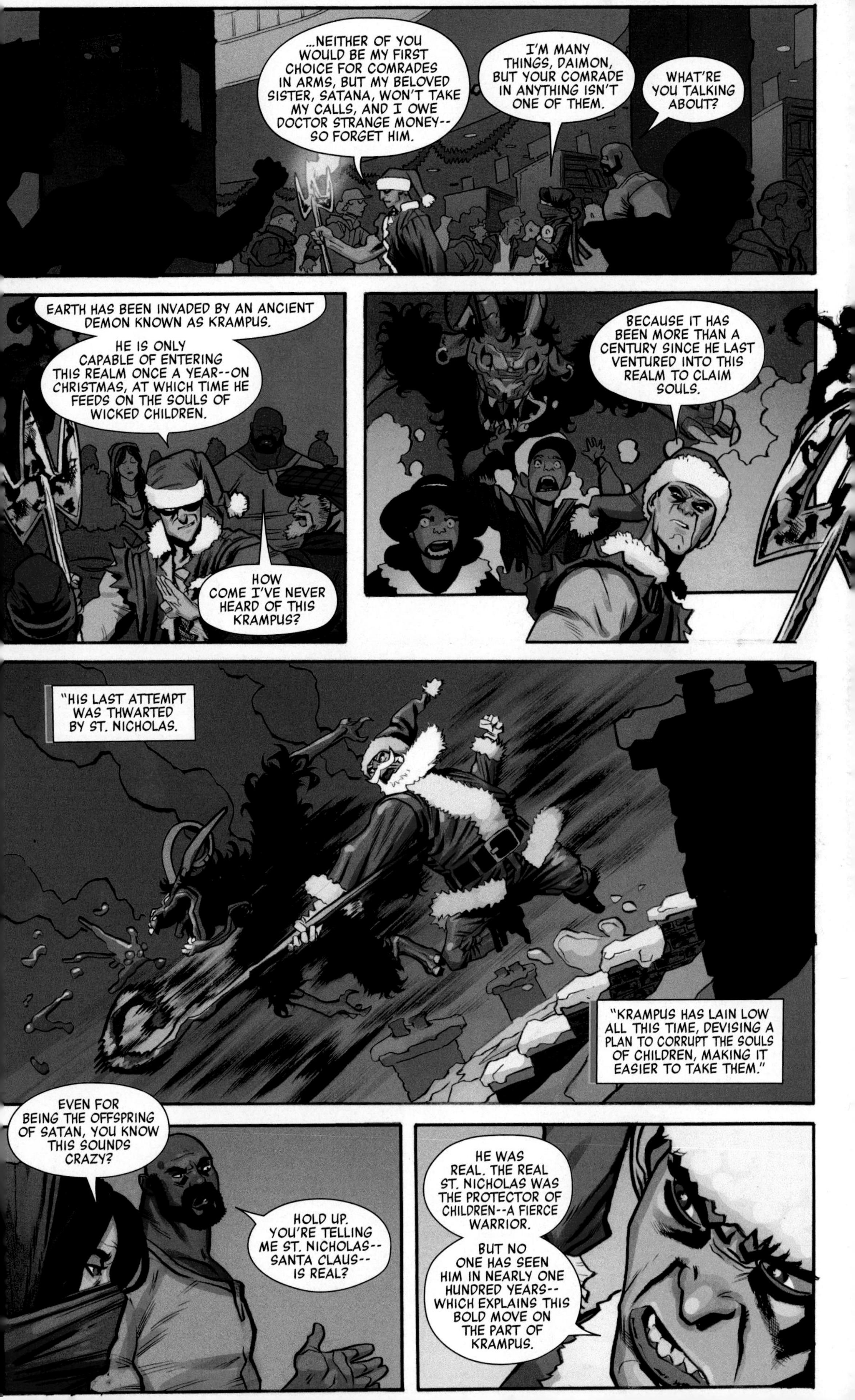
...NEITHER OF YOU WOULD BE MY FIRST CHOICE FOR COMRADES IN ARMS, BUT MY BELOVED SISTER, SATANA, WON'T TAKE MY CALLS, AND I OWE DOCTOR STRANGE MONEY-- SO FORGET HIM.
I'M MANY THINGS, DAIMON, BUT YOUR COMRADE IN ANYTHING ISN'T ONE OF THEM.
WHAT'RE YOU TALKING ABOUT?
EARTH HAS BEEN INVADED BY AN ANCIENT DEMON KNOWN AS KRAMPUS.
HE IS ONLY CAPABLE OF ENTERING THIS REALM ONCE A YEAR--ON CHRISTMAS, AT WHICH TIME HE FEEDS ON THE SOULS OF WICKED CHILDREN.
HOW COME I'VE NEVER HEARD OF THIS KRAMPUS?
BECAUSE IT HAS BEEN MORE THAN A CENTURY SINCE HE LAST VENTURED INTO THIS REALM TO CLAIM SOULS.
"HIS LAST ATTEMPT WAS THWARTED BY ST. NICHOLAS.
"KRAMPUS HAS LAIN LOW ALL THIS TIME, DEVISING A PLAN TO CORRUPT THE SOULS OF CHILDREN, MAKING IT EASIER TO TAKE THEM."
EVEN FOR BEING THE OFFSPRING OF SATAN, YOU KNOW THIS SOUNDS CRAZY?
HOLD UP. YOU'RE TELLING ME ST. NICHOLAS-- SANTA CLAUS-- IS REAL?
HE WAS REAL. THE REAL ST. NICHOLAS WAS THE PROTECTOR OF CHILDREN--A FIERCE WARRIOR.
BUT NO ONE HAS SEEN HIM IN NEARLY ONE HUNDRED YEARS-- WHICH EXPLAINS THIS BOLD MOVE ON THE PART OF KRAMPUS.

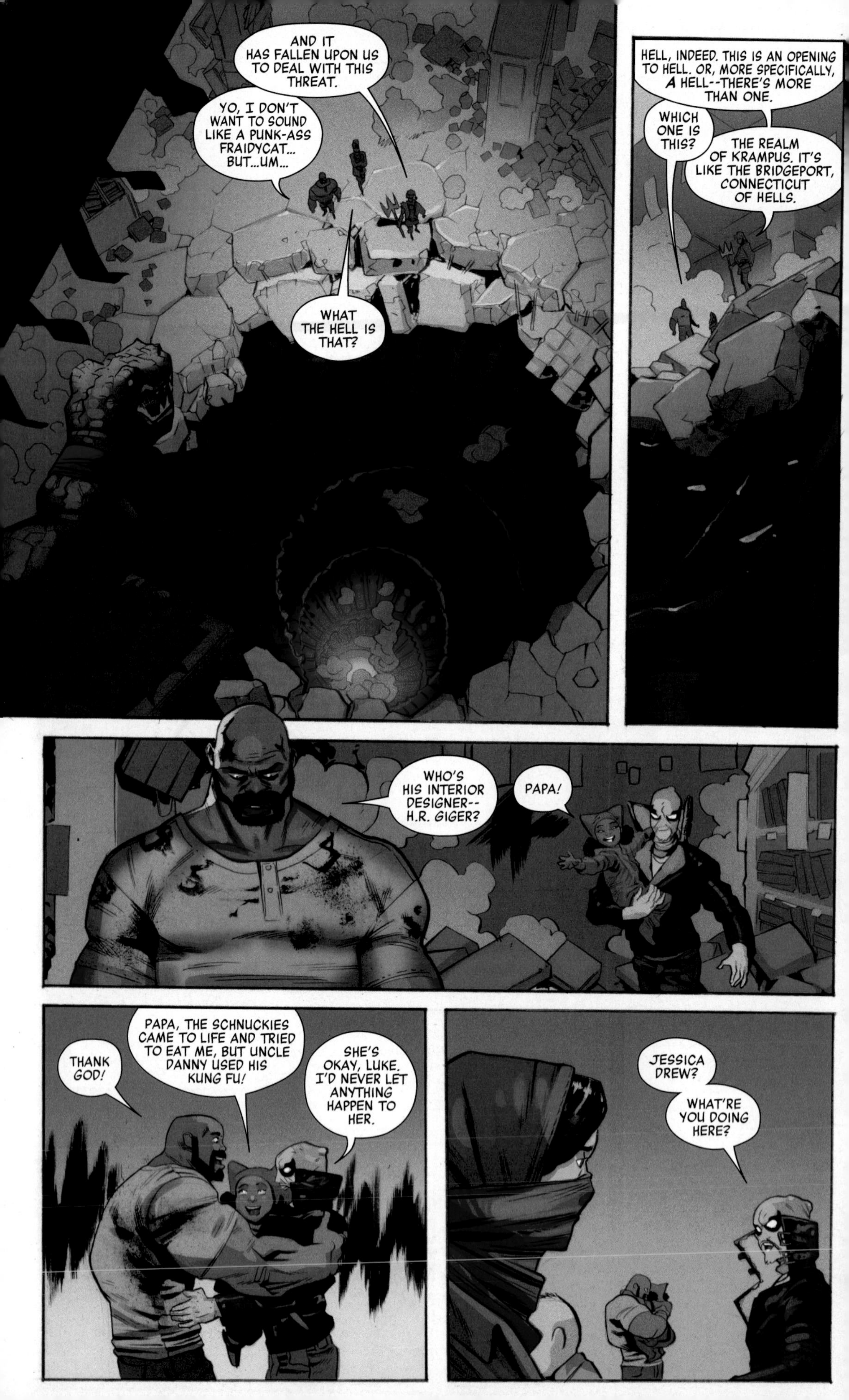
AND IT HAS FALLEN UPON US TO DEAL WITH THIS THREAT.
YO, I DON'T WANT TO SOUND LIKE A PUNK-ASS FRAIDYCAT... BUT...UM...
WHAT THE HELL IS THAT?
HELL, INDEED. THIS IS AN OPENING TO HELL. OR, MORE SPECIFICALLY, A HELL--THERE'S MORE THAN ONE.
WHICH ONE IS THIS?
THE REALM OF KRAMPUS. IT'S LIKE THE BRIDGEPORT, CONNECTICUT OF HELLS.
WHO'S HIS INTERIOR DESIGNER-- H.R. GIGER?
PAPA!
THANK GOD!
PAPA, THE SCHNUCKIES CAME TO LIFE AND TRIED TO EAT ME, BUT UNCLE DANNY USED HIS KUNG FU!
SHE'S OKAY, LUKE. I'D NEVER LET ANYTHING HAPPEN TO HER.
JESSICA DREW?
WHAT'RE YOU DOING HERE?

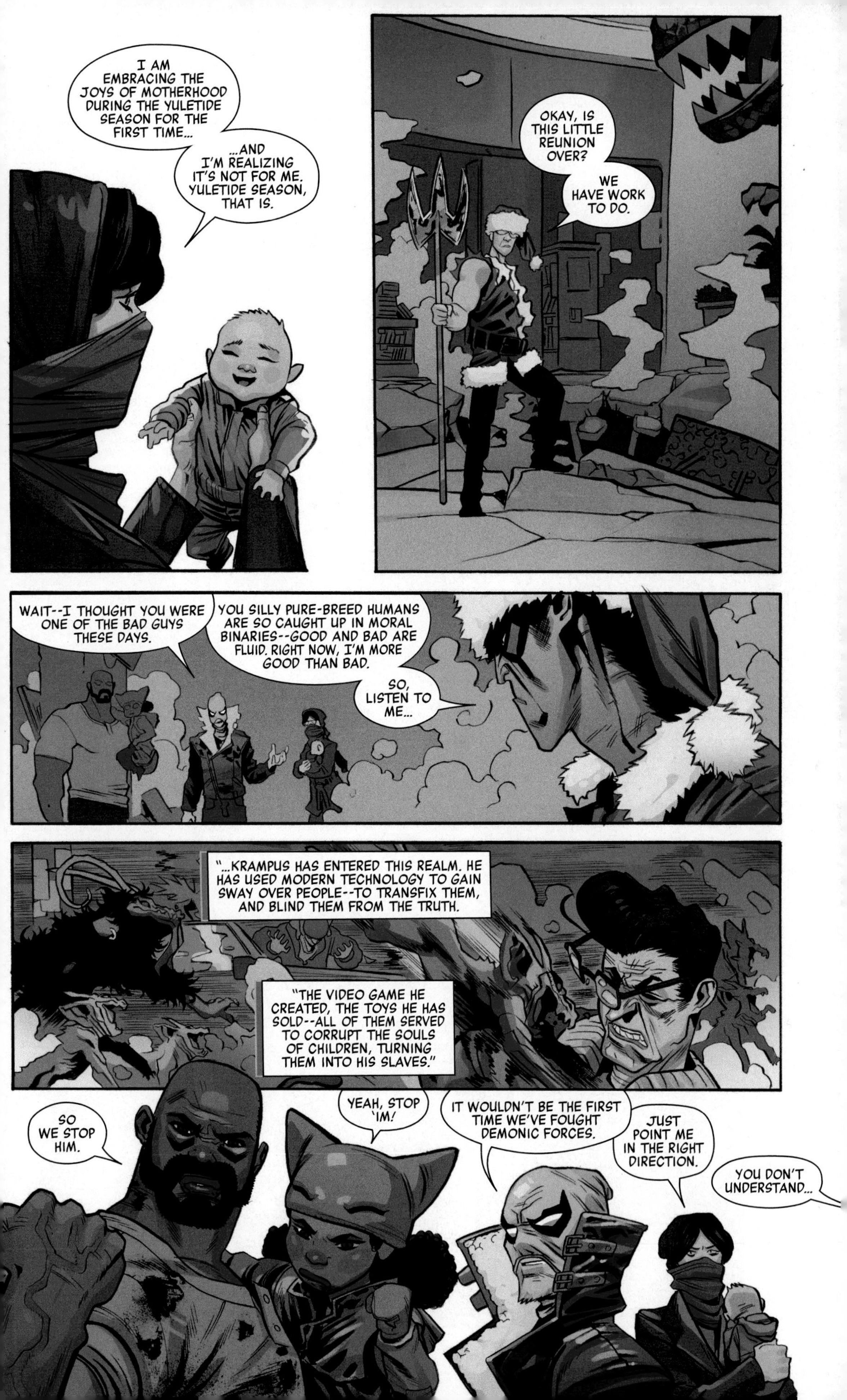
I AM EMBRACING THE JOYS OF MOTHERHOOD DURING THE YULETIDE SEASON FOR THE FIRST TIME...
...AND I'M REALIZING IT'S NOT FOR ME. YULETIDE SEASON, THAT IS.
OKAY, IS THIS LITTLE REUNION OVER?
WE HAVE WORK TO DO.
WAIT--I THOUGHT YOU WERE ONE OF THE BAD GUYS THESE DAYS.
YOU SILLY PURE-BREED HUMANS ARE SO CAUGHT UP IN MORAL BINARIES--GOOD AND BAD ARE FLUID. RIGHT NOW, I'M MORE GOOD THAN BAD.
SO, LISTEN TO ME...
"...KRAMPUS HAS ENTERED THIS REALM. HE HAS USED MODERN TECHNOLOGY TO GAIN SWAY OVER PEOPLE--TO TRANSFIX THEM, AND BLIND THEM FROM THE TRUTH.
"THE VIDEO GAME HE CREATED, THE TOYS HE HAS SOLD--ALL OF THEM SERVED TO CORRUPT THE SOULS OF CHILDREN, TURNING THEM INTO HIS SLAVES."
SO WE STOP HIM.
YEAH, STOP 'IM!
IT WOULDN'T BE THE FIRST TIME WE'VE FOUGHT DEMONIC FORCES.
JUST POINT ME IN THE RIGHT DIRECTION.
YOU DON'T UNDERSTAND...

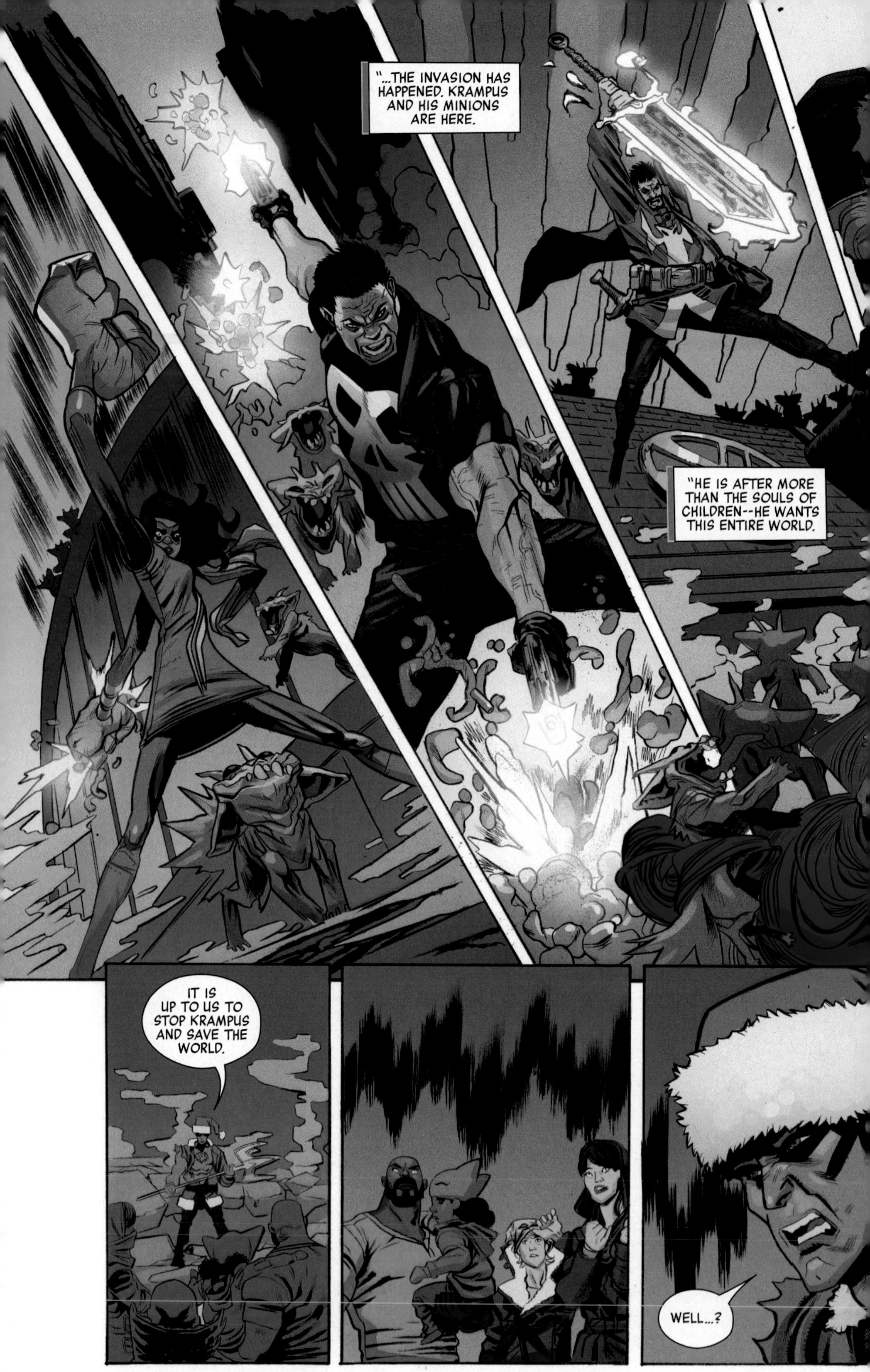
"...THE INVASION HAS HAPPENED. KRAMPUS AND HIS MINIONS ARE HERE.
"HE IS AFTER MORE THAN THE SOULS OF CHILDREN--HE WANTS THIS ENTIRE WORLD.
IT IS UP TO US TO STOP KRAMPUS AND SAVE THE WORLD.
WELL...?

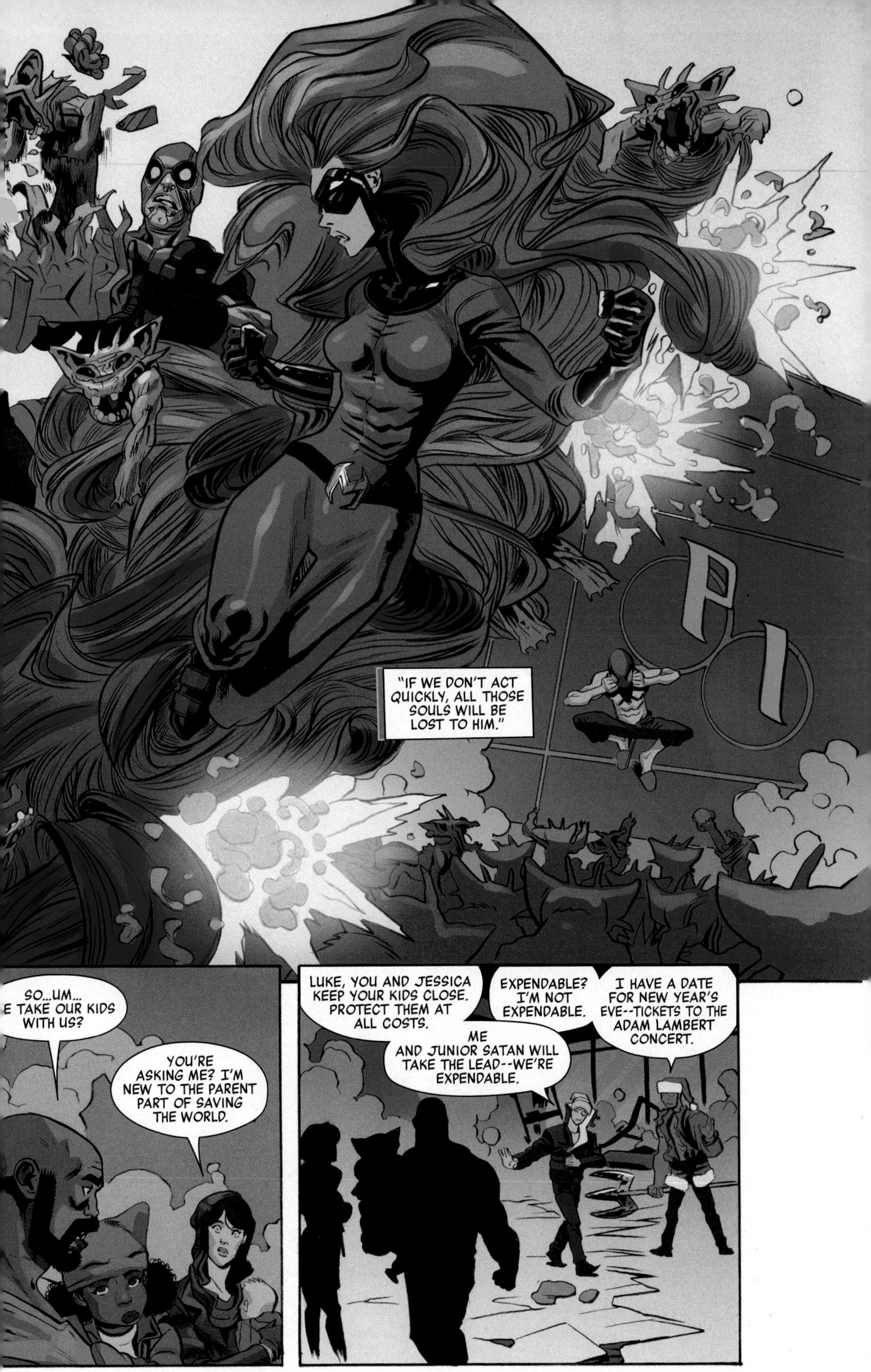
"IF WE DON'T ACT QUICKLY, ALL THOSE SOULS WILL BE LOST TO HIM."
SO...UM... E TAKE OUR KIDS WITH US?
YOU'RE ASKING ME? I'M NEW TO THE PARENT PART OF SAVING THE WORLD.
LUKE, YOU AND JESSICA KEEP YOUR KIDS CLOSE. PROTECT THEM AT ALL COSTS.
ME AND JUNIOR SATAN WILL TAKE THE LEAD--WE'RE EXPENDABLE.
EXPENDABLE? I'M NOT EXPENDABLE.
I HAVE A DATE FOR NEW YEAR'S EVE--TICKETS TO THE ADAM LAMBERT CONCERT.

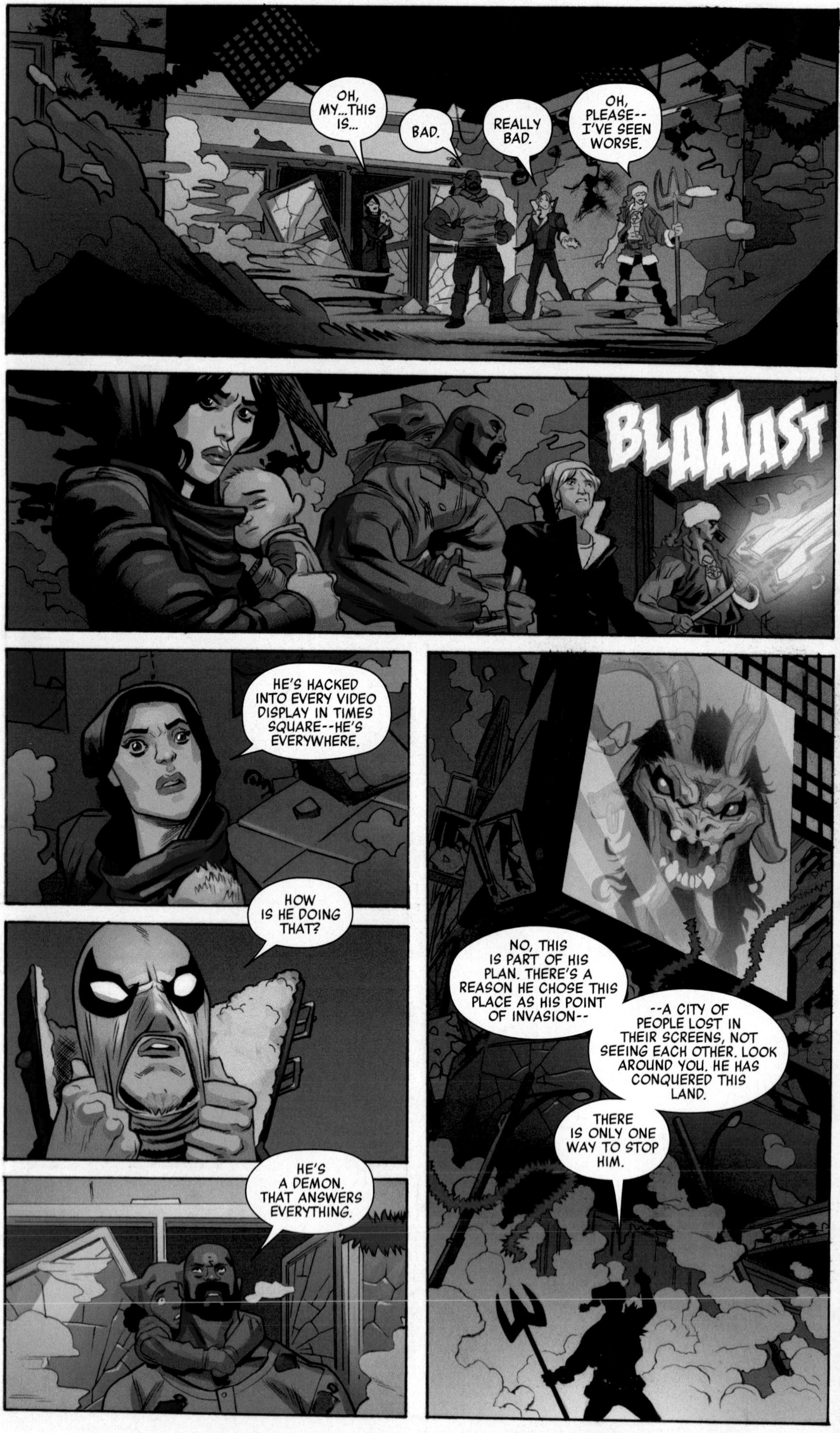
OH, MY...THIS IS...
BAD.
REALLY BAD.
OH, PLEASE-- I'VE SEEN WORSE.
BLAAAST
HE'S HACKED INTO EVERY VIDEO DISPLAY IN TIMES SQUARE--HE'S EVERYWHERE.
HOW IS HE DOING THAT?
HE'S A DEMON. THAT ANSWERS EVERYTHING.
NO, THIS IS PART OF HIS PLAN. THERE'S A REASON HE CHOSE THIS PLACE AS HIS POINT OF INVASION--
--A CITY OF PEOPLE LOST IN THEIR SCREENS, NOT SEEING EACH OTHER. LOOK AROUND YOU. HE HAS CONQUERED THIS LAND.
THERE IS ONLY ONE WAY TO STOP HIM.

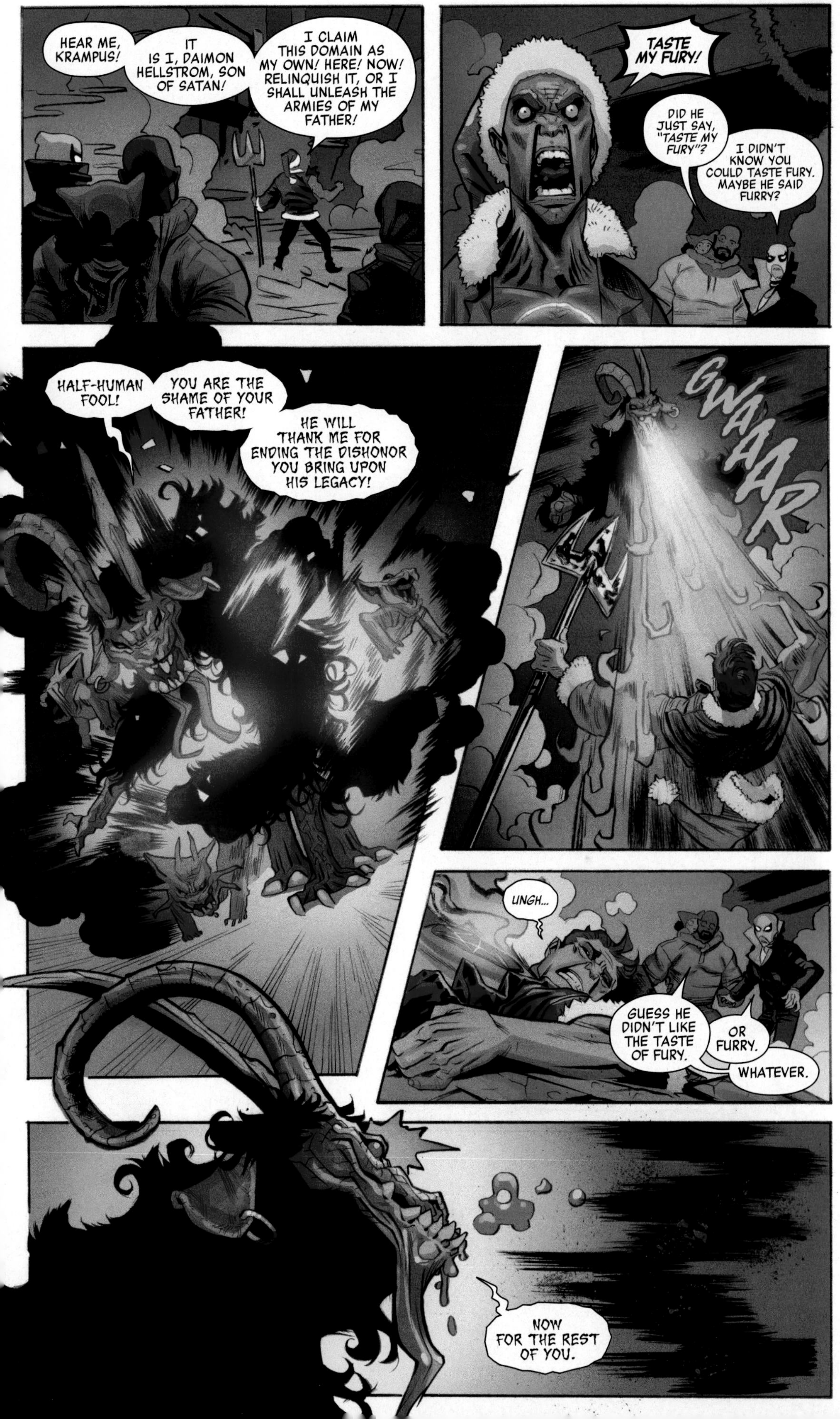
HEAR ME, KRAMPUS!
IT IS I, DAIMON HELLSTROM, SON OF SATAN!
I CLAIM THIS DOMAIN AS MY OWN! HERE! NOW! RELINQUISH IT, OR I SHALL UNLEASH THE ARMIES OF MY FATHER!
TASTE MY FURY!
DID HE JUST SAY, "TASTE MY FURY"?
I DIDN'T KNOW YOU COULD TASTE FURY. MAYBE HE SAID FURRY?
HALF-HUMAN FOOL!
YOU ARE THE SHAME OF YOUR FATHER!
HE WILL THANK ME FOR ENDING THE DISHONOR YOU BRING UPON HIS LEGACY!
GWAAAAR
UNGH...
GUESS HE DIDN'T LIKE THE TASTE OF FURY.
OR FURRY.
WHATEVER.
NOW FOR THE REST OF YOU.

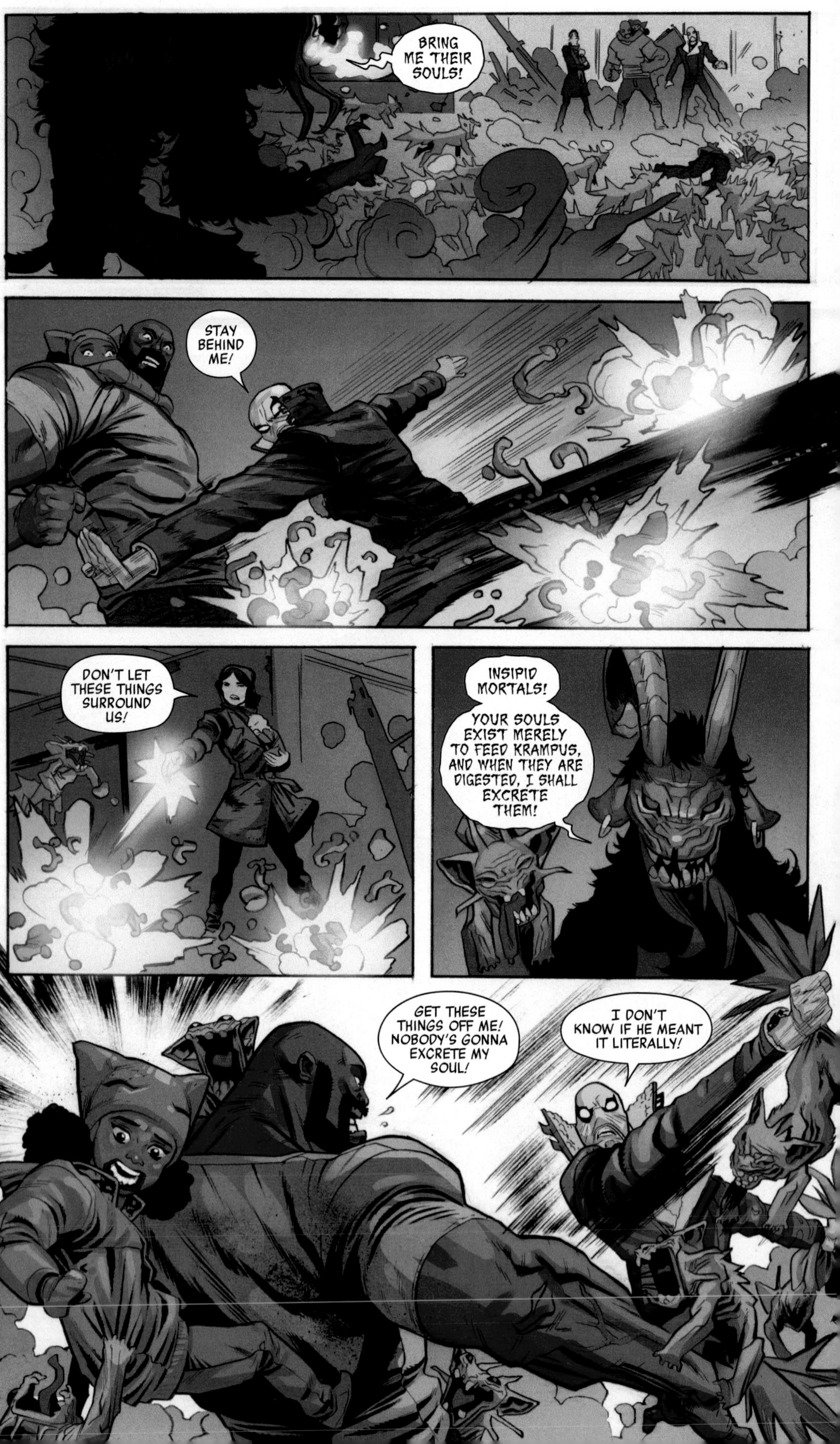
BRING ME THEIR SOULS!
STAY BEHIND ME!
DON'T LET THESE THINGS SURROUND US!
INSIPID MORTALS!
YOUR SOULS EXIST MERELY TO FEED KRAMPUS, AND WHEN THEY ARE DIGESTED, I SHALL EXCRETE THEM!
GET THESE THINGS OFF ME! NOBODY'S GONNA EXCRETE MY SOUL!
I DON'T KNOW IF HE MEANT IT LITERALLY!

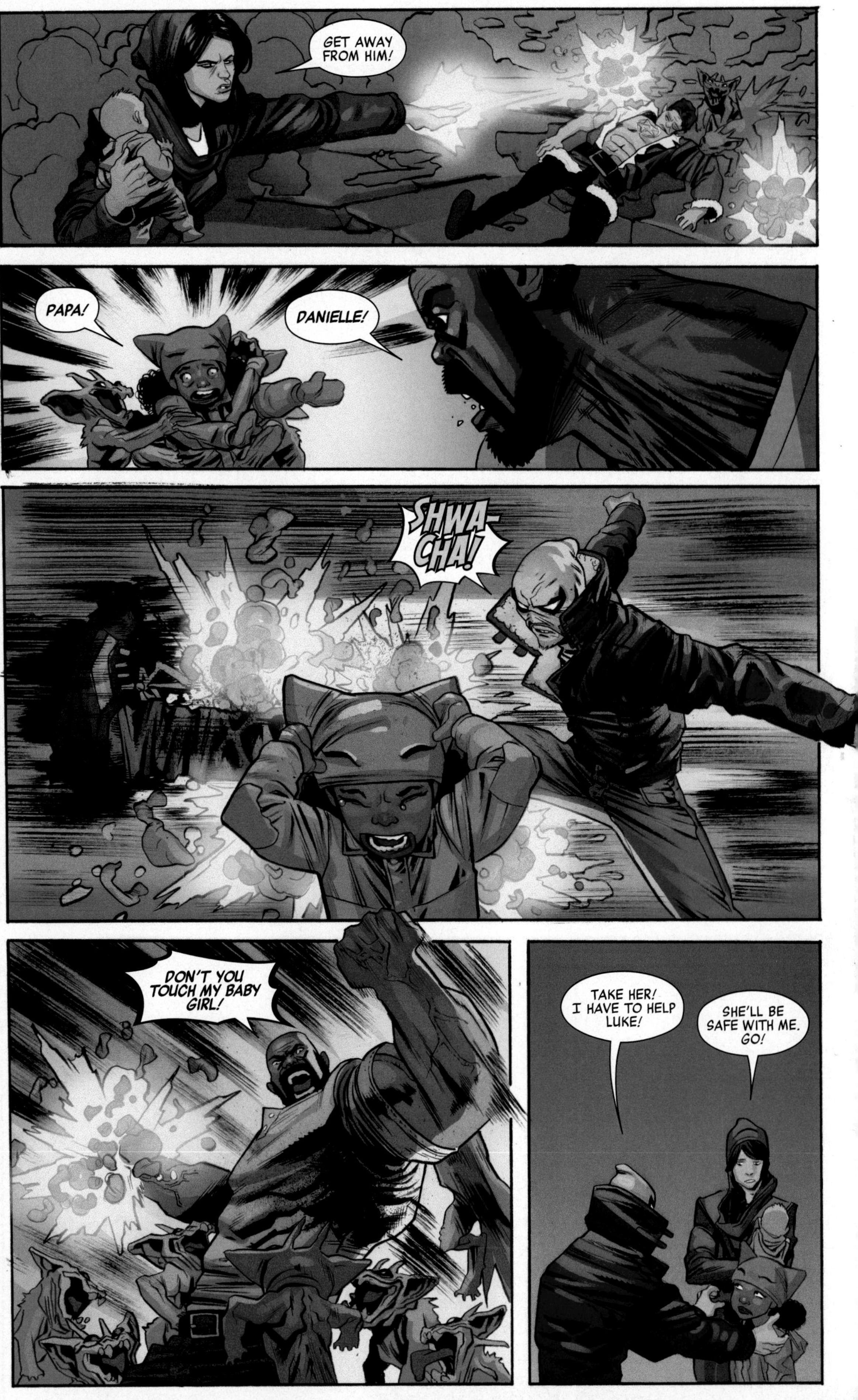
GET AWAY FROM HIM!
PAPA!
DANIELLE!
SHWA-CHA!
DON'T YOU TOUCH MY BABY GIRL!
TAKE HER! I HAVE TO HELP LUKE!
SHE'LL BE SAFE WITH ME. GO!

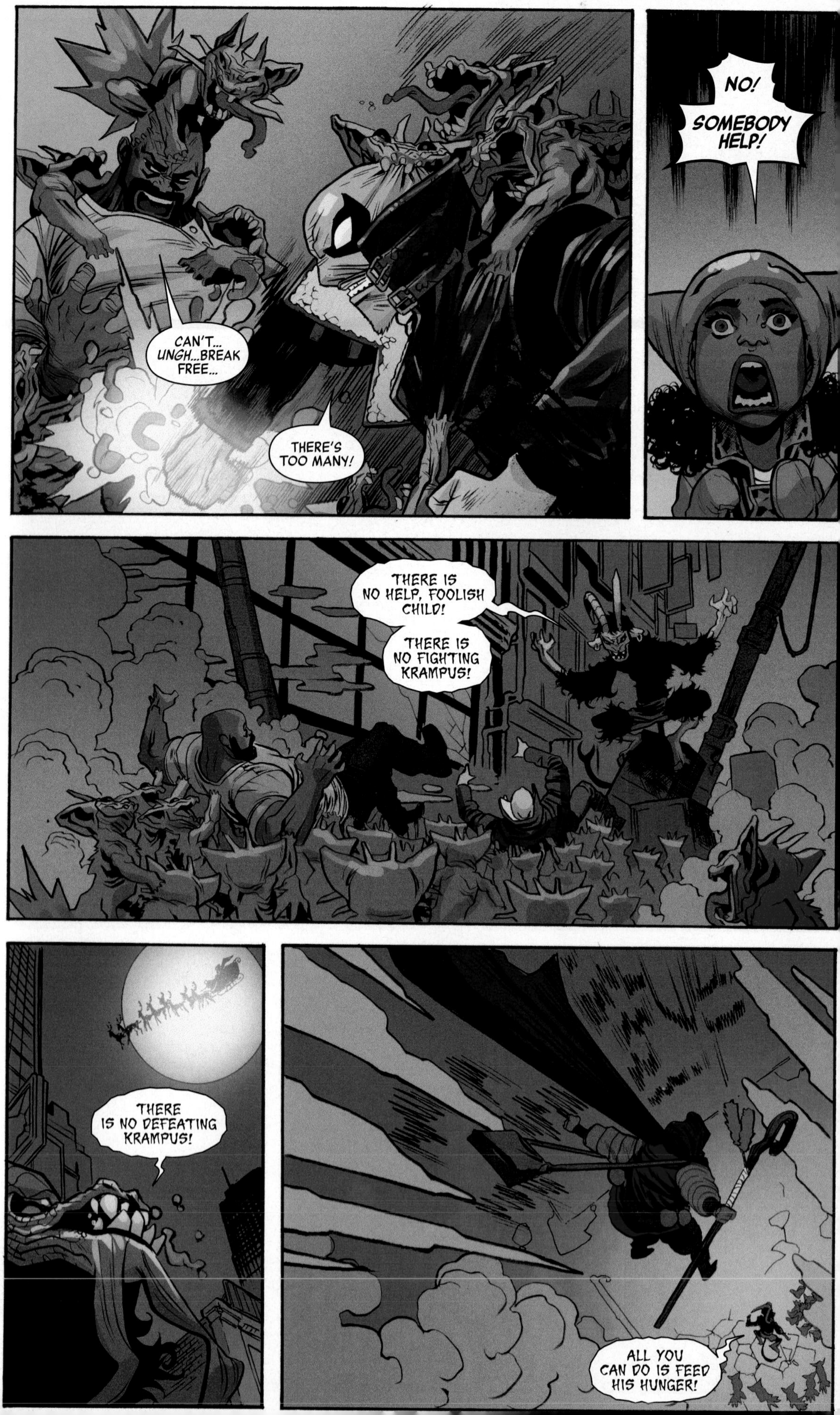
CAN'T... UNGH...BREAK FREE...
THERE'S TOO MANY!
NO!
SOMEBODY HELP!
THERE IS NO HELP, FOOLISH CHILD!
THERE IS NO FIGHTING KRAMPUS!
THERE IS NO DEFEATING KRAMPUS!
ALL YOU CAN DO IS FEED HIS HUNGER!

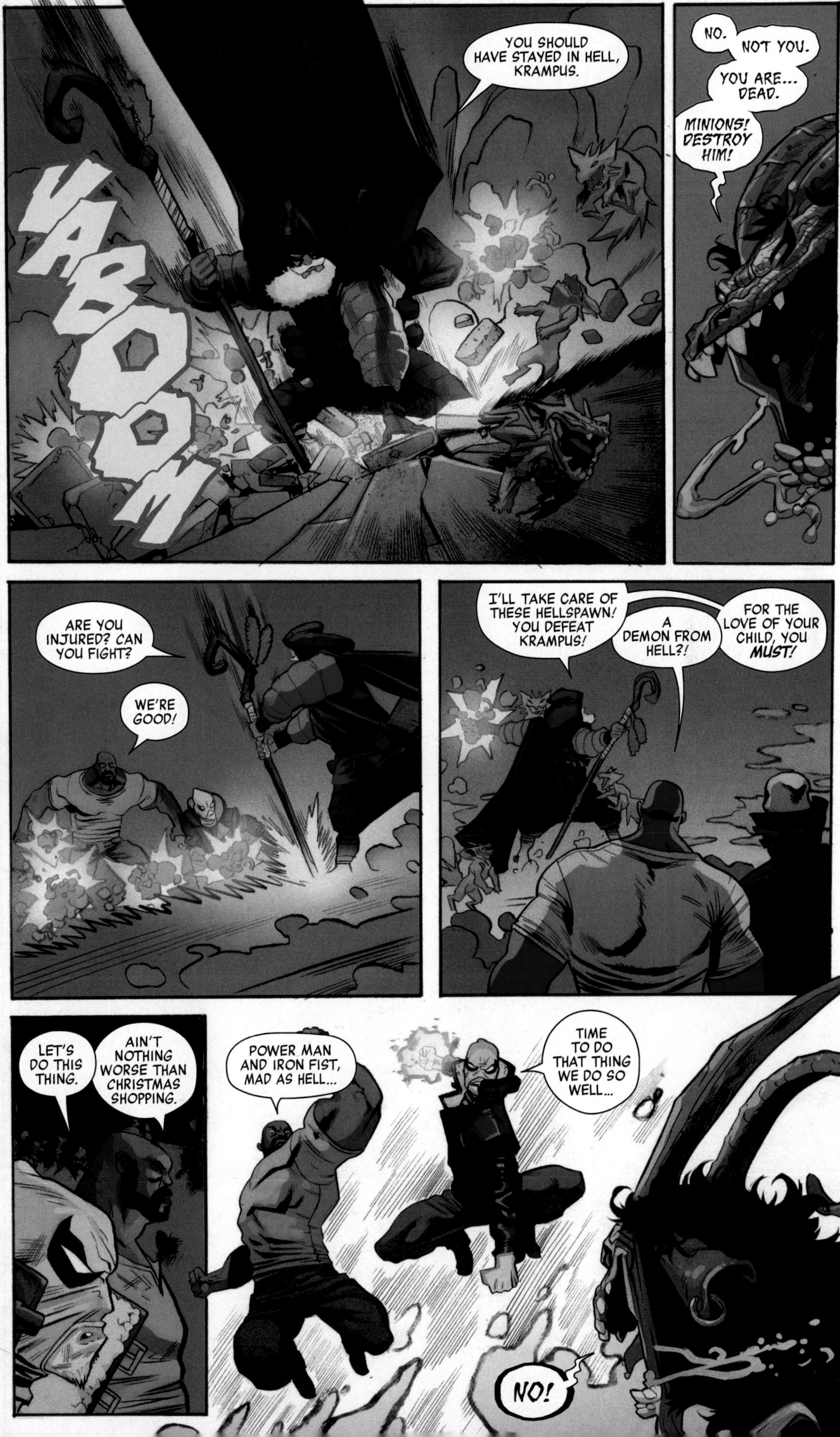
YOU SHOULD HAVE STAYED IN HELL, KRAMPUS.
KABOOM
NO.
NOT YOU.
YOU ARE... DEAD.
MINIONS! DESTROY HIM!
ARE YOU INJURED? CAN YOU FIGHT?
WE'RE GOOD!
I'LL TAKE CARE OF THESE HELLSPAWN! YOU DEFEAT KRAMPUS!
A DEMON FROM HELL?!
FOR THE LOVE OF YOUR CHILD, YOU MUST!
LET'S DO THIS THING.
AIN'T NOTHING WORSE THAN CHRISTMAS SHOPPING.
POWER MAN AND IRON FIST, MAD AS HELL...
TIME TO DO THAT THING WE DO SO WELL...
NO!

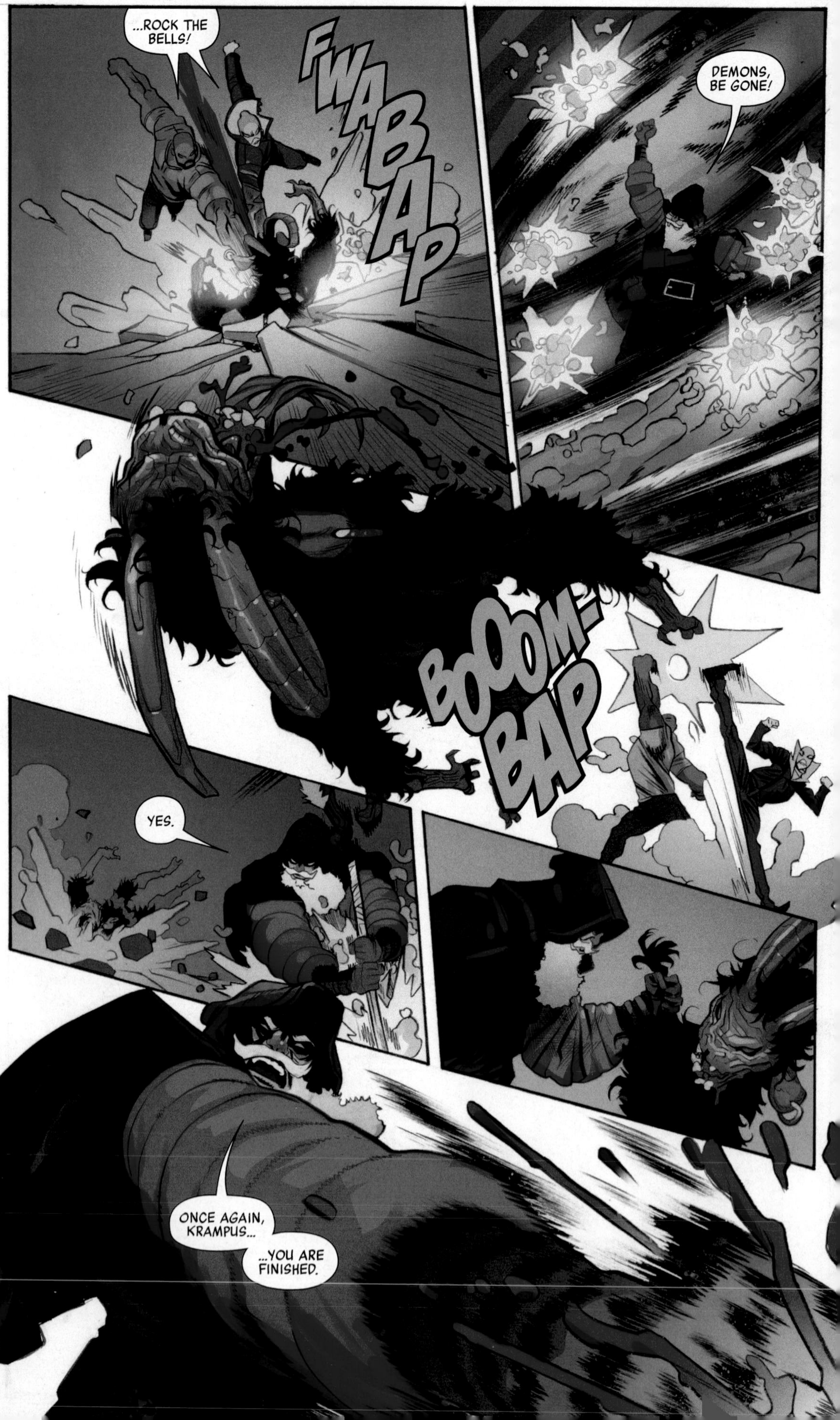
...ROCK THE BELLS!
FWABAP
DEMONS, BE GONE!
BOOOOM-BAP
YES.
ONCE AGAIN, KRAMPUS...
...YOU ARE FINISHED.

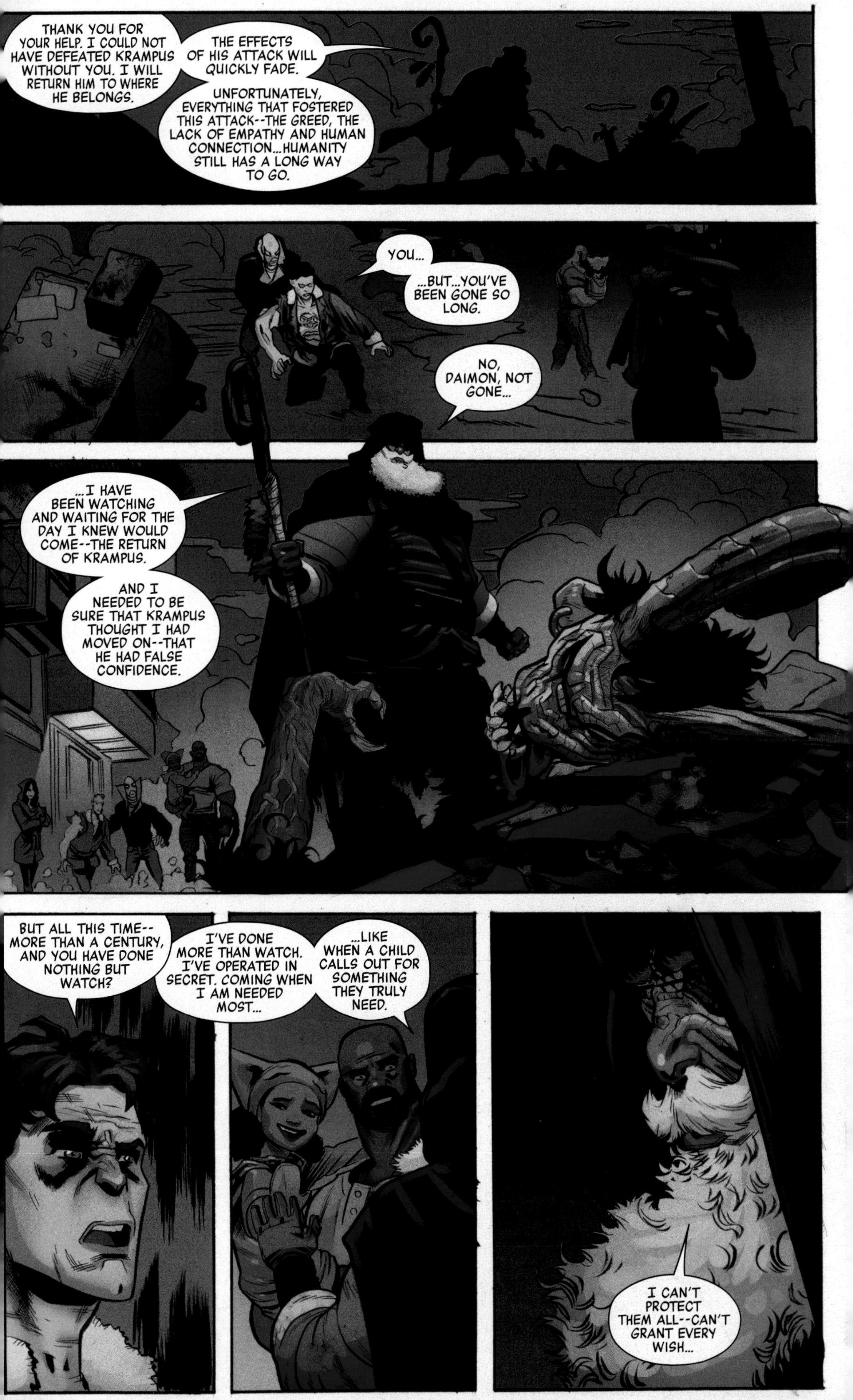
THANK YOU FOR YOUR HELP. I COULD NOT HAVE DEFEATED KRAMPUS WITHOUT YOU. I WILL RETURN HIM TO WHERE HE BELONGS.
THE EFFECTS OF HIS ATTACK WILL QUICKLY FADE.
UNFORTUNATELY, EVERYTHING THAT FOSTERED THIS ATTACK--THE GREED, THE LACK OF EMPATHY AND HUMAN CONNECTION...HUMANITY STILL HAS A LONG WAY TO GO.
YOU...
...BUT...YOU'VE BEEN GONE SO LONG.
NO, DAIMON, NOT GONE...
...I HAVE BEEN WATCHING AND WAITING FOR THE DAY I KNEW WOULD COME--THE RETURN OF KRAMPUS.
AND I NEEDED TO BE SURE THAT KRAMPUS THOUGHT I HAD MOVED ON--THAT HE HAD FALSE CONFIDENCE.
BUT ALL THIS TIME--MORE THAN A CENTURY, AND YOU HAVE DONE NOTHING BUT WATCH?
I'VE DONE MORE THAN WATCH. I'VE OPERATED IN SECRET. COMING WHEN I AM NEEDED MOST...
...LIKE WHEN A CHILD CALLS OUT FOR SOMETHING THEY TRULY NEED.
I CAN'T PROTECT THEM ALL--CAN'T GRANT EVERY WISH...

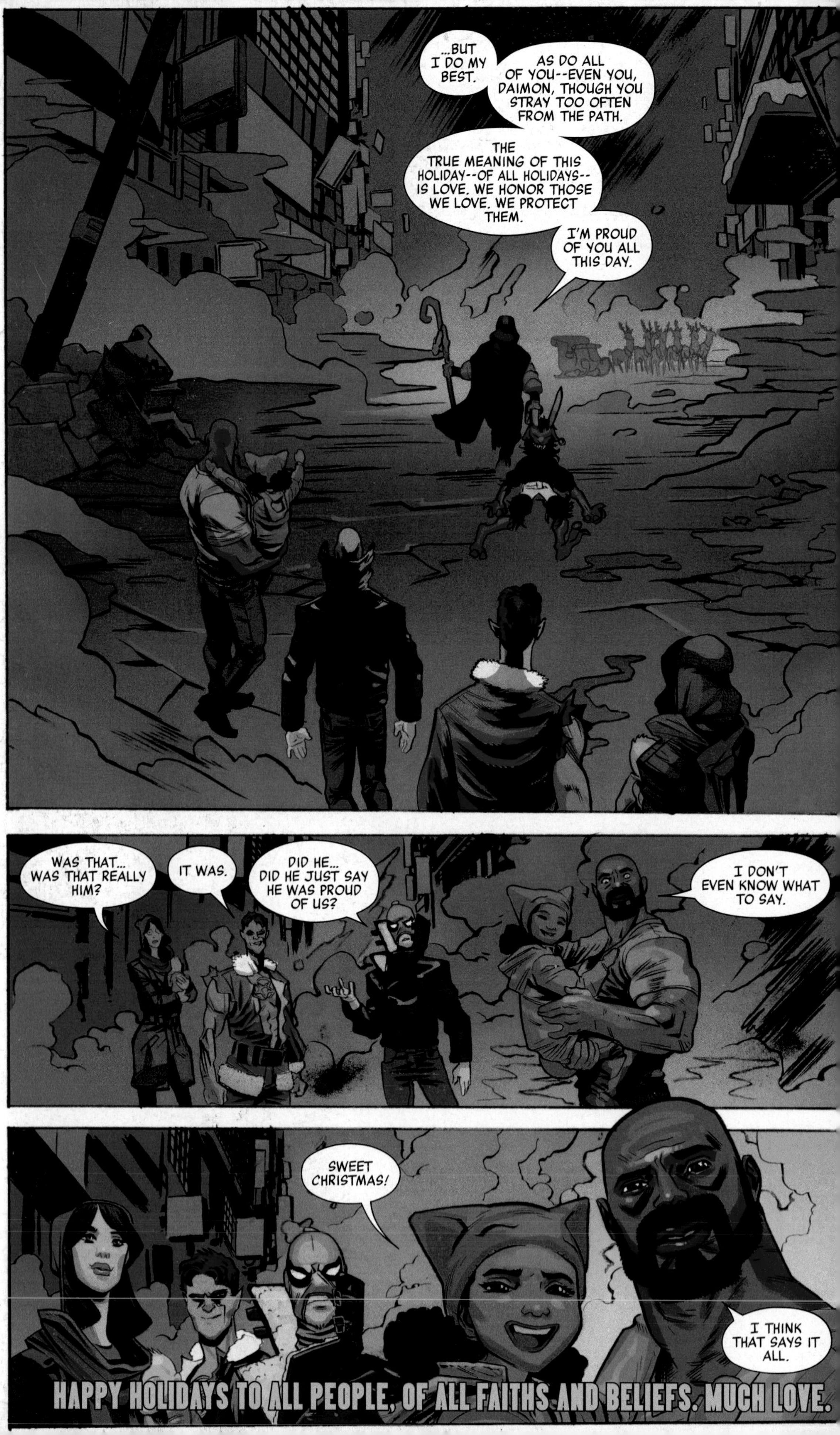
...BUT I DO MY BEST.
AS DO ALL OF YOU--EVEN YOU, DAIMON, THOUGH YOU STRAY TOO OFTEN FROM THE PATH.
THE TRUE MEANING OF THIS HOLIDAY--OF ALL HOLIDAYS--IS LOVE. WE HONOR THOSE WE LOVE. WE PROTECT THEM.
I'M PROUD OF YOU ALL THIS DAY.
WAS THAT... WAS THAT REALLY HIM?
IT WAS.
DID HE... DID HE JUST SAY HE WAS PROUD OF US?
I DON'T EVEN KNOW WHAT TO SAY.
SWEET CHRISTMAS!
I THINK THAT SAYS IT ALL.
HAPPY HOLIDAYS TO ALL PEOPLE, OF ALL FAITHS AND BELIEFS. MUCH LOVE.